The Multicultural Cookbook for Students

The Multicultural Cookbook for Students

by Carole Lisa Albyn
and
Lois Sinaiko Webb

Oryx Press
1993

The rare Arabian Oryx is believed to have inspired the myth of the unicorn. This desert antelope became virtually extinct in the early 1960s. At that time several groups of international conservationists arranged to have 9 animals sent to the Phoenix Zoo to be the nucleus of a captive breeding herd. Today the oryx population is over 800, and nearly 400 have been returned to reserves in the Middle East.

20 19 18 17 16 15 14 13 12 11

Oryx Press, 88 Post Road West, Westport, CT 06881
An imprint of Greenwood Publishing Group, Inc.
www.oryxpress.com

Published simultaneously in Canada

Children should always have adult supervision when working in the kitchen. Please see "Getting Started" on page xiii for more information.

Printed and bound in the United States of America

⊚ The paper used in this publication meets the minimum requirements of American National Standard for Information Science—Permanence of Paper for Printed Library Materials, ANZI Z39.48, 1984.

Library of Congress Cataloging-in-Publication Data

Albyn, Carole Lisa.
    The multicultural cookbook for students / by Carole Lisa Albyn and Lois Sinaiko Webb.
        p. cm.
    Includes index.
    Summary: Presents a collection of recipes from over 120 countries and briefly discusses the culture and culinary habits of each country.
    ISBN 0-89774-735-6
    1. Cookery. International—Juvenile literature.   2. Food habits—Juvenile literature.   3. Food crops—Juvenile literature.
[1. Cookery, International. 2. Food habits.]   I. Webb, Lois Sinaiko.   II. Title.
TX725.A1A34   1993
641.59—dc20   92-41634
                                                        CIP
                                                        AC

This book is dedicated to the child, who, in a very small voice, so small that I had to lean over to hear, asked for a recipe from "Yemen, South Yemen." This is my way of apology for sending you off without anything because all I had to offer was a coffee recipe from "South Yemen."

C.L.A.

My share of this book is dedicated to my granddaughter Paulina Rose Belsky, along with all children on this great earth whose grandparents, for generations, furnished the recipes in this book.

I am donating my share of royalties to charities helping to feed the children of the world.

L.W.

Contents

Preface

The food that is grown and produced throughout the world, and the many varieties of dishes into which it is fashioned, can be overwhelming to think about. The reason that we decided to think about it, and to collect our thoughts in this book, is to answer the questions of the student who is studying a country, and who is approaching that study through the production and preparation of its food—a wonderful way to learn about people and their cultures. Actually, the *Multicultural Cookbook for Students* should be useful and enlightening for anyone interested in authentic recipes from around the world.

We begin our cooking journey in Africa, an area where the oldest human remains have been discovered, and travel around the world, linking countries and peoples through their natural resources, agriculture, and methods of preparing food. In selecting from the many available recipes, our intent was to gather a good variety, using inexpensive ingredients wherever possible, including both easy-to-prepare and more ambitious recipes, depending on what the cook is looking for. The book is divided into seven broad sections, based, loosely, on the continents of the world. The introductions to these sections often include recipes that are common to all of the countries that you will read about in that section. If you can't find a recipe that you like for the individual country you are studying, you might wish to select one of the general recipes for the region.

Many teachers request that students bring food from an area being studied to class, which helps get a better feel for the country. If you have been given such an assignment, here are a few things to keep in mind:

- **Be sure to have an adult help you** and involve him or her with the assignment from the beginning.
- Select a few recipes that you and your adult helper may choose among.
- Read the selected recipe carefully and note what you need to buy, and how much time is needed to prepare it.
- Schedule a shopping time with whoever is helping you to buy the necessary items to complete your recipe.

- Schedule a time in the kitchen to prepare your recipe when your adult helper can assist you.

If cooking equipment is available at school, you may ask your teacher to demonstrate or supervise the preparation of some of these recipes for a social studies unit. Some recipes do not even require cooking equipment or might be prepared simply in, for example, an electric frying pan.

We cannot overemphasize the need for caution in the kitchen. Even the most experienced cook has accidents, and so it is essential that you have an adult help you through the completion of the recipe. Please read "Common Sense, Safety, and Cleanliness Tips for Cooks," on page xiii. These recipes were designed to teach you about countries, not introduce you to cooking methods in general. We have had to include some recipes that you may want to take to school but will need refrigeration. Check with your teacher to see if there is a refrigerator at your school which you can use. Then, store your prepared item in something easily transportable, and refrigerate it. After all, you don't want to be known as the kid who sent everyone in your class to the hospital!

WHAT'S INCLUDED

The Multicultural Cookbook for Students contains 337 recipes from 122 countries. We have made a special effort to include as many recipes as possible from countries in Africa, the Middle East, Asia, the Caribbean, and Latin America, because recipes from these areas are not as easy to find as recipes from Europe and North America are. As noted above, the book is arranged geographically, with recipes from countries arranged within these seven continents or regions: Africa, the Middle East, Europe, Asia and the South Pacific, the Caribbean, Latin America, and North America. We have tried to keep countries with similar cooking traditions together. The book moves from country to country much as a person traveling from country to country by motorcycle or car would.

Each of the seven sections opens with an introductory description of the continent or region and gives general information on the types of recipes offered. We briefly describe each country and list general information about the kinds of foods and meals that the people of the country grow, enjoy, and prepare. Outline maps accompany each country's description; most maps show where the country is located in relation to the countries around it.

The Recipes

In almost all cases, we have provided at least two recipes for each country listed. Some countries have more recipes, and a few have fewer. Each recipe includes the following:

- *Yield,* stating how many people the recipe will serve.
- *Ingredients,* listing how much of which food items you need to make the recipe.

- *Equipment*, listing the cooking equipment, such as pans, bowls, spoons, etc. you need.
- *Instructions*, telling you exactly how to make the recipe.
- *Serving suggestions*, describing how to serve the food you have prepared.

All recipes have been tested by the authors or by PTA groups, Girl and Boy Scout groups, or other children in the Houston, Texas area.

Special Features

The Multicultural Cookbook for Students includes a glossary of terms to explain certain words that may be unfamiliar to you. Terms included in the glossary are highlighted in bold type throughout the book. They include names of food that may be unfamiliar to U.S. students (such as **cassava**), cooking techniques (such as **blanching**), and cooking equipment (such as **serrated knife**).

The book ends with a comprehensive index, listing recipe names, major ingredients, countries, and other terms.

Getting Started

Important
Please read the following before you begin
to use this book

Safety, Common Sense, and Cleanliness Tips for Cooks

This book will *not* teach you *how* to cook. There are a number of good books that teach young people cooking techniques, please check your local library for titles.

To make cooking an enjoyable experience it's a good idea to follow a few rules. These rules apply to all cooks, from beginners to professional executive chefs, and they will stay with you throughout your life. They are about safety, attention to detail, and cleanliness in the kitchen. Attention to detail means simply, use "common sense" and think before you act.

Safety:

1. **Make sure that an adult helps you as you select and work on your recipe.** Even apprentice or beginner chefs in restaurants never cook alone; there is always an experienced chef present to answer questions and help explain how to operate electrical devices and other cooking equipment. It is also important to keep food at the proper temperature at all times, and it takes an experienced eye and nose to tell if something is usable or has spoiled and should be discarded.

2. The stove-top burners are the kitchen's most dangerous equipment and where most home accidents happen. A safety precaution we recommend is a fire extinguisher (designed for stove fires), in good working condition and hanging within easy reach if an accident should occur. Accidents do happen, and so a first aid kit with burn and cut medication is also good to have on hand. To prevent accidents follow a few simple rules.

- Never ever turn your back or walk away from a skillet or pan of hot cooking oil. Have the necessary equipment and ingredients ready to fry before heating the oil in the skillet or saucepan.
- If the oil should begin to smoke or seems too hot, quickly turn off the heat. *Do not move the pan.* And *do not* throw water in the pan. Allow it to cool down and begin again.
- Never leave food cooking unattended. All cooking food must be checked from time to time, so that you are sure it isn't sticking and burning. If the phone rings or there are other distractions while you're cooking, turn the heat off, and using a potholder, slide the pan to a cold burner and double check to make sure you pushed the correct **off** button before you leave the kitchen. It is very easy to forget you left something cooking on the stove once you walk away from it. When you return, if it hasn't been more than a few minutes, just continue where you left off and give your cooking project your undivided attention.
- When you finish cooking, before you leave the kitchen, check to be sure the oven and stove top dials are "OFF."

3. In each recipe we recommended the approximate cooking heat and time. This can vary, based on the thickness of the pan you are using, the heat controls on your stove, and how thickly you cut the cooking ingredients.
4. Keep dry, heat-proof oven mitts or pot holders handy. All-metal spoons get hot, and so use wooden mixing spoons or plastic-handled metal spoons instead. Do not use all-plastic spoons for mixing hot food; they will melt. Never transfer very hot food to plastic containers, because some are not made to hold hot food and might melt.
5. Tilt the cover of a pan full of cooking food away from you as you take it off. This way, the steam that comes out can't burn you.
6. Dull knives are sometimes more dangerous than sharp knives. A dull knife might slip off food, causing accidents. Always cut food on a cutting board, never while you're holding the food. Have an adult standing by to help you. Always carry a knife by the handle with the blade pointing toward the floor. Never pass a knife to another person blade first. Never put utility knives in a dishwasher or in a sink full of soapy water with other cooking utensils. It is not only dangerous but not good for the knives. Wash them by hand and keep in a safe place.

Cleanliness:

1. Tie your hair back or wear something on your head, such as a bandana.
2. Roll up your sleeves and wear an apron or some protection to keep your clothes clean.
3. Wash your hands with soap and dry them with a clean towel or paper towels before you touch food. Wash your hands as often as necessary while you are handling food. This will prevent cross-contamination.

4. Wash all fresh fruits and vegetables before cutting them.
5. Cooking in a clean kitchen makes the job more pleasant.
6. Make sure all your equipment is ready and in good working order before you begin.
7. Good cooks clean up after themselves and leave the kitchen spotless. Clean up any spills and drips when they happen.

We have made every effort to keep the cooking instructions and procedures throughout this cookbook as simple and easy to follow as possible. Before you start cooking, read the recipe through and make sure you understand it. Have the ingredients prepared according to the instructions, and have the necessary cooking equipment ready before you begin.

Equipment and Methods You Need to Know About

Almost every recipe you will use from this book will require the following basic equipment:

- A set of **measuring cups**. You will probably need nested cups in different sizes for measuring dry items such as flour, and you will probably need a liquid measuring cup, with lines drawn on the sides to tell you how much liquid you have.
- A set of **measuring spoons** for measuring small amounts of liquid and dry items.
- A **work surface**, such as a counter top or table top, where you can put all of your equipment as you prepare your food.
- A set of **sharp knives** for cutting and dicing ingredients.

Each recipe will tell what other equipment you will need—such as bowls, pans, or spoons—to make the food described.

Glossary

All of the following terms are highlighted throughout this book, wherever you see them, in bold, dark type.

Acidophilus is the name of the live bacteria (or lactic culture) that turns warm milk into yogurt. (See recipe for yogurt making page 94, Bulgaria). It is available at most supermarkets and health food stores.

Al dente is Italian and means "to the tooth." It is a descriptive term used for cooking pasta. "Pasta should be cooked al dente," means the pasta should be firm to the bite, chewy, not mushy and overcooked.

Baste means to moisten food by spooning liquid over it while cooking. It prevents meat or other food from drying out.

Blanch means to put fruit or vegetables in boiling water to soften them, to set color, to peel off skin, or to remove the raw flavor. The fruit or vegetables are first dropped in boiling water for a minute or two and then plunged into cold water to stop the cooking action. (See also **Peeling tomatoes**).

Bouillon is the broth made from meat, poultry, or vegetables boiled in liquid. The concentrated form of this broth or bouillon comes in dry cubes or granules and is **reconstituted** with liquid, such as water.

Buffet is a style of food service. An assortment of prepared dishes are set out on a table. The food is either self-service or served by serving people.

Bulgur is a cracked wheat grain. The nutty-textured cereal is ground fine or coarse for use in different Middle Eastern dishes. It is available at health food and Middle East stores.

Bundt pan is a baking utensil with scalloped edges and a tube in the center. It is used mostly for cake baking.

Candy thermometer is a calibrated instrument that registers up to 400° F. It shows the exact temperature of a cooking mixture. To properly use the thermometer, the bottom end should be immersed below the surface of the cooking mixture, but not touching the pan bottom. Candy thermometers are available at most supermarkets.

Capers are the tiny olive-green buds of a bush native to North Africa and the Mediterranean region. They are salted and pickled in vinegar. They add a zesty flavor to sauces and salads.

Cardamom is a spice made of the dried, ripe seeds of the cardamom plant. The aromatic seeds are ground and used in many dishes, especially curries, breads, and tea. Scandinavians love to add the fragrant spice to pastries. It is an old Chinese custom to chew on a few seeds to sweeten the breath.

Cassava (also called **manioc**) is an edible root. It is almost pure starch, easily digestible and nutritious. Cassava comes from tropical yucca plants. There are two kinds: sweet cassava, eaten as a vegetable; and bitter cassava, which is made into tapioca and manioc, a meal used in cooking. Tapioca is used for thickening soups and in puddings. Manioc flour is used extensively in South American cooking. Brazil is the world's largest grower of cassava. It is available at some supermarkets and all Latin American food stores.

Chickpeas are round legumes (beans), also known as garbanzo beans, used extensively in Mediterranean, Middle Eastern, Indian, and Mexican cooking. They are available dried or cooked and canned at most supermarkets.

Chutney is the name for a condiment (relish) always served with curries. There are hundreds of chutneys made with different fruit or vegetable and spice combinations cooked with vinegar and sugar. Chutneys are easy to make and are also available at most supermarkets.

Cilantro/Coriander are found in either fresh leaf form, which is an herb, or as dried seeds, a spice. Both are used extensively in Asian, Indian, and Spanish cooking. Cilantro is the Spanish name for fresh coriander.

Coarsely chop means to cut into large bite-size pieces, about 1/2 to 1-inch square, see also **Finely chop**.

Colander is a perforated utensil for draining food. It usually has a rounded bottom and feet to stand on.

Core means to cut out and discard the hard center part and the stem of fruits and vegetables, such as apples.

Coriander see **Cilantro/Coriander**

Crushed or finely ground nuts are sold in jars and can be purchased in the candy department of most supermarkets. They are a popular topping for ice cream. The finely ground nuts needed for recipes in this cookbook can also be finely chopped. You can grind your own peanuts by hand, putting the nuts in the **mortar** and pressing on them with the pestle, or by finely chopping them with a knife. If you have an electric nut grinder or a food processor, nuts can be finely ground in just seconds. Electric blenders might work if the nuts are very dry; otherwise, we do not recommend them. In a blender, oil is released from the nuts making them gummy and hard to grind. A hand or electric meat grinder can also be used.

Cube means to cut something into small (about 1/2 inch) squares; compare with **Dice**.

Devein means to remove the vein, usually associated with peeled shrimp. It is a black, (sometimes white) vein running down the back of shrimp from the head to the tail. It is easily visible and can be removed by cutting the thin membrane covering it, while rinsing the shrimp under cold running water. Use either the tip of a finger nail or tip of a knife to gently pull it out in one piece. It is removed for appearance sake only. It is always eaten in very tiny shrimp and is perfectly harmless to eat.

Dice means to cut something into very small (about 1/4 inch) squares; compare with **Cube**.

Dollop means a small amount or lump.

Double boiler is one pan fitted on top of another. The upper pan holds food that must be cooked at a temperature lower than direct heat. It is cooked by the steam heat of boiling water. The amount of water in the bottom pan is important; it must be enough to cook the food and not boil away. If it is too full it can boil over and be dangerous. A double boiler can be made out of any 2 pans that fit together with room between them for the water and steam. A heat-resistant bowl can also be fitted over the pan of water.

Dutch oven is a large heavy cast-iron pot with a tight fitting dome cover. It is ideal for slow, stove-top cooking.

Durum wheat also called "hard wheat," is high in gluten. Gluten gives dough its tough, elastic quality. **Semolina** flour is made from the hard portion of wheat that remains after the flour, bran and chaff have been removed. There are two types of semolina—one is made from hard berries of both hard and soft wheat. When it is coarsely milled into granules, it is used for soups, groats, and puddings. The other kind of semolina comes from hard durum wheat and is used for all good-quality homemade or commercial pasta. Durum wheat semolina flour is particularly suitable for pasta because it contains a high proportion of protein, which prevents the starch from breaking down during cooking, producing pasta that stays firm and resilient.

Egg beater is a hand or kitchen tool used to whip, mix, and/or beat food.

Eggs, hard cooked or hard boiled means to carefully put eggs into the pan and cover with cold water. Bring them to a boil over high heat and quickly reduce to simmer. Cover and cook for about 12 to 15 minutes. Remove from heat, uncover, and place under cold running water to chill eggs before peeling. This prevents the green ring from forming around the yolk.

Eggs, separated means that the egg yolk has been put in one container and the white in another. It is very important to keep the whites free of any yolk. Break and separate each egg, one at a time, into small individual bowls before putting them together with other whites or yolks. If an egg is spoiled it can be discarded, or if the yolk breaks into the white it can be refrigerated to use at another time.

Fillets are boneless cuts or slices of meat, poultry, or fish.

Finely chop means to cut in very tiny pieces. It is the same as to **mince**.

Finely ground nuts see **Crushed or finely ground nuts**

Fish: Opaque white and easily flakes means fish is fully cooked. The flesh appears solid white (versus translucent light grey when raw). When you poke it with a fork it easily separates into small chunks (flakes).

Flake (fish) see **Fish: Opaque white and easily flakes**

Fluff (rice or grains) means using a fork to stir in a top to bottom circular motion, to separate the grains.

Fold refers to gently and slowly mixing (using a whisk or mixing spoon), in a rotating top to bottom motion, allowing air to be incorporated into the mixture.

Frothy describes something that has been beaten or whipped (such as egg whites) just until the surface is covered with small bubbles.

Ghee in India is used for cooking and is made from butter or vegetable oils. **Usli ghee** is made from clarified pure butter made from the milk of water buffalo or yak. The advantages of cooking with ghee is it tastes good, it will not burn and turn brown, and it keeps indefinitely even when left unrefrigerated.

Ground peanuts or **ground nuts** see **Crushed or finely ground nuts**

Hard-cooked eggs see **Eggs, hard cooked**

Hungarian paprika is a powder condiment made from dried pods of red bonnet peppers. The peppers grow throughout Europe and the best are said to grow in Hungary where they are the national spice. Paprika has a rich deep red color.

Knead means to work a dough until smooth and elastic, preferably with the hands. It is especially important in bread-making. Shape the dough into a ball. Push the "heels" of your hands against the dough, fold the upper half over, and turn it a little bit. Then push the heels of your hands against the dough and repeat the whole procedure many times until dough is smooth.

Lentils are very nutritious legumes (beans). Many varieties of lentil have been a staple in the Middle East and Central Asia for thousands of years. They are available at most supermarkets and all Middle East food stores.

Mace is a spice ground from the outer covering of the nutmeg. The flavor and uses of mace and nutmeg are similar.

Manioc see **Cassava**

Marble effect is created when two colors of batter are swirled, but not fully mixed together, resembling marble stone.

Marinade is the sauce in which food is marinated.

Marinate means to soak in a sauce made up of seasonings and liquids.

Melting chocolate requires very little heat. Put chocolate chips in a pan over boiling water or put in heat-proof bowl in warm oven until melted (about 3 to 5 minutes, depending on quantity).

Millet is the name for several different plant species that are grown as grain for human food in different parts of the world, such as Africa, Asia, and India. It seems to grow where nothing else can and has been cultivated in dry, poor soil for over 1,000 years as an important high-protein food staple. To this day millet nourishes about one-third of the world's population and is said to equal rice in food value. Millet is available at most health food stores either in the form of meal, groats, or flour. Millet is a "nonglutinous" grain. Gluten gives the elasticity to wheat flour needed in bread baking. Adding some millet to wheat flour makes excellent tasting bread. Millet has an important place in our economy even though it is not a popular food grain. In the United States, it is cultivated mostly as a forage grass, poultry feed, and is especially suitable for chicks and pet birds.

Mince means to finely chop or pulverize.

Mortar and pestle refers to a bowl (called the mortar) and a grinding tool (called the pestle). Both are made of a nonbreakable, hard substance. The mortar holds something that must be mashed or ground to extract its flavor. The pestle is held in the hand and is used to do the mashing or grinding. You can make a mortar and pestle; simply use a metal bowl for the mortar and for the pestle use a clean, small, smooth-surfaced rock, the head of a hammer, or wooden mallet.

Opaque white see **Fish: Opaque white and easily flakes**

Peeling tomatoes is made easy by dropping them in boiling water for about 1 or 2 minutes. Remove with a slotted spoon and hold under cold water to stop the cooking action. If the skin has not already cracked open, poke the tomato with a small knife and the skin easily peels off. (This is also called **blanching**.)

Pestle see **Mortar and Pestle**

Pimento or **pimiento** are heart-shaped sweet-tasting peppers that are almost always canned because they spoil rapidly.

Pith is the spongy tissue between the skin and meat of fruit such as oranges, lemons, and grapefruit.

Pitted means the stony seeds or pits from fruit or vegetables, such as avocados, have been removed.

Plantains or **platanos** come in all sizes and are green, yellow, and black. They are cooking bananas with a squash-like taste. They are good boiled, baked, fried, and broiled and are either sliced or mashed. They are available year-round from Ecuador and Mexico and are sold in some supermarkets and Latin American food stores.

Prepared mustard refers to any creamy mustard spread, readily available at all supermarkets. For the recipes in this book, unless otherwise stated, the mustard can be either regular or Dijon-style.

Pulp is the edible solid part of fruit or vegetable.

Punch down is an action performed in bread making. When the prepared yeast mixer is added to flour it begins to ferment and gases (carbon dioxide) develop, causing the dough to rise. The gases are forced out of the dough by a process known as "punching down"; this helps to relax the gluten and equalizes the temperature of the dough. To punch down, take your fist and flatten the dough against the bowl. The best time to "punch down" the dough is when it has doubled in size through fermentation. After the dough is punched, it must rise a second time before it can be made into bread or rolls.

Reconstitute means to restore to a former condition by adding liquid such as water.

Rose water is an extract distilled from fresh rose petals. It is an important flavoring in the Middle East and India. It is available at Middle East food stores and most pharmacies.

Seed means to remove and discard seeds before cutting or chopping, usually in a fruit or vegetable.

Semolina see **Durum wheat**

Separated eggs see **Eggs, separated**

Serrated knife has saw-like notches along the cutting edge, such as on a bread knife.

Shredded describes food, such as cabbage, that has been torn into strips. A grater is often used to shred food. (To shred coconut, see recipe on page 208.)

Sift means to shake a dry, powdered substance (such as flour, baking powder, etc.) through a strainer/sifter to remove any lumps and give lightness. See also **Sifter**.

Sifter is a sieve-like container that holds something that needs to be sifted or strained. A flour sifter is used to remove lumps and separate the particles.

Sorghum is a grain related to millet and used in Asia and Africa for porridge, flour, beer, and molasses.

Springform pan is a round baking pan with a removable bottom. The sides open by means of a spring hinge, allowing the cake to be easily removed from the pan.

Steamer pan or **basket** is made of wire mesh or has small holes and sits above a pan of boiling water, allowing food to cook by the steam of boiling water. Steam cooking preserves most of the food's nutrients. A steamer can be made by fitting a wire rack, strainer, or colander into a large saucepan, allowing room between for the water and steam. Aluminum foil can be scrunched up into a ball and used as a prop to keep the container with food above the water level. The cover must fit tightly over the basket to keep as much steam in as possible.

Stewed means food that is slowly cooked in a small amount of liquid at low heat in a covered container. This allows flavors to blend and cook together.

Stir-fry food means to cook it quickly using very little hot oil. The food is continually stirred, keeping it crisp and firm. Stir-fry originated in China where it is done in a **wok**.

Strain means to put food through a sieve or strainer so that liquid or small parts of food pass through small holes, and the large parts are left in the strainer.

Tapioca see **cassava.**

Taro is the name given to several different tropical plants with similar edible starchy tubers and spinach-like leaves. Taro is an important staple in African, Asian, and Caribbean cooking. The root has a nutty, potato-like flavor and texture. The leafy green tops are chopped and cooked in vegetables stews. Taro root or flour is available at most Latin American food stores.

Tenderize means to make meat tender by using a process, such as pounding with a kitchen mallet or adding a marinade to soften the tissue.

Trimmed means that the stem or core, or any tough and inedible parts, brown spots, or discoloration of skin or flesh on vegetables or fruit has been removed. To **trim** meat means to remove fat, gristle, or silver skin.

Turmeric is a spice, used more for its bright yellow color than flavor. It is used to color curries, pickles, margarine, and cloth.

Whisk means to beat in a fast circular motion. This makes the mixture lighter by beating in air. A **whisk** is also a light-bulb-shaped kitchen tool made of fine wires held together by a long handle.

Wok is a bowl-shaped metal pan used in Asian countries to cook foods. It is especially useful for quickly frying foods and the **stir-fry** method of cooking.

The Multicultural Cookbook
for Students

Africa

Africa is a large continent with a wide variety of soils, climates, people, and economic conditions. For these reasons, there are many foods and styles of eating in Africa, although there are a few foods that cut across borders and nationalities. Dried meat, such as the jerky recipe found in the section for the United States, and *fo* (a kind of stew) are common foods found throughout Africa. If you can't find a suitable recipe for the African country that you are interested in, try one of these recipes common to many nations.

In most African countries serving utensils are simple things from nature. Dried gourds are made into bowls of all shapes and sizes and are great for holding and serving food. Much of the cooking is performed over open fires. Frying is a very popular method of cooking all over Africa. Baking is done, but not in ovens with temperature gauges and plugged into electricity or gas; rather, covered bar-b-que pits are used.

One important point to remember as you read these recipes is that many of the people in Africa depend on their crops in order to eat. Natural disasters such as bad weather, or other catastrophies such as war, may create frightful shortages of food, which will require some sort of help or relief. The recipes we recommend here are to show you the kinds of foods people like to eat when food is available.

Tanzania

Tanzania is located on the eastern coast of Africa. The country's residents are fortunate to have many natural resources and a climate suited to agriculture. Many people are involved with agriculture both to provide their own food and to produce cash crops. The staple foods grown are **cassava,** corn, **sorghum, millet,** bananas, **plantains,** rice, potatoes, wheat, sweet potatoes, and papayas. One-pot meals are created from combining these foods, and a little spiced meat is usually added whenever possible. Usually, though, the people combine grains and beans or peas, such as millet with **lentils,** to replace meat. These combinations make protein-rich meals.

Cash crops include coffee, cloves, cashews, and tea. People in Western countries, such as those in Europe and the United States, love the flavor of Tanzanian coffee. The money Tanzanians gain from these exports is very important since it helps them buy goods that they cannot grow or make on their own.

The rivers, lakes, and coastal waters are great for fishing. Fish is very important in the Tanzanian diet, providing a great source of protein. Fish is used in sauces, soups, and stews, and is fried or plainly grilled.

Spiced Papaya

This dish is commonly eaten as a side dish to meat.

Yield: 6 servings

2 papayas, about 1 pound each, firm to the touch
2 to 4 tablespoons butter, margarine, or vegetable oil
salt to taste
1 teaspoon freshly ground nutmeg or 1/2 teaspoon ground nutmeg

Equipment: Steamer pan and rack or large-size saucepan with cover, strainer, or **colander;** large-size skillet

1. Using a sharp knife, cut papayas in half and discard seeds. Place cut side down on work surface and cut papayas crosswise into 1-inch wide slices. Using the knife, peel slices and cut each slice into 1-inch **cubes.** Repeat until all papaya meat is cut into cubes.
2. Fill bottom pan with just enough water to not boil dry yet not touching the steamer rack. Fit steamer rack, strainer, or colander into large saucepan, add papaya cubes, and cover tightly. Bring water to a boil over high heat, reduce to medium, and cook for about 10 minutes, until papaya is tender, not mushy.
3. Heat 2 tablespoons butter, margarine, or vegetable oil in skillet, add nutmeg, and mix well. Add steamed papaya and salt to taste. Add more butter, margarine, or vegetable oil, if necessary, and carefully toss to coat.

Serve hot as a side dish with meat.

Meatcakes

The small amount of meat used in this recipe demonstrates how meat can be stretched to feed many people, and the frying technique for cooking is representative of the most common way of cooking in Africa.

Yield: serves 6

1 pound ground meat
4 cups grated potatoes
1 cup grated carrot
1 egg, beaten
1/2 cup milk
1/2 cup flour
2 tablespoons sugar
1/2 teaspoon salt
1 teaspoon curry powder, or more to taste
1 teaspoon baking powder
2 to 4 tablespoons vegetable oil

Equipment: Grater, skillet, large-size mixing bowl, medium-size mixing bowl, mixing spoons, spatula

1. Put meat, potatoes, and carrots in large mixing bowl, add egg and milk, and using mixing spoon or clean hands, blend well.
2. Mix together flour, sugar, salt, 1 teaspoon curry powder, and baking powder in medium mixing bowl. Slowly add flour mixture to meat mixture, mixing continually with clean hands.
3. Heat 2 tablespoons oil in skillet over medium-high heat. Using clean hands, shape mixture into patties (about 1/2 cup size) and place side-by-side in hot skillet. Allow room to turn patties. Fry for about 5 minutes each side, or to desired doneness Continue frying patties until all the mixture is used. Add more oil if necessary. Keep patties in warm place until serving time.

Serve as the main dish, in a sandwich, or as a light snack.

Kenya

Nomadic herders live in the northern part of Kenya where most of the livestock is raised. There is a coastal strip to the south, and to the west are highlands that aren't good for farming. The eastern plateau is the most usable land for farming. Kenyans see livestock as a form of wealth. For this reason meat is not traditionally a major factor in the Kenyan's diet. People instead consume grains and vegetables and by-products of their livestock, such as milk. British settlers established Western farming and ranching methods in the fertile agricultural region of the eastern plateau which are still in use today. Corn was introduced to Africa over 100 years ago by Europeans and is now an important food throughout most of Africa. It is one example of European influence on the foods that Africans consume today.

Ugali   Cornmeal Porridge

The national dish of Kenya is a cornmeal mush called *Ugali*. It is cornmeal cooked with water to a thick consistency and poured out onto a board or plate for everyone to eat from. The following recipe for *ugali* could be made over an open fire outside, or in a kitchen. Beef broth with vegetables can be poured over it, and on special occasions chunks of meat are added to the broth.

Yield: serves 4 to 6

1 cup cold water
1 cup yellow cornmeal
1 teaspoon salt, more or less to taste
3 cups boiling water

Equipment: Medium-size saucepan, mixing spoon or **whisk**

1. Put cold water in saucepan, and, mixing continually, add cornmeal and salt. Bring to a boil over high heat, and, mixing continually, slowly add 3 cups boiling water to prevent lumps.
2. Reduce to simmer, cover, and cook for about 8 minutes, mixing frequently to prevent sticking. Add salt to taste and mix well.

Serve *ugali* in individual bowls with cream, sugar, syrup, **ghee** (see recipe page 163), or butter poured over it.

Sukuma Wiki   Collard Greens

Green vegetables are important to the African diet. In Kenya, collard greens are both cheap and popular. The dish *sukuma wiki* literally translates to "stretch the week." In Africa the following recipe would also be made with **cassava** leaves or potato leaves if collard greens were not available. Any other greens can be substituted. "Doing your own thing" is typical in African cooking—follow the basic recipe using what is on hand and easily available.

Yield: serves 4 to 6

6 cups tightly packed, chopped collard greens (or other available greens), fresh, washed and drained; or frozen, thawed
2 to 4 tablespoons vegetable oil
1 onion, **coarsely chopped**
1 cup chopped **stewed** tomatoes
1 green chili pepper, **seeded** and **finely chopped** or 1 teaspoon ground red pepper
3 tablespoons lemon juice
1 tablespoon all-purpose flour
1/2 to 1 cup water
salt and pepper to taste

Equipment: **Steamer** or medium-size saucepan with a cover, fitted with metal **colander** or strainer; mixing spoon; large-size skillet

1. Fill bottom of steamer or saucepan with about an inch of water. Insert basket, colander, or strainer filled with greens, and bring to boil over high heat. Turn down heat if necessary so that water boils but doesn't evaporate. Cover and steam for about 8 minutes.
2. Heat the 2 tablespoons of oil in a skillet over medium high heat. Add onion, tomatoes, and pepper and cook about 3 minutes or until onion is soft. Mix well. Reduce heat to low and add remaining oil, if necessary, to prevent sticking.
3. Mix lemon juice, flour, and 1/2 cup water in cup until well blended. Pour into onion mixture and mix well. Add remaining 1/2 cup water, cooked greens, salt and pepper to taste, and mix well. Increase heat to medium, cover, and cook for 3 minutes to heat through.

Serve the greens as a side dish with meat stew.

Somalia

Somalia is a poor country in northeastern Africa that suffers frequent droughts and is poorly suited for farming. As this book is going to press, the Somalis are particularly suffering and starving, not only from lack of food to eat but also from warring tribes who are preventing relief shipment of food from being distributed within Somalia. Somalis are nomadic herders of camels, which are a major source of pride and wealth. They drink camel milk, eat camel meat, and use camels to carry necessities. Camel's milk is a food most basic to them. During the wet season two camels can provide enough milk to feed 10 people; four camels during the dry season will feed 10 people. Herding animals is a long-standing tradition in Somalia because the land to the north is dry, arid, and grassy. Growing crops is not easy in this area; instead people trade their sheep, goats, and camels in the cities for money to purchase the other items they need such as tea. Much trade is conducted with Arabic nations.

To the south, however, the land is more fertile. Somalis who moved into this area changed their occupations from herding to farming. Along the Jubba and Shabeelle rivers people grow bananas, sugar cane, corn, vegetables, and **sorghum**. Fishing is being developed as an industry. Interestingly, Somali nomads despise eating fish; the farmers to the south are the nation's fish consumers, and what they don't eat is exported.

Somalis are Sunni Muslim. This is important to note because no form of alcohol is allowed. Instead Somalis drink tea or milk.

Curry in a Hurry Dish

The main meat or vegetable of this dish is whatever is on hand. Precooked ingredients are needed, and this is a good dish for using up leftovers. Because it uses precooked food this dish assembles fast, just right for someone in a hurry or someone cooking over a wood fire who needs to conserve fuel.

Yield: 6 servings

2 to 4 tablespoons vegetable oil
1 onion, **coarsely chopped**
2 tablespoons curry powder
1/2 cup all-purpose flour
1/2 cup cold water
3 cups beef or chicken broth, homemade or canned
3 cups cooked beef, pork, lamb, chicken, turkey, or combination, cut into bite-size **cubes**
3 cups cooked vegetables, such as carrots, celery, eggplant, zucchini, tomatoes
salt and pepper to taste

Equipment: Large saucepan, mixing spoon

1. Heat 2 tablespoons oil in saucepan over medium-high heat, add onions, and, mixing continually, fry until limp, about 3 minutes. Add curry powder and mix well. Add more oil if necessary.
2. Mix flour with 1/2 cup cold water, blend to a smooth paste, and add to skillet, mixing continually to prevent lumps. Cook for about 3 minutes. Add broth, mix well, and bring to a boil. Reduce heat to simmer.
3. Slowly add cubed meat, vegetables, and salt and pepper to taste, mix well, and cook to heat through, about 5 minutes.

Serve with *injera* bread (see recipe page 8).

Ethiopia

Ethiopia is an independent nation on the coast of east central Africa. Ethiopians have their own unique, world-famous style of cooking that has remained independent of European influence.

Ethiopia has a variety of terrains ranging from high plateaus to lowland valleys. The best areas for agriculture are the plateaus. These plateaus provide a fertile soil and a year-round growing season, which allows most people to farm in Ethiopia. Crops include **millet**, **sorghum**, barley, wheat, corn, **plantains**, potatoes, peanuts, sugar cane, and peas. An important cash crop is coffee, which grows wild and is cultivated here. It comes from the Kaffa province, which is where coffee got its name. In fact, the first known coffee plant was found in this area. *Teff*, a millet unique to Ethiopia, is what the bread *injera* is made from. *Wats*, fiery hot stews, are served on *injera*.

The national dish of Ethiopia is *doro wat*, made with chicken and **hard-cooked eggs**. *Wats* (stews) can also be made of beef, fish, **lentils**, or **chickpeas**. These last two ingredients are used during the religious days when meat is forbidden. Here we have a chicken *wat* that you can spice up to the level you will enjoy.

Yield: serves 4 to 6

1/2 cup butter or margarine
2 cups chopped onions
3 cloves garlic, **finely chopped**, or 1 teaspoon garlic granules
1 cup tomato paste
3 cups water or chicken broth, homemade or canned
1 teaspoon ground ginger
1/2 teaspoon ground cinnamon
1/4 teaspoon ground cloves
1 teaspoon ground red pepper, more or less to taste
1 chicken, cut into serving-size pieces
6 peeled, **hard-cooked eggs**
salt and pepper to taste

Equipment: Large-size saucepan or **Dutch oven,** mixing spoon

1. Melt butter or margarine in saucepan or Dutch oven over medium high heat. Add onions and garlic, and, stirring frequently, fry until onions are golden brown, about 5 minutes. Reduce heat to simmer, add tomato paste, water or broth, ginger, cinnamon, cloves, and red pepper to taste, and mix well.
2. Add chicken pieces and coat well with sauce. Increase heat to high, bring to a boil, reduce to simmer, cover, and cook for about 45 minutes. Turn chicken pieces over to prevent sticking, add eggs, cover with sauce and continue cooking for about 10 minutes more, or until chicken is tender. Remove from heat and add salt and pepper to taste.

To serve, place the pot of stew in the middle of the table and have guests help themselves, using the fingers of the right hand. Serve with hot rice and *injera* bread.

Injera   *Thin Round Ethiopian Bread*

Teff, the **millet** used by Ethiopians, is not easy to find outside of this region, so we have adapted a recipe that closely resembles real *injera*. Baked on a griddle or in a skillet, this thin pancake-like bread makes a perfect scoop for Ethiopian *wats* (stews).

Yield: about 18 (pancakes)

4 cups self-rising flour
1 cup whole wheat flour
1 teaspoon baking powder
2 cups club soda
4 to 4 1/2 cups water
2 to 8 tablespoons vegetable oil

Equipment: Large-size mixing bowl, mixing spoon, 9-inch skillet, clean kitchen towel, 12-inch-square aluminum foil

1. Put self-rising and whole wheat flours in bowl, add baking powder, and mix well. Add club soda and 4 cups water, and mix into a smooth, thin batter.
2. Heat 2 tablespoons oil in skillet over medium high heat. Thinly spread 1/2 cup of the batter into skillet. Remove from heat and swirl batter so that it makes a very thin pancake; return to heat. When moisture evaporates and small holes appear, as in a pancake, remove from heat. Do not brown or make too crisp (adjust heat accordingly). Cook one side only.
3. Flip skillet over to release thin pancake onto clean kitchen towel spread out to cover work surface. If pancake sticks to skillet, lightly tap rim against work surface top. If breads are too pasty, add a little water to thin batter. Add a little oil to the skillet for each pancake to prevent sticking, and repeat until all batter is used. When pancakes are cool, stack, and cover with foil to prevent drying out.

To serve, set platter of pancake breads on the table and have your guests help themselves. Tear off pieces of *injera* and use them to scoop up the food.

Uganda

Uganda is a land-locked country that sits on the Equator in east central Africa. In Uganda almost everyone cultivates the land and grows their own food. **Cassava**, sweet potatoes, corn, **millet**, **sorghum**, beans, and peanuts are among the important crops of this country. The bulk of the crops are grown in the fertile area south of Lake Kyoga.

Peanut Butter Candy

One of the principal crops of Uganda, as well as most of Africa, is peanuts. They are nutritious and hardy, making them a first-rate survival food. In this recipe peanuts and highly prized honey are combined to make a sweet treat.

Yield: 36 pieces

1 cup peanut butter, either smooth or chunky
1 cup honey, slightly warm
1 to 2 cups powdered milk or toasted wheat germ, or combination
1/2 cup finely grated coconut

Equipment: Medium-size mixing bowl, flat pan (such as pie pan), flat dish covered with wax paper

1. Put peanut butter and honey in bowl and blend well using clean hands. Add 1 cup powdered milk or wheat germ and, using clean hands, blend into a stiff dough, adding more powdered milk or wheat germ as needed.
2. Form mixture into small 1-inch balls or patties. Put coconut in flat pan. Roll balls or patties in coconut to coat. Place side by side on dish covered with wax paper, cover with another wax paper sheet, and refrigerate.

Serve as a sweet snack treat.

Ground Nut Sauce with Greens

Yield: serves 4 to 6

2 tablespoons vegetable oil
1 onion, **finely chopped**
2 tomatoes, finely chopped
1 cup chopped okra, fresh or frozen
1 cup finely chopped peanuts
1/4 cup sesame seeds
4 cups water or chicken broth, homemade or canned
1 teaspoon curry powder
salt to taste
4 cups chopped collard greens or spinach, fresh, washed, **trimmed**, and **blanched**; or frozen and thawed

Equipment: Large-size skillet with cover, mixing spoon

1. Heat oil in skillet over medium high heat. Add onion, tomatoes, okra and fry, stirring frequently, until onions are soft (about 3 minutes). Add nuts, seeds, and water or chicken broth. Increase heat to high, bring to a boil, reduce to simmer, and cook for about 10 minutes, stirring frequently, until mixture slightly thickens. Add curry powder and salt to taste and mix well.
2. Add blanched or thawed greens to mixture and mix well to coat the greens with the sauce. Cover and cook for 10 minutes or until greens are heated through and limp.

Serve greens as a side dish with meat or beans.

Mozambique

Mozambique, an independent nation in east Africa, was formerly called Portuguese East Africa, and Portuguese people have greatly influenced the food. Portugal set up outposts in Mozambique beginning in 1505, colonized the country, and were forced to leave after an independence movement took power in 1974. The Portuguese imported a vast assortment of fruits and vegetables to Mozambique and cultivated them in climates and soils similar to those in the plants' homelands. Among these foods are oranges, lemons, limes, pineapples, chilies, peppers, corn, tomatoes, sweet potatoes, **cassavas**, and bananas.

Arroz de Coco   Coconut Milk Rice

Yield: serves 4 to 6

2 tablespoons vegetable oil
1 green bell pepper, **seeded, finely chopped**

1 cup finely chopped onion
1 cup uncooked rice
3 cups coconut milk, canned, frozen, or homemade (see recipe page 208)
2 tomatoes, **peeled**, finely chopped or 1 cup canned stewed tomatoes
salt to taste
1/2 teaspoon ground red pepper, more or less to taste

Equipment: Large-size skillet with cover or **Dutch oven**, mixing spoon

1. Heat oil in skillet or Dutch oven over medium heat. Add bell pepper and onion, stirring frequently, and cook for about 5 minutes or until vegetables are soft but not brown.
2. Reduce heat to low, add rice, and stir continually until grains are evenly coated. Add coconut milk and tomatoes, increase heat to high, and bring to a boil; reduce heat to simmer, cover, and cook for 20 minutes or until liquid is absorbed and rice is tender.
3. Remove skillet or Dutch oven from heat and mix in salt and ground red pepper to taste. Cover mixture and set aside for 10 minutes to allow flavors to blend.

To serve, **fluff** the rice with a fork and serve directly from the skillet or Dutch oven, or transfer to serving bowl.

Ovos Moles de Mango   Mango and Egg Pudding

Mangos were introduced to Africa by way of India, where they are thought to have originated. They are nutritious and delicious.

Yield: serves 4 to 6

2 ripe mangos, peeled, **seeded**, and **coarsely chopped**
1/4 cup *each* fresh lemon juice, strained, and water
2 cups sugar
1 teaspoon *each* ground cinnamon and ground clove
5 egg yolks (refrigerate egg whites to use at another time)
whipped cream or prepared whipped topping for garnish

Equipment: Large-size mixing bowl, potato masher or electric blender, medium-size saucepan, wooden mixing spoon, **egg beater** or electric mixer

1. Mash mangos, lemon juice, and water in mixing bowl using potato masher, or place in electric blender and blend until smooth and lump-free.
2. Pour mixture into saucepan. Add sugar, cinnamon, and cloves, and, stirring continually, bring to a boil over high heat. Reduce heat to simmer and cook until mixture thickens (about 10 minutes—mix frequently to prevent sticking). Remove from heat.
3. Put egg yolks into large mixing bowl, and, using the mixer, mix yolks until slightly thick, about 1 minute. Continue beating while slowly pouring hot mixture into yolks. Beat until smooth and thick (about 5 minutes). Cool to room temperature and refrigerate for 2 hours before serving. The dessert will thicken as it cools.

Serve pudding in small individual bowls as dessert. Top with whipped cream.

Yield: 10 to 12 slices

1 1/2 cups cake flour
2 teaspoons baking powder
1 teaspoon ground cinnamon
1/2 teaspoon ground cloves
1 cup butter or margarine at room temperature
2 cups sugar
4 eggs, **separated**
1/2 cup heavy cream
1 cup cooked mashed potatoes, fresh or instant
1 cup **finely chopped** nuts—cashews, **blanched** almonds, or pecans
4 teaspoons finely grated lemon peel
1 teaspoon almond extract

Equipment: **Sifter**, medium-size mixing bowl, large-size mixing bowl, electric mixer, mixing spoon, **whisk**, greased 9-inch **springform pan**

Preheat oven to 350° F

1. Sift flour, baking powder, cinnamon, and cloves into medium-size mixing bowl.
2. Using mixer, blend butter and sugar in large mixing bowl. Add egg yolks (one at a time) mixing continually until smooth and creamy. Stirring continually, add cream, mashed potatoes, flour mixture, nuts, lemon peel, and extract until mixture is smooth and lump-free.
3. Put egg whites into clean, dry, medium-size mixing bowl, and beat with electric mixer until they are stiff and form peaks.
4. Gently **fold** whites into batter until well blended, using spoon or whisk.
5. Pour mixture into springform pan and bake in oven for about 60 minutes, until a toothpick inserted into center of cake comes out clean.

Serve cake while still slightly warm or at room temperature.

Madagascar

Madagascar is a large island (the fourth largest in the world) in the Indian Ocean just off the east coast of Africa. In Madagascar many different kinds of crops can be raised because of the wide variety of climates and soils. Agriculture is very important to Madagascar's economy. Two-thirds of the world's vanilla is produced in Madagascar, and it helps bring money to the country. Rice, however, is the staple crop and is grown on over one-half of the cultivated land. In fact, to the Merina, the predominate ethnic group in Madagascar, rice is the only real food, and everything else is considered flavoring. Guards are posted 24 hours a day to drive birds away during the last two growing months of the rice. There is such a large bird population that there soon wouldn't be any rice left for the people to eat if it were not guarded!

Because France colonized Madagascar from 1896 to 1960, there are very strong French influences in Madagascar's cooking, as reflected in the following two recipes. The vegetables in these recipes would actually be mashed together in Madagascar, but we suggest that you finely chop them; the result will be almost the same with less work and better texture.

Soupe a la Malgache   Soup of the Malagasies

Yield: serves 6 to 8

2 pounds veal or beef bones
8 cups water
2 cups **stewed** tomatoes with juice
3 white potatoes, peeled and **finely chopped**
2 onions, peeled and finely chopped
3 carrots (trim tops) peeled and finely chopped
1 turnip, peeled and finely chopped
1 leek, finely chopped, washed, and drained
1 cup finely chopped string beans, fresh (**trimmed**) or frozen
salt and pepper to taste
4 cups cooked rice (cooked according to directions on package)

Equipment: Large-size saucepan with cover, mixing spoon

1. Put meat bones in saucepan, add water, bring to a boil, reduce to simmer, and cook for 1 hour.
2. Add tomatoes, potatoes, onions, carrots, turnip, leek, and string beans; cover and continue simmering for 1 hour more. Add salt and pepper to taste and mix well.

Serve *soupe* thick and hot over large servings of cooked rice.

Tomatoes Rougaille   Tomato Sauce

Yield: serves 4 to 6

2 cups **finely chopped** green bell peppers, **trimmed** and **seeded**
2 cups **stewed** tomatoes with juice
1 onion, finely chopped
few drops liquid hot pepper sauce, more or less to taste
salt and pepper to taste
6 cups cooked rice (cooked according to directions on package); keep warm

Equipment: Medium-size bowl, mixing spoon

Put green peppers, tomatoes, onion, hot sauce, and salt and pepper to taste in the bowl. Mix well, adjust seasonings (salt and pepper), and refrigerate.

Serve *rougaille* over warm cooked rice.

South Africa

In South Africa, the long domination of Europeans has had a lasting effect on the foods and cooking of the people, both black and white, who reside there. South Africa's location on the tip of Africa has made it a major resupply point for trade ships. The Dutch East India Company founded a settlement in 1652 on the cape precisely for this reason. They organized and stocked farms with the intention of supplying their ships with good food. A blending of East Asian, Malay, and Indian cooking styles and ingredients with the European touch has created a unique South African style of cooking which can be seen in the following recipes.

Bobotje
Meat Curry Casserole with Custard Topping

Bobotje is the popular national dish of South Africa. It can be made with any meat, or combination of meats, cooked or uncooked. It's a great way of using leftovers. The use of curry demonstrates an Indian (India) influence.

Yield: serves 6 to 8

4 cups **finely chopped** cooked beef or poultry
1 cup crumbled soft white bread
2 cups milk
4 eggs
1 onion, finely chopped
1 apple, **cored** and finely chopped
1 tablespoon *each* curry powder and sugar
1/2 cup *each* chopped almonds and raisins
2 tablespoons white vinegar
salt and pepper to taste
6 bay leaves
sprinkle of paprika for garnish

Equipment: Large-size mixing bowl, mixing fork or clean hands, greased oven-proof 2-quart casserole, baking pan larger than casserole, small-size saucepan, small-size mixing bowl, **whisk** or fork

1. Put meat, crumbled bread, 1 cup milk, 1 egg, onion, apple, curry powder, almonds, raisins, vinegar, and sugar into large mixing bowl, and mix well using fork or clean hands. Add salt and pepper to taste and blend well. Transfer mixture to casserole and pat smooth.
2. Preheat oven to 350° F.
3. Put remaining 1 cup milk in small saucepan, add bay leaves, and heat over medium high heat to boiling, remove at once and allow to cool to room temperature; remove bay leaves and discard.

4. Put remaining 3 eggs in small bowl and beat with whisk or fork. Add milk, mix well, and pour egg mixture over meat. Set casserole in larger pan with 1 inch of water, and bake in oven until contents are firm (about 45 minutes).

To serve, cut into squares. Serve with side dishes of rice and **chutney**.

Geel Rys   Yellow Rice

Geel rys (yellow rice) gets its name from the **turmeric** added for both color and taste.

Yield: serves 4 to 6

3 cups water
1 1/2 cups uncooked rice
1 cup seedless raisins
1/2 teaspoon turmeric
1 teaspoon cinnamon
3 tablespoons light brown sugar
5 tablespoons butter or margarine

Equipment: Medium-size saucepan with cover, mixing spoon

1. Bring water to a boil over high heat, add rice, reduce heat to simmer, cover, and cook for 20 minutes or until rice is tender. Remove from heat.
2. Add raisins, turmeric, cinnamon, brown sugar and butter or margarine; mix well, cover, and reduce heat to warm for 10 minutes.

Serve *geel rys* as a side dish with stews, meat, poultry, or fish.

Engelegte   Curry Pickled Fish

Combining curry seasonings with pickling spices is an easy and tasty way to preserve fish. It keeps for several days without refrigeration. Sailors on the Dutch spice ships learned of this preserving process from the Malaysians. When the South Africans heard about a new way of preserving food, curry pickled fish soon became very popular.

Yield: serves 6 to 8

3 to 6 tablespoons vegetable oil
6 skin-on fish **fillets**, fresh or frozen, washed and patted dry
3 cups vinegar
1 teaspoon *each* curry powder, **turmeric**, salt
3 tablespoons sugar
2 onions, thinly sliced

Equipment: Large-size skillet, pancake turner or spatula, glass or earthenware bowl with lid or plastic wrap, small-size saucepan, mixing spoon

1. Heat 3 tablespoons oil in skillet over medium heat, add fish fillets and fry on both sides until fish is done (about 8 minutes per side—the flesh becomes **opaque** white and easily **flakes** with a fork). Add more oil if necessary. With pancake turner or spatula, carefully transfer fillets to bowl. Slightly overlap fillets to cover the bottom of bowl.

2. Heat vinegar, curry powder, turmeric, salt, and sugar in saucepan over high heat, mix well, and bring to a boil. Add onion slices, reduce to simmer, cover, and cook for 8 minutes. Remove from heat and cool to room temperature.
3. Pour vinegar mixture over fillets, cover with lid or plastic wrap, and refrigerate for about 12 hours before serving.

Serve *engelegte* cold, with onion slices, on a bed of lettuce as an appetizer or salad.

Lesotho

Lesotho is a small independent country surrounded by South Africa. Food has to be imported because of the overworked and poor soil in Lesotho. Small gardens are kept by most households and add greatly to the imported foods the people must live on. Most workers go to South Africa to earn money to purchase food for their families; more than 100,000 work in South African mines.

Setjetsa

Cereals are important to the diet of the people of Lesotho because they are inexpensive and nutritious. This recipe makes good use of garden vegetables and cereal.

Yield: 6 to 8

4 cups pumpkin, peeled, washed, and cut into small pieces or canned
3 cups water
1 tablespoon sugar
1 tablespoon butter, margarine, or vegetable oil
2 cups cornmeal
1/2 teaspoon salt, more or or less to taste

Equipment: Medium-size saucepan, mixing spoon

1. Combine pumpkin and water in saucepan and cook on medium heat until pumpkin is soft.
2. Add sugar and butter, margarine, or vegetable oil and mix well. Slowly add cornmeal, mixing continually, until mixture is well blended and smooth.
3. Reduce heat to low and continue cooking for 30 minutes. Add salt to taste.

Serve as a side dish with meat and vegetables.

Fried Ripe Plantains

Yield: serves 4 to 6

4 to 6 ripe (black-skin) **plantains**
1 cup vegetable oil

Equipment: Sharp knife, medium-size skillet, slotted spoon or metal spatula, paper towels

1. Peel ripe plantains and cut slices on an angle about 1 inch thick.
2. Heat oil in skillet over medium-high heat, add plantain slices, a few at a time, and fry on both sides until golden brown (about 3 minutes). Remove from oil with slotted spoon or spatula and drain on paper towels.

Serve ripe plantains hot as a side dish with meat, fish, or poultry.

Cornmeal Flatbread

Corn is an important crop in Lesotho, and the following recipe is a simple way to make a cornmeal flat bread.

Yield: serves 6 to 8

2 cups boiling water
1/2 cup cornmeal
1/2 teaspoon salt
4 strips fried bacon, finely crumbled with drippings

Equipment: Nonstick or lightly greased 10 x 15-inch baking sheet with raised edges, oven mitts, medium-size mixing bowl, mixing spoon or **whisk**, heat-proof surface, spatula

Preheat oven to 425° F.
1. Put greased baking sheet in oven to preheat for 5 minutes.
1. Put cornmeal in mixing bowl. Add boiling water, salt, and crumbled bacon and drippings, stirring continually
2. Using oven mitts, remove baking sheet and place on heat-proof surface. Pour mixture over the hot baking sheet. Using the spatula, spread mixture evenly, wafer-thin, completely covering pan bottom. Return to oven and bake until lightly browned, about 5 minutes. Remove from oven and cut into 2- or 3-inch squares.

Serve flatbread warm for best flavor. It is excellent with soups or stews.

Zimbabwe

Zimbabwe, formerly Rhodesia, is landlocked in south central Africa. The Shona people of Zimbabwe make up 80 percent of the population. They are moving from farming and cattle raising to feed their families to living in town-ships to earn money, but farming is still an important part of their survival. Corn is a major factor in their diets as in other African countries; meat is eaten but plays a lesser role. The land is sandy, unfertile, and hard pressed to support the population; overuse has hurt agriculture in Zimbabwe. Among the crops grown are corn, yams, pump-
kins, peanuts, and papaya (also know as paw-paws). Fish from lakes and rivers are enjoyed both fresh and in dried form. Drying fish allows people who live away from lakes to eat this rich form of protein.

The Ndebele people, another group in Zimbabwe, traditionally lived by growing **millet** and hunting. Cattle were used for milk. Hunting has declined in recent years, and so cattle now provide the meat for the Ndebele. Meat is a main ingredient in their diet, along with cereals. They make a thick porridge called *isitshwala* that they serve with soured milk or mix with wild greens found locally. Corn has taken the place of millet. When ground, it makes a flour used in mealies also called *sadza*, the national food of Zimbabwe. Stews of beef, chicken, or vegetables are poured on top of the *sadza*.

There are strong English influences in Zimbabwe cities because of years of English rule, and native Zimbabweans love their tea almost as much as the English do; a pot is kept brewing on the stove at all times. City dwellers are very European in their food preferences and eating habits. They make sure that their supermarkets carry a worldwide assortment of foods.

Breedie   Beef Stew

Yield: serves 4 to 6

2 to 4 tablespoons vegetable oil
1 pound lean stewing beef, **cubed**
2 onions, **finely chopped**
2 cups **stewed** tomatoes, homemade or canned
1 cup corn kernels, fresh (cut from the cob) or frozen (thawed)
1/2 pound green beans, fresh or frozen, cut in 1/2-inch pieces
1/2 cup seedless raisins
3 teaspoons sugar
salt and pepper to taste

Equipment: Large-size saucepan with cover or **Dutch oven**, mixing spoon

1. Heat 2 tablespoons of oil in a saucepan or Dutch oven over medium-high heat. Add meat and cook until brown, about 8 minutes, stirring frequently. Reduce heat to medium, add onions, and fry until soft (about 5 minutes). Add more oil if necessary.
2. Add tomatoes, corn, green beans, raisins, sugar, and salt and pepper to taste. Mix well and reduce to simmer. Cover and cook for 30 minutes or until meat is tender.

Serve *breedie* hot over a mound of snowy white rice.

Cornmeal Cake

Yield: serves 6

1 cup yellow cornmeal
4 cups hot boiled milk
2 eggs, beaten
3/4 cup butter or margarine
1/2 cup sugar
1 tablespoon vanilla extract
1/2 cup sour cream

Equipment: Medium-size saucepan, wooden mixing spoon, 8-inch cake pan, spatula

1. Put milk, eggs, 1/2 cup butter or margarine, and sugar in saucepan. Bring to a boil over high heat, remove from heat, and add cornmeal, stirring continually to prevent lumps. Turn heat to low and continue cooking for 20 minutes or until thickened; stir frequently to prevent sticking. Add vanilla and mix well.
2. Preheat oven to 350° F.
3. Melt remaining 1/4 cup butter and pour into cake pan. Swirl pan to coat bottom and sides, and add mixture. Bake for 30 minutes, until cake is golden brown and a toothpick inserted in the center comes out clean. Remove from oven; then using spatula, carefully cover top with sour cream, and return to oven for 15 minutes more or until top is bubbly and lightly browned.

Serve cake for dessert while still warm, cut into squares.

Botswana

Botswana is a popular country for tourists because of the large herds of big animals that still survive in the mixed tree and grass savanna land of Botswana. Botswana is prosperous financially because minerals such as diamonds and gold are exported. Therefore, people eat better and have better health. Agriculture is very difficult in Botswana because it is a dry country. Botswanans do grow corn, **sorghum**, **millet**, black-eyed peas, and beans, however. Cattle raising is the most important food-producing activity in Botswana; the country is the continent's largest cattle exporter.

Dodo
Green or Yellow Plantain Chips

Yield: serves 4 to 6

6 green or yellow **plantains**
2 to 4 cups vegetable oil
salt to taste

Equipment: Vegetable knife, medium-size skillet, slotted spoon or metal spatula, paper towels

1. Peel plantains by cutting through the skin lengthwise and opening with your finger. Slice on an angle into 1/4-inch-thick ovals.
2. Heat about 1/4-inch oil in skillet over medium heat. Fry plantain slices, a few at a time, turning frequently, until brown, about 5 minutes. Use slotted spoon or spatula to turn over and remove from oil; drain on paper towels. Add more oil to the skillet if necessary. Sprinkle chips with salt to taste.

Serve the chips as an accompaniment to everything from breakfast eggs to dinner steak or eat as a midday snack. *Dodo* are eaten either hot or cold.

Namibia

Namibia, also known as South West Africa, was administered by the Republic of South Africa. Namibia is mostly high desert plateau land that supports cattle raising but little agriculture. Namibians live in rural communities. Cattle raising goes on mostly in the northern and central parts of Namibia. White Namibians, mostly descendants of Germans who ruled for many years, dominate this cattle-raising region. These people maintain the customs and eating habits of old Germany, adapting them to their surroundings; for example, ostrich eggs are used instead of chicken eggs at times. Can you imagine using an ostrich egg? Only one is needed to stir up a pan full of scrambled eggs! The San, a dwindling group of people who still forage for food, also eat ostrich eggs, and then use the shell to carry water. Sheep and goat raising is concentrated in the arid southern region. Fishing along the coast provides food and export income. Milk is important to Namibians' diets and is drunk both fresh and soured. Ovambo tribe people, who live both in Namibia and Angola, raise **millet** as a staple crop. The millet is pounded into a flour, then made into a thick porridge (recipe follows). They also grow corn for beer and grow beans and gourds as secondary crops.

Thick Millet Porridge

Yield: serves 4

1 cup **millet**, available at most health food and Asian food stores
3 cups water
1/4 teaspoon salt
Milk and honey or sugar to taste

Equipment: Electric blender, mixing spoon, saucepan

1. Grind millet in blender until powdered (or buy in powdered form).
2. In saucepan boil water and salt. When it reaches a gentle boil, stir in millet "flour," and turn heat down to medium low. Continue to stir until lump-free. Cook for 10 minutes more.

Serve porridge in bowls with milk and sugar. This recipe makes a nice alternative to breakfast cereals.

Angola

Angola, formerly known as Portuguese West Africa, is located on the southwest coast of Africa. The Portuguese dominated Angolans throughout this century until independence was granted in 1975. The cities reflect the Portuguese influence on cooking, where you can find baked goods and hot spices of Portuguese liking (see following recipe). Life is changing slowly for the rural people. Agriculture is still practiced by hand, as it has always been. The land is fairly good for agriculture, although oil has become the primary export. **Cassava** is a staple crop. The leaves are made into a spinach-like dish that is nutty flavored; the roots are dried and pounded into flour. Many garden vegetables are grown including eggplant, corn, rice, peas, and tomatoes.

Galinha Muamba — Angolan Chicken Dish

Yield: serves 6

1 teaspoon red pepper flakes
1 teaspoon ground ginger
1 onion, **finely chopped**
3 cloves garlic, finely chopped or 1 teaspoon garlic granules
salt and pepper to taste
1/2 cup lemon juice
2 to 3 cups water
2 to 4 tablespoons vegetable oil, more or less as needed
2 pounds chicken, cut into serving pieces

Equipment: Small-size mixing bowl, mixing spoon, gallon-size plastic baggie or bowl with cover, paper towels, large-size skillet, tongs, 9 x 12 baking sheet, aluminum foil

1. Put red pepper flakes, ginger, onion, garlic, salt and pepper to taste, lemon juice, 2 cups water, and 2 tablespoons vegetable oil in small bowl and mix well to blend. Pour into baggie and add chicken pieces. Seal baggie and shake vigorously to coat chicken. Refrigerate for about 4 hours. Rotate baggie frequently to coat chicken. If no baggies are available, put chicken in a large bowl and cover with mixture, making sure all pieces are coated. Cover and refrigerate for about 4 hours. Rotate chicken pieces in **marinade** frequently.
2. Remove chicken from marinade, pat dry with paper towels, and place on paper-towel-covered work surface. Set aside marinade.
3. Heat 2 tablespoons oil in skillet over medium-high heat. Add chicken pieces, a few at a time, and brown on both sides. Add more oil if necessary. Use tongs to turn pieces. Place browned pieces side-by-side in baking pan.
4. Preheat oven to 350°F.
5. Pour marinade over chicken in pan, cover tightly with foil, and bake for about 35 minutes until tender.

Serve chicken with vegetables and rice.

Zambia / Zaire

The Ndembu tribe lives both in Zambia and Zaire, and so the recipes that follow can be used for both countries. The Ndembu subsist on **cassava** and hunting. Cash crops and the canning of pineapples and tomatoes have changed their economy in the recent past. Changing subsistence farming, where people are only able to raise enough food to feed their families, to commercial farming, where people raise enough extra food to sell to others, is difficult. Most villagers grow **millet**, corn, **sorghum**, and **cassava**. Other food crops include sweet potato, **taro**, yams, peanuts, peas, beans, pumpkins, sugar cane, bananas, and rice. The cattle-killing tse-tse fly prevents cattle raising in northern Zaire. The people who live there hunt and fish to supplement their meat diet. They also keep chickens. Just imagine trotting home from a fishing trip to the Zaire River with a nice mess of fish for the family to use in the following recipe.

Fish and Greens

Yield: serves 6

1/4 cup vegetable oil
4 onions, **finely chopped**
1 1/2 cups **stewed** tomatoes with juice, homemade or canned
1 cup water
1/2 teaspoon ground red pepper
2 cups tightly packed chopped greens, fresh, washed and stemmed: mustard greens, kale, spinach, turnip greens, dandelion greens, or collard greens
6 fish **fillets**, about 6 ounces each and cut each into 3 pieces
1 teaspoon paprika
salt and pepper to taste

Equipment: Large-size saucepan with cover, mixing spoon

1. Heat oil in saucepan over medium-high heat, add onions, and cook until tender (about 3 minutes). Add tomatoes, water, and red pepper, and mix well. Add greens, increase heat to boil, and mix well. Reduce to simmer, cover, and cook for 5 minutes.
2. Lay fish on top of greens. Sprinkle with paprika, add salt and pepper to taste, and increase heat to boil. Reduce to simmer, cover, and cook for about 16 minutes, until fish **flakes** easily with a fork.

Serve fish and greens right from the pan. A large bowl of rice or beans can be served with it. In Zaire, this dish is served with yams or sweet potatoes.

Chicken Moambe   *Chicken Stew*

In the Congo/Zaire River region the favorite dish is *chicken moambe.* There are many ways of making it, but all include onions, celery, and tomato sauce. Most African countries are now growing and canning tomatoes. It is not unusual to find them now being added to many native dishes.

Yield: serves 6 to 8

3 to 4 pounds chicken, cut into serving pieces
6 cups water
2 tablespoons vegetable oil

1 cup **finely chopped** onion
1 cup finely chopped celery
1 cup tomato sauce, canned
1 teaspoon ground nutmeg
salt and pepper to taste

Equipment: Large-size saucepan with cover, medium-size skillet, mixing spoon

1. Put chicken pieces and water in saucepan. Bring mixture to a boil over medium-high heat, reduce to simmer, cover, and cook until chicken is tender, about 40 minutes.
2. Heat oil in skillet over medium-high heat. Add onions and celery, fry until soft (about 5 minutes), and mix well. Reduce heat to simmer, add tomato sauce, nutmeg, salt and pepper to taste, and mix well. Add mixture to chicken, mix well, and continue simmering for about 20 minutes, until flavors are well blended.

Serve *chicken moambe* with side dishes of rice and beans.

Central African Republic

Central African Republic takes its name in part from its location, smack in the middle of Africa. The land consists of a high plateau that covers most of the country with rain forests in the south. Even though Central African Republic is just north of the Equator, the high altitudes of the plateau keep it for the most part from being a hot country. Agricultural work is done by 85 percent of the people, mostly livestock raising and subsistence farming. The most common method of farming is the slash and burn technique. Staples grown are **millet**, rice, **cassava**, peanuts, beans, sesame, and corn. Bananas are grown in the rain forests. Cassava is served at almost every meal for many Central Africans. Cassava roots are pounded, grated, and dried to make flour and then mixed with water to make the sour-tasting dough. Dried cassava keeps several weeks. Even though cassava grows easily and well, it does not have the nutritional value that other harder-to-grow crops have, such as peanuts. **Millet** porridge is made from pounded millet (see index for millet recipes). People who live in the cities have a more balanced diet including meat and fruits and assorted vegetables. Fishing along the rivers provides a needed source of protein for the people, who supplement their diets through hunting as well.

Sesame Cakes

Yield: serves 4 to 6

1 cup roasted sesame seeds, ground (use blender, mortar/pestle, or food processor to grind). Buy seeds in bulk at outlets such as health food stores.
1/4 cup water or less (just enough to make flour stick together)
salt to taste
1 to 3 tablespoons oil

Equipment: **Mortar and pestle**, electric blender, or food processor; medium-size mixing bowl, mixing spoon, wax paper, medium-size skillet, metal spatula

1. Using mortar and pestle, electric blender, or food processor, grind seeds to flour consistency.
2. Put sesame flour in mixing bowl and add just enough water to make a firm dough. Add salt to taste. Shape into ping-pong-size balls and place side-by-side on wax paper.
3. Heat oil in skillet over medium-high heat. Slightly flatten balls into patty shape and fry on both sides in skillet until golden brown, about 6 minutes.

Serve either warm or cold as a snack with honey or peanut butter.

Cameroon

Cameroon is located in western Africa and is divided by different land forms. To the north are dry plains; the south and central regions are savanna-covered plateaus, and the western region is dominated by highlands and mountains. The coastal region consists of swamps and dense rain forests. Cameroon has a diversified economy and, in terms of food, is self-sufficient. It is a major exporter of cocoa and other cash crops.

Millet and Honey Balls

Yield: 40 balls

2 cups **millet**, available at most health food and Asian food stores
5 cups water
1 teaspoon salt
3/4 cups raw honey

Equipment: Medium-size saucepan, wooden mixing spoon, medium-size mixing bowl, wax-paper-covered serving tray

1. Place millet, water, and salt in medium saucepan. Bring water to boil over high heat, then reduce heat to low and simmer for almost 30 minutes, or until all water has evaporated.
2. Pour cooked millet into bowl and let cool to the point that you can easily handle it. Drizzle honey over it and mix well. Form ping-pong-sized balls and place on wax-paper-covered serving tray for serving.

Sudan

Sudan is in northeastern Africa, just south of Egypt. One of the most notable features of Sudan is the Nile river, which flows through the country from south to north.

Sudanese grow **sorghum**, **millet**, wheat, and sesame as their chief crops. Other important crops are onions, sugar cane, dates, mangos, guavas, oranges, bananas, and peanuts. Peanuts are an important protein-rich crop throughout Africa. The livestock that the nomads to the north raise are camels, goats, sheep, chickens, and cattle. Fish, mostly Nile perch, is eaten in regions bisected by the Nile and its tributaries. The Red Sea is also a source of fish. The Sudanese people in the north are Sunni Muslim, while those in the south follow traditional African beliefs. Yogurt is a favorite food among the nomadic people.

Fatayer Bil-leban   Yogurt Pancakes

Yield: serves 4 to 6

3 eggs, **separated**
2 tablespoons corn syrup
2 cups plain yogurt
1 teaspoon baking soda
1 1/2 cups all-purpose flour
2 teaspoons baking powder
1 cup butter—melt 1/2 cup and set aside remaining 1/2 cup

Equipment: Large-size mixing bowl, **egg beater** or electric mixer, mixing spoon or **whisk**, flour **sifter**, griddle or large-size skillet, pancake turner or metal spatula

1. Beat egg whites in medium-size mixing bowl, using egg beater or mixer, until stiff but not dry, and set aside.
2. Combine egg yolks, corn syrup, yogurt, and baking soda in large mixing bowl, and mix well. **Sift** flour and baking powder into egg mixture, stirring continually to blend. Add melted butter and mix well. Fold in egg whites using mixing spoon or whisk.
3. Melt 2 tablespoons remaining butter on griddle or in skillet over medium high heat, and reduce heat to medium. Spoon enough batter onto the hot skillet to make thin pancakes about 4 inches wide. Cook until small bubbles appear on surface, about 1 minute, and then flip over and cook second side. When done, transfer to platter, and keep warm. Continue making pancakes, adding more butter to the skillet as needed.

Serve warm with side dishes of yogurt, chopped fruit, and jam or jelly.

Chicken and Potatoes

On special occasions, such as religious holidays or when company arrives, chicken is served.

Yield: 6 servings

2 to 3 pound chicken, cut up into pieces
salt and pepper to taste
4 to 6 tablespoons butter

2 onions, chopped
3 garlic cloves, **finely chopped** or 1 teaspoon **garlic granules**
1 small can tomato paste (1/2 cup tomato paste)
1 1/2 cups water
4 large potatoes, peeled and quartered, or 8 small, peeled

Equipment: Skillet with cover, bowl

1. Rub chicken with salt and pepper, and then set aside.
2. Heat butter or margarine in skillet over medium heat, add onions and garlic, and fry until soft, about 3 minutes. Add chicken pieces in batches and fry until golden, about 5 minutes each side. Add more butter or margarine as needed. Keep pieces in warm place. Return chicken pieces to skillet, slightly overlapping if necessary, and heat over medium-low heat.
3. In a bowl, add water to tomato paste, and then add mixture to chicken. Simmer covered for 30 minutes.
4. Add potatoes to skillet, increase heat to medium, cover, and simmer an additional 20 to 30 minutes. Chicken and potatoes should be very tender.

Chad

Chad is located in central Africa, completely surrounded by other nations. Chadians raise their own food; they fish, and they raise stock. Southern Chad has grassy, wooded savanna land. Most of the farming is done in the southern region. Crops include **millet**, **sorghum**, peanuts, rice, sweet potatoes, **cassava**, and yams. Yams and sweet potatoes are often confused because they are very similar, but yams originate from Africa and are botanically different from the North American sweet potato.

Islamic nomads live to the north where the climate is too dry to grow crops well. People herd cattle, sheep, camels, and goats.

Chadians also export smoked and dried fish. Lake Chad supplies large quantities of fish to the Buduma people, who inhabit the lake area. They fish from boats made of reed. The same style and construction has been in use for thousands of years. Everyone uses them, and even young children are trained to navigate around in them!

Sugar cane was introduced by the French in the 1970s. Children of all ages walk around chewing on a length of it to satisfy their sweet tooth.

Peanuts are among the biggest exports of Chad. Here are two recipes that use this important food.

Sweet Potato Salad

Yield: serves 6

4 cooked sweet potatoes, fresh, peeled; or canned, drained, cut into 1/4-inch slices
1/2 onion, chopped

1/2 cup lemon juice
2 tablespoons peanut or vegetable oil
1 cup shelled, roasted peanuts
salt and pepper to taste
3 tomatoes cut in 4 wedges each, for garnish

Equipment: Medium-size bowl, cup, mixing spoon

1. Put potato slices in bowl, add chopped onion, and lightly toss to mix.
2. Mix lemon juice and oil in cup and pour over potato mixture; mix well. Add peanuts and salt and pepper to taste, lightly toss, and transfer to serving bowl. Garnish with tomato wedges around the edge of bowl and chill.

Serve salad as a side dish along with stew.

Squash with Peanuts Dessert

Yield: serves 4 to 6

2 to 4 tablespoons butter or margarine
1 cup shelled and **coarsely chopped** peanuts
3 to 6 tablespoons dark brown sugar
3 cups cooked acorn squash, fresh or frozen, mashed and thawed

Equipment: Medium-size skillet, mixing spoon

1. Melt 2 tablespoons butter or margarine in skillet over medium-high heat. Add peanuts and cook for 3 minutes until lightly brown. Add 3 tablespoons brown sugar and mix well; add squash and remaining 2 tablespoons butter or margarine and mix well. Taste to adjust sweetness and add more sugar if necessary.
2. Cook over low heat for 5 minutes to heat through.

Serve as dessert in individual bowls.

Niger

Niger is a landlocked country in central Africa, and large areas are semidesert or part of the Sahara Desert. The desert in the north is inhabited mostly by the Tuareg, nomadic herders. The majority of the people live along a band of land that follows the Niger River in the southeast tip of the country. In this river basin irrigation makes it possible to raise food and livestock with a little more assurance of success. To the west, dry farming techniques are employed, utilizing seasonal rains that make temporary lakes. Live-stock is the mainstay of the economy. **Millet** and **sorghum** are the bases of the Niger diet; other food crops include **cassava**, beans, peanuts, black-eyed peas, rice, corn, and onions. Reliance on rain is important, and so during drought, famine is always a threat. Past droughts have killed off much of the livestock, hurting the people and their economy badly.

Millet and Onions

The best eating **millet** is the whole grain yellow proso variety available at most health food stores.

Yield: serves 4

3 tablespoons butter or margarine
1 cup whole **millet**
2 cups hot water
2 onions, **coarsely chopped**
salt to taste

Equipment: Medium-size skillet with cover or **Dutch oven**, wooden mixing spoon, small-size skillet

1. Melt 1 tablespoon butter or margarine in medium skillet or Dutch oven over medium-high heat. Add millet and, mixing continually, toast gently until grains are light brown (about 5 minutes). Add 1 tablespoon more of butter or margarine, if necessary, to prevent sticking. Reduce heat to medium and slowly add hot water. Mix well, bring to simmer, cover, and cook for about 25 minutes, until water is absorbed. Millet has a nutty aroma as it cooks. The grains stay separate and they do not get mushy.
2. Melt remaining 1 tablespoon butter or margarine in small skillet over medium heat. Add onions and fry, mixing continually until limp and golden brown (about 5 minutes).

To serve, pour millet into a serving bowl and cover with fried onions. Add salt to taste.

Nigeria

Nigeria, on the west coast of Africa, is the world's sixth-leading producer of oil, and it has one of the strongest economies in Africa. Despite its production of oil, however, more than 70 percent of the population is involved in agriculture. Palms are very important to this agricultural nation. Every bit of the palm is used, including the oil for cooking, stalk juice for palm wine, fronds for thatch roofs, and stalk fibers for house construction material. Nigerians also grow food crops of yams, **taro**, **cassava**, **sorghum**, **millet**, black-eyed peas, corn, peanuts, and cocoa. Cocoa is exported, but all other agricultural products are consumed in Nigeria. Livestock raised include goats, sheep, pigs, and donkeys.

Pepper Soup

Pepper soup is popular all through western Africa and is tasty yet simple to make. The soup can be made with firm skinless fish **fillets** instead of meat. If using fish, cut each fillet into 3 pieces and reduce cooking time to 40 minutes.

Yield: serves 4 to 6

1 pound lean stewing beef, cut into bite-size pieces
6 cups water
2 green chili peppers, **seeded** and **finely chopped** or 1/2 teaspoon ground red pepper,
    more or less to taste
1 onion, peeled and finely chopped
4 new red potatoes (leave skins on), washed and cut into bite-size pieces
2 tomatoes, **peeled** and **cubed**
1/2 cup tomato paste
3 sprigs fresh thyme or 1 teaspoon dried crushed thyme
salt and pepper to taste
2 cups cooked rice for serving (cooked according to directions on package)

Equipment: Large-size saucepan with cover or **Dutch oven**, mixing spoon

1. Put meat, water, peppers, onion, potatoes, tomatoes, tomato paste, thyme, and salt
    and pepper to taste in saucepan with cover or Dutch oven. Bring to a boil over high
    heat, reduce to simmer, and mix well.
2. Cover and cook for about 1 hour or until meat is very tender.

To serve, put cooked rice in the bowls and cover with soup.

Toasted Corn and Peanuts

Yield: about 4 cups

1 to 2 tablespoons vegetable oil
2 cups corn kernels, fresh (cut from about 4 ears), or frozen (thawed)
2 cups shelled peanuts
salt to taste

Equipment: Medium-size heavy bottom skillet, mixing spoon, covered bowl or jar

1. Heat 1 tablespoon oil in skillet over medium heat. Swirl oil to completely coat pan
    bottom. Pour corn kernels in the pan and cook, stirring continually until lightly
    browned. Reduce heat to low and cook about 5 minutes. (Do not add more oil
    unless necessary to prevent sticking). The corn should be on the dry side.
2. Remove from heat, add peanuts, season with salt to taste, and mix well. Transfer to
    covered bowl or jar and refrigerate.

Serve and eat as a trail mix snack; it is very filling, chewy, and nourishing.

Ogede Sise   Boiled Bananas

Bananas and **plantains** are plentiful and nourishing. In Africa they are usually cooked,
either deep fried or boiled. They make a delicious side dish with meat.

Yield: serves 2 to 4

6 cups water
4 skin-on bananas (allow 1 or 2 bananas per person)

Equipment: Medium-size saucepan, tongs or slotted spoon, sharp knife

1. Put water in saucepan, bring to a boil over high heat. Add skin-on bananas, bring water up to boiling again, reduce to simmer, and cook for 15 minutes. Remove from water with tongs or slotted spoon and set on platter.
2. Slit skins with a sharp knife and serve.

Serve the hot bananas at once. Each person is served one or two and eats it out of the skin. The bananas also can be cut in bite-size pieces.

Ghana

Ghana is an agriculturally wealthy country situated on the west coast of Africa. Its varied soils and climates make it possible to grow a wide variety of foods. Ghanaians have developed their own national cuisine that is derived both from the variety of fresh foods available and from the different people who invaded and traded there, such as the Dutch and the British. Ghana is famous for growing high quality cocoa beans and dominates the cocoa market. Other food crops are coffee, yams, corn, **cassava**, sweet potatoes, cashew nuts, pepper, **sorghum**, **millet**, peanuts, rice, ginger, and assorted garden vegetables. Almost everyone is involved in some aspect of farming, and nearly every household has a little kitchen garden.

Fishing is a big industry and employs many people in Ghana. Fish is available to everyone throughout Ghana because of coastal fishing, fish farms, inland waters, and Lake Volta, one of the largest man-made lakes in the world. Cattle are raised in the savanna of the northern territory, and many Ghanaians raise chickens and cows on their farms.

Fufu   *Plantain, Yam, or Sweet Potato Balls*

Fufu is a national dish of Ghana.

Yield: about 12 to 18 balls

1 pound skin-on **plantains**, yams, or sweet potatoes
6 cups water
1 teaspoon ground nutmeg
1 teaspoon ground red pepper, more or less to taste
salt and pepper to taste

Equipment: Medium-size saucepan with cover, large-size mixing bowl, potato masher or electric blender, mixing spoon

1. Put plantains, yams, or sweet potatoes in saucepan with water, and bring to a boil over high heat. Reduce to simmer, cover, and cook for about 40 minutes or until tender. Remove from heat and allow to cool enough to peel and cut into chunks. Using potato masher or electric blender, mash into smooth paste. Add nutmeg, red pepper, and salt and pepper to taste.

2. Shape mixture into ping-pong-size balls; moisten your hands and roll mixture in the palms of your hands. Repeat, each time wetting your hands, until all of the mixture is used. Place balls side-by-side on serving platter. Keep at room temperature until ready to eat.

Serve as you would dumplings on top of stew or in soup. *Fufu* is also served as a side dish with meat or chicken.

Hkatenkwan — One-pot Meal with Ginger Chicken and Okra

Yield: serves 6

1 chicken, cut into pieces
1 tablespoon peeled and **finely chopped** fresh ginger or 1 teaspoon ground ginger
1 onion, chopped
8 cups water
2 tablespoons tomato paste
1 cup tomatoes, chopped
1 cup chunky peanut butter
1 teaspoon ground red pepper
1 cup eggplant, peeled and **cubed**
10 whole okra, fresh or frozen, **trimmed**
salt and pepper to taste

Equipment: Large saucepan with cover or **Dutch oven**, slotted spoon

1. Put chicken, ginger, onion, and water in saucepan or Dutch oven and bring to boil. Reduce heat to simmer, cover, and cook for 1 hour or until chicken is tender. With slotted spoon remove chicken pieces and set aside.
2. Increase heat to medium and add tomato paste, tomatoes, peanut butter, red pepper, eggplant, and okra. Cook for 5 minutes, stirring frequently. Reduce heat to simmer, cover, and cook 10 minutes more.
3. Return chicken to the pan, laying the pieces on top of the vegetables. Cover and simmer for 15 minutes or until chicken is heated through. Add salt and pepper to taste.

To serve set the saucepan in the middle of the table and have your guests help themselves.

Joffof Ghana — Chicken and Rice Ghana

Joffof rice is originally from Senegal, but the people of Ghana have adopted it. *Joffof* means that the rice is cooked in the same pot with all other ingredients.

Yield: serves 6 to 8

3 to 4 pounds chicken, cut into pieces
4 cups **stewed** tomatoes, homemade or canned
2 onions, **coarsely chopped**
6 to 8 cups water
1 cup uncooked rice
1/4 teaspoon ground cinnamon

1/2 teaspoon ground red pepper
1 cup *each* cooked and **cubed** ham and sausage
3 cups coarsely chopped cabbage
1 cup green beans, cut in 1-inch pieces, fresh, frozen (thawed), or canned
salt and pepper to taste

Equipment: Medium-size roasting pan with cover or **Dutch oven**, mixing spoon

1. Put chicken, tomatoes with juice, onions, 6 cups water, rice, cinnamon, and red pepper in roasting pan or Dutch oven. Bring to a boil over high heat, reduce to simmer, cover, and cook for 30 minutes.
2. Preheat oven 350°F.
3. Layer ham, sausage, cabbage, green beans, and salt and pepper to taste over chicken mixture. Cover and bake in oven for about 45 minutes. Add more water if necessary to prevent sticking.

To serve, bring roasting pan or Dutch oven directly to the table and have your guests help themselves.

Akwadu   Banana-coconut Bake

This refreshing dessert is a welcome relief at the end of a spicy Ghana meal. Bananas and coconuts are plentiful and inexpensive all year long in Ghana.

Yield: serves 4 to 6

5 bananas, peeled and cut in half, lengthwise
5 tablespoons butter or margarine, melted
2 tablespoons lemon juice
1 cup orange juice
1/2 cup light brown sugar
1 cup **shredded** coconut

Equipment: 9- x 9-inch baking pan, small-size bowl, spoon

Preheat oven to 375°F.
1. Place banana slices side-by-side in baking pan and sprinkle with butter or margarine.
2. Mix lemon and orange juice in small bowl and pour over bananas. Sprinkle with brown sugar and coconut.
3. Bake for about 10 minutes or until coconut is golden.

Serve warm; spoon bananas and juice into individual bowls.

Peanut Milk

Many children around the world have never tasted a nice, cool glass of milk. There are often no (or hardly any) cows, goats, or sheep to milk in their countries, and even in some countries with available livestock, the thought of drinking milk is quite unpleasant. Milk drinking is not part of their culture. Such nonmilk-drinking countries are in Africa, Asia, and some of South and Central America. It has been discovered that even one cup of milk can cause a terrible stomachache or even send someone to the hospital. Extensive research has been done, and scientists have found lactose-deficient people are lacking the body chemicals needed to digest milk. When a protein-rich drink is needed, it is often made with peanuts.

Yield: serves 4 to 6

1/2 cup peanut butter
4 cups water
1/2 teaspoon salt
sugar to taste (optional)

Equipment: Medium-size saucepan, mixing spoon, **whisk** or **eggbeater**

1. Put peanut butter, water, and salt into saucepan, and bring to a boil over high heat, stirring until blended. Reduce heat to simmer and cook for 10 minutes, stirring occasionally.
2. Remove from heat, add sugar to taste, and mix well.

Serve either cold or hot in a glass or cup; mix well before drinking.

Ivory Coast

Côte d'Ivoire is a remarkable nation on the west coast of Africa that has prospered since gaining independence from France in 1960. Some French influences can still be seen, especially in the cooking done in the cities. Modern shops, French restaurants, and most of the conveniences found in large European cities are found in the large cities. Most people of the Ivory Coast are spread fairly evenly throughout the country, growing food for themselves and the world. Food crops include corn, **millet**, yams, rice, and garden vegetables. Coffee and cocoa are major exports  and contribute to the success of the economy. Livestock raised include goats, sheep, cattle, and pigs. Interestingly, saltwater fish is not traditionally liked by the people of this coastal nation, so their catch is exported for the most part.

Calalou   *Eggplant and Okra Stew*

Stews, like this *calalou*, are important one-pot-meals in Africa. Everything to be eaten for the day can be thrown in a pot with some water and oil and placed over a fire. Everything cooks together until it is tender and tasty.

Yield: serves 6

1/4 cup peanut or vegetable oil
1 cup **finely chopped** onion
2 tablespoons flour
1/2 cup water
2 cups **stewed** tomatoes, homemade or canned
1/2 teaspoon ground red pepper, more or less to taste

1/2 teaspoon thyme
2 bay leaves
1 medium-size eggplant, **cubed** (about 5 cups)
2 cups okra, fresh or frozen, stemmed and cut in 1/2-inch slices
salt and pepper to taste

Equipment: Large-size skillet with cover, mixing spoon, cup

1. Heat oil in skillet over medium-high heat. Add onions, mix well, and fry for 3 minutes or until soft.
2. In cup, add flour to water and mix well to dissolve any lumps. Add flour mixture to cooked onions, stirring continually, and cook over medium heat for about 3 minutes until it starts to thicken. Reduce heat to simmer, add tomatoes, red pepper, thyme, and bay leaves, and mix well. Cover and cook for 10 minutes.
3. Add the eggplant and okra, cover, and simmer for 40 minutes more. Add salt and pepper to taste. Remove bay leaves and discard before serving.

Serve in individual bowls as a main dish over rice or as a side dish with meat or chicken.

Chicken a la n'gatietro   Fried Chicken in Peanut Sauce

The Ivory Coast is a great producer of peanuts and peanut oil. Peanuts, called groundnuts in Africa, are nutritious and flavorful.

Yield: serves 6

2 to 3 pounds of chicken cut for frying
3 tablespoons peanut or vegetable oil
1 cup chopped onion
4 green onions, **finely chopped**
1 large tomato, chopped
2 tablespoons tomato paste
1 teaspoon paprika
1 bay leaf
2 cups water
1/2 cup chunky peanut butter
salt and pepper to taste

Equipment: Large-size deep skillet or **Dutch oven**, medium-size mixing bowl, mixing spoon

1. Heat oil in skillet or Dutch oven over medium heat. Add chicken pieces and brown on both sides (about 10 minutes per side). Fry in batches if necessary. Return all chicken pieces to the skillet or Dutch oven, stacking if necessary.
2. Put onions, green onions, tomato, tomato paste, paprika, bay leaf, water, and peanut butter in bowl, and mix well. Pour mixture over chicken and bring to a boil; reduce at once to simmer, and cook until chicken is tender, about 30 minutes. (Turn chicken pieces once while cooking.) Season with salt and pepper to taste.

Serve on large platter with a side dish of rice.

Tiba Yoka   Baked Bananas

A wide variety of bananas grow all through Africa, from tiny ones just a couple inches long to enormous specimens several feet in length. Many African-grown bananas are only good to eat when cooked, either fried or baked.

Yield: serves 4 to 6

6 bananas, peeled
1 cup **crushed** or **finely ground peanuts**
1/2 cup orange marmalade
1/3 cup melted butter

Equipment: Shallow 9-inch baking pan, small-size mixing bowl, mixing spoon

Preheat oven to 350° F.
1. Roll the bananas in the peanuts and set in baking pan.
2. Mix orange marmalade with melted butter in the bowl. Pour over bananas and bake in oven until bubbly and hot, about 15 minutes.

Serve warm and spoon the syrup over the bananas. For an added treat, serve with ice cream.

Kyekyire Paano   Toasted Cornmeal Cookies

Yield: about 24 cookies

1 cup yellow or white cornmeal
1 1/2 cups all-purpose flour, **sifted**
1/2 teaspoon salt
1/2 cup sugar
1/2 teaspoon ground or grated nutmeg
1/2 cup butter or margarine
2 eggs, beaten
1 teaspoon grated lemon rind

Equipment: Shallow 8-inch baking pan, oven mitts, mixing spoon, large-size mixing bowl, clean hands, greased or nonstick cookie sheet

Preheat oven to 350° F.
1. Spread cornmeal in baking pan and place in oven for about 20 minutes, or until lightly brown. Using oven mitts, stir or shake pan often so the cornmeal toasts evenly. Remove from oven and mix with flour, salt, sugar, and nutmeg in mixing bowl. Blend in butter or margarine with mixing spoon or clean hands.
2. Add eggs and lemon rind and mix well. Drop dough by spoonsful on cookie sheet; make each cookie about the size of a ping-pong ball.
3. Increase oven heat to 375° F.
4. Bake in oven for about 15 minutes or until golden brown.

Serve cookies as a snack with milk.

Sierra Leone / Liberia

Rice and oil palm trees are two important food crops in both Sierra Leone and Liberia. Rice is eaten almost three times a day. In fact, rice has to be imported to meet the needs of the people even though it's grown in both countries. Other food crops include **cassava**, coffee, cocoa, and oil palm products. The heart of the palm tree is favored by Liberians, who eat it as we would a salad. You may find heart of palm canned in the specialty section of your supermarket. Palm oil is extracted from palm nuts and is exported from this region. Palm oil is used for cooking throughout western Africa. It gives the food fried in it a reddish color.

Rice Bread

No festive occasion is complete without this tasty heavy bread, favored in Sierra Leone and Liberia.

Yield: 12 servings

1/4 cup oil
1/2 cup water
1/3 cup currants or raisins
3/4 cup sugar
1 cup mashed bananas
1 3/4 cup rice flour (use instant cream of rice cereal if you can't find rice flour; it makes the bread crunchier but is a good alternative)
2 1/2 teaspoons baking powder
1/2 teaspoon baking soda
1/2 teaspoon salt
1/2 teaspoon nutmeg

Equipment: Two mixing bowls, **sifter**, mixing spoon, spatula, greased 9-inch cake pan

Preheat oven to 325°F.

1. Mix oil, water, currants or raisins, sugar, and bananas in one of the mixing bowls. Beat mixture well and set aside.
2. In separate bowl, **sift** flour, baking powder, baking soda, salt, and nutmeg. Stir into banana mixture and beat until mixture is smooth.
3. Pour into prepared pan, place in oven, and bake approximately 50 minutes. Cake will be heavy, as a fruit cake is.

Serve small slices with a glass of milk.

Dried Seeds for Snacking

Melon, pumpkin, sunflower, and squash seeds are popular snacks throughout western Africa. Dried watermelon seeds are very popular and are frequently ground and used to thicken soups and sauces. You can try this recipe with any seed in season. The seeds are often combined with peanuts or cashew nuts, seasoned, and toasted on a cookie sheet in a 300° F oven until seeds and nuts turn light golden color, about 50 to 60 minutes.

Yield: about 2 cups

2 cups seeds: melon, pumpkin, sunflower, or squash
3 cups water
1 1/2 teaspoons salt

Equipment: **Colander** or strainer, medium-size saucepan, mixing spoon, nonstick cookie sheet, oven mitts

1. Put seeds in a colander or strainer and rinse off any fibers on them.
2. Transfer seeds to saucepan, add water and salt, and bring to a boil over high heat. Boil for 3 minutes, reduce heat, and simmer for 1 hour. Drain seeds in colander or strainer.
3. Preheat oven to 300° F.
4. Spread seeds out on cookie sheet and bake in oven for about 1 hour or until dry. Shake seeds several times during baking. Remove from oven, sprinkle with salt, and cool to room temperature; store in dry place.

Dried seeds are fun to chew on, but they are even better if seasoned with sprinkles of garlic salt or granules, red pepper, curry powder, or even sugar.

Abala   *Savory Steamed Rice*

The countries along the west African coast are so small and similar it is not unusual to find many eating the same foods and observing the same cooking customs. *Abala* is a favorite dish among most of the west African countries, and this recipe can be used for other west African countries. It is a dough-like mixture formed into balls, wrapped in warmed banana leaves, and steamed. The banana leaves are not eaten; they simply act as a casing to hold the balls of creamed rice. **Blanched** cabbage or lettuce leaves also work well, as do squares of aluminum foil, which we suggest. Sometimes chopped tomatoes or other chopped vegetables, headed and peeled shrimp, or peeled crayfish tails are added. The traditional cooking oil of West Africa is palm oil, which gives everything cooked in it a red color. We suggest using vegetable oil for its availability and for health reasons, as palm oil is high in saturated fats and is not readily available.

Yield: serves 6

1 cup cream of rice cereal
3/4 to 1 cup boiling water
1 green chili pepper, **seeded** and **finely chopped**
1 onion, finely chopped
1/2 cup vegetable oil
1 teaspoon salt

Equipment: Medium-size mixing bowl, mixing spoon, 6 squares (8-inch size) of aluminum foil, vegetable steamer

1. Pour cream of rice in mixing bowl and, while stirring continually, slowly add boiling water until mixture is thick and free of lumps. Add chili pepper, onion, oil, and salt, and mix well. Cool to room temperature.
2. Using clean hands, make 6 balls of the mixture and wrap each securely in a square of foil.
3. Fill the bottom pan of the steamer or deep saucepan with water so that the water is just below and not touching the basket or strainer. Bring water to a boil over high heat. Place foil-wrapped mixture in the basket, strainer, or colander. Cover tightly to keep as much steam in as possible. Reduce heat to simmer and cook for 2 hours. Check frequently to make sure the bottom pan does not dry out; if it does, add more boiling water.

To serve, each person is given an *abala*. Each opens his or her own and eats out of the wrapping like eating a candy bar.

Kanya   Peanut Bars

Possibly the most popular sweet treat in west Africa is a peanut mixture known as *kanya*, *kayan*, or *kanyan*. The candy can be made with either fresh roasted peanuts or peanut butter. *Kanya* is usually sold by child street peddlers for just pennies. It is an easy to make sweet and crunchy candy.

Yield: about 15 pieces

1/2 cup smooth peanut butter
1/2 cup sugar
1/2 cup cream of rice cereal, more or less, as needed

Equipment: **Mortar and pestle,** small-size metal bowl, mixing spoon or electric blender, nonstick 9-inch cake pan, clean hands

1. Put peanut butter and sugar in mortar or small mixing bowl. Using the pestle or the back of a mixing spoon, beat them together until well mixed.
2. Slowly add cream of rice, stirring continually and adding more cream of rice, if necessary, to make a firm dough.
3. Transfer dough to cake pan, and using back of spoon or clean hands, press evenly to cover bottom. Chill in refrigerator to set.

To serve, cut into small rectangular bars and eat as a candy.

Ginger Cookies

These cookies have a somewhat unusual ingredient, red pepper.

Yield: about 24 cookies

2 cups flour
6 tablespoons sugar
3 teaspoons ground ginger
1/2 teaspoon salt
1/4 teaspoon ground red pepper, more or less to taste
6 tablespoons butter or margarine
4 tablespoons water or milk

Equipment: Flour **sifter**, large-size mixing bowl, mixing spoon, floured work surface, rolling pin, cookie cutter or water glass, greased or nonstick cookie sheet

Preheat oven to 350° F.
1. **Sift** flour, sugar, ginger, salt, and red pepper together in mixing bowl.
2. Blend in butter or margarine, using mixing spoon or clean hands. DO NOT RUB YOUR EYES; RED PEPPER IN MIXTURE CAN BE IRRITATING.
3. Add water or milk to make a firm dough, transfer dough to work surface, and, using floured rolling pin, roll the dough about 1/2-inch thick.
4. Using a cookie cutter or the top edge of a water glass, press into dough, cutting out round cookies. Place them side-by-side on cookie sheet. Bake in oven for about 15 minutes, until golden brown.

Serve ginger cookies as a snack.

Guinea

The land of Guinea along the west coast of Africa consists of four regions: the coastal, the inland savanna, the mountainous Fouta Sallon region, and the southeastern forest region. Guinea is a humid tropical country that receives a lot of rain, up to 169 inches a year. Most Guineans are involved in agriculture, raising food crops of **cassava**, rice, **millet**, corn, and sweet potatoes, with rice being the main subsistence crop. Cash crops include coffee, bananas, palm products, peanuts, citrus fruits, and pineapples. Nomadic and semi-nomadic herders
raise livestock. Poor sanitation is a problem in Guinea, which leads to unsanitary drinking water. This first recipe uses peanuts, a staple crop of Guinea, and is simple and fun to make.

Peanut Balls

Yield: about 36 balls

1 cup **crushed** or **finely ground peanuts**
2 1/4 cups all-purpose flour
1 cup butter or margarine, at room temperature
1/2 cup confectioners' sugar (powdered sugar)
2 teaspoons vanilla
36 whole peanuts as garnish

Equipment: Medium-size mixing bowl, mixing spoon, large-size mixing bowl, mixing spoon or electric mixer, nonstick or greased cookie sheet

Preheat oven to 375° F.
1. Blend peanuts and flour in medium-size mixing bowl.
2. Combine the butter or margarine in large-size mixing bowl with the sugar, and, using mixing spoon or mixer, mix until well blended. Add vanilla and mix well.

3. Add peanut mixture to large bowl and mix well. Using clean hands, divide dough into ping-pong-size balls and place side-by-side on cookie sheet, leaving about 1 inch between. Stick a peanut in the center top of each ball for garnish.
4. Bake in the oven for about 10 minutes or until the balls are golden brown.

Serve peanut balls as a snack.

Groundnut Chicken

Chicken in peanut sauce is eaten with a variety of side dishes: sliced banana, *foo foo*, grated coconut, and sliced red onions that are sprinkled with sugar and vinegar.

Yield: serves 6

2 cups shelled, **blanched, finely ground peanuts**
2 cups boiling water
1 cup coconut milk, homemade (see recipe page 208) or canned
2 to 4 tablespoons vegetable oil
1 chicken, cut in pieces
1 onion, **finely chopped**
3 tomatoes, **peeled** and sliced
1 clove garlic or 1/2 teaspoon garlic granules
salt and pepper to taste
4 **hard-cooked eggs**, peeled and quartered

Equipment: Small-size saucepan, mixing spoon, large-size skillet or **Dutch oven**, tongs or fork

1. Combine the peanuts and boiling water in the saucepan. Bring to a boil over medium-high heat, reduce heat, and simmer for 5 minutes or until sauce is thick but still liquid. Stir in the coconut milk, remove from heat, and set aside.
2. Heat 2 tablespoons oil in the skillet or Dutch oven over medium heat and fry chicken pieces until golden brown on both sides. Use the tongs or fork to turn the pieces and then remove them from the pan. Set aside.
3. Add onion, tomatoes, and garlic to the skillet or Dutch oven and fry until onions are soft (about 3 minutes). Add more oil if necessary. Stir in peanut mixture and salt and pepper to taste. Add the chicken pieces and simmer for 30 minutes, or until chicken is tender. Stir frequently to prevent sticking. Transfer to serving platter and place eggs around the mixture.

Serve groundnut chicken with boiled rice.

Senegal

Senegal, on the west coast of Africa, is mostly low lying and covered with savanna. Most of the Senegalese people live in small villages, farming and raising stock. The best agricultural areas are to the west because the land is more fertile than in the east and north, where the land becomes poorer. The major food and cash crop produced in Senegal is peanuts, but **millet, sorghum, manioc,** corn, and rice are also grown. Some food is imported because Senegal does not produce enough to feed its people.

Because fish is plentiful and cheap, fishing is becoming big industry in Senegal. In the following recipe, rice, a Senegalese favorite, is combined with fish in the national dish *ceeb u jen*. "Ceeb joints" have sprung up in crowded urban areas where city workers can go to eat ceeb on their lunch breaks. Ceeb joints are small makeshift kitchens outside homes, where the only cooking equipment is a huge iron caldron that sits atop a brush or a wood-burning *brazier* (a large metal pan with room on the bottom for wood to burn, similar to a simple U.S. barbeque oven). Here the housewife cooks for her family then sells what's left to passersby. The ceeb is served to customers in plastic bowls, and the "joint" consists of a couple of benches to sit on.

Tiebou Dienn [also *Ceeb u Jen*]   *Fish Stew*

Any combination of in-season vegetables with rice and fish can be used for this hearty dish. Preparing the fish is a little unusual. Deep slits are cut into thick fish steaks or **fillets**, which are then stuffed with herbs and spices. There are three steps to making *ceeb*: making the fish stuffing (Senegalese call it *roof*), cooking the vegetables, and cooking the rice. In Senegal the rice is cooked after the vegetables in the same caldron. A brown crust of rice called *xoon* forms on the bottom of the pot. This crust is a delicacy and is served with the ceeb. To shorten the cooking time, the rice in our recipe will be cooked separately.

Yield: serves 4 to 6

1/2 cup **finely chopped** flat-leaf parsley
4 green onions, finely chopped
1/4 teaspoon ground red pepper, more or less to taste
3 cloves garlic, finely chopped, or 1 teaspoon garlic granules
4 (6 to 8 ounces each) fish steaks, cut 1-inch thick, or 4 fillets (any firm fish will do)
4 to 6 tablespoons vegetable oil
1 cup tomato paste
4 cups water
1/2 cup tapioca or 1/2 cup all-purpose flour mixed into a paste with 1/2 cup water
4 cups coarsely chopped vegetables, fresh or frozen (thawed), or any combination:
    carrots, turnips, cauliflower, eggplant, okra, green beans, pumpkin, or squash
1/4 small head cabbage, cut into 4 wedges
salt and pepper to taste
3 cups cooked rice (cooked according to directions on package)
2 limes, cut in wedges for garnish

Equipment: **Mortar and pestle** or metal bowl, paper towels, large-size saucepan with cover or **Dutch oven**, mixing spoon, slotted spoon, large-size skillet

1. *Prepare roof:* put parsley, onions, red pepper, and garlic in the mortar or metal bowl and grind them together using the pestle, rock, hammer head, or mallet. Add a few drops of water at a time to make a paste.
2. Rinse fish and pat dry with paper towels. Using a sharp knife, cut 1 or 2 deep slits into each piece and fill with the parsley mixture.

3. Heat 2 tablespoons oil in saucepan or Dutch oven over medium-high heat; brown fish on both sides, about 6 minutes per side. Add more oil if necessary to prevent sticking. Remove with slotted spoon and set aside in warm place.
4. *Prepare vegetables:* using the same saucepan or Dutch oven, add tomato paste, water, tapioca, and all vegetables. Mix well and bring to a boil over high heat. Reduce heat to simmer, cover, and cook for about 45 minutes or until very tender. Season with salt and pepper to taste.
5. *Prepare rice:* heat 2 tablespoons oil in skillet over medium-high heat. Add cooked rice and fry (DO NOT STIR) for about 15 minutes or until bottom becomes crusty brown.

To serve, flip the rice over with crusty bottom side up in the middle of a large platter. Surround rice with fish and vegetables. Serve with lime wedges to sprinkle on fish. Using a clean right hand, pull off pieces of crusty rice and scoop up bite-size amounts of vegetables and fish. Squeeze them together in a ball and pop in your mouth.

Burkina Faso

In West Africa Burkina Faso, formerly known as Upper Volta, was known as a "paradise of meat" because big game hunting was so popular there. Currently the citizens export livestock and many other food stuffs. The people of Burkina Faso live by growing their own food, and any extra is sold as a cash crop. Food crops include peanuts, **shea nuts**, sesame, **sorghum**, **millet**, corn, and rice. They also raise goats, sheep, pigs, and donkeys. Agricultural conditions are hard in Burkina Faso because of frequent droughts and the terrible tse-tse fly which kills cattle. Foods such as grains have to be imported when droughts strike.

Fo   *Meat Stew*

Stews are popular throughout West Africa, and Burkina Faso is no exception. The national dish is called *fo*. It always contains beef, onions, tomatoes, and okra, but it is up to the individual cooks to add their own special touches. Try adding your own special touch to this recipe. That's what African cooking is all about.

Yield: serves 6

1 1/2 pounds beef, **cubed** (use inexpensive stewing meat)
4 cups water
1 teaspoon salt
1/4 teaspoon *each* ground ginger and ground red pepper
2 onions, **coarsely chopped**
4 tomatoes, coarsely chopped
2 cups coarsely chopped okra
2 cups peeled, coarsely chopped squash
salt and pepper to taste.

Equipment: Large-size saucepan with cover or **Dutch oven**, mixing spoon, medium-size saucepan with cover, potato masher

1. Put beef, 2 cups water, salt, ginger, red pepper, and onions in large saucepan and, over high heat, bring to a boil. Reduce heat to simmer, cover, and cook 1 hour. Add tomatoes and okra, mix well, cover, and simmer for 20 minutes more.
2. Put remaining 2 cups water and squash in medium saucepan, bring to a boil over high heat, reduce heat to simmer, and cook for 15 minutes, until tender. Remove from heat.
3. Mash squash in cooking liquid, using potato masher. Add to meat mixture, and mix well. Simmer uncovered for about 15 minutes to thicken and add salt and pepper to taste.

Serve *fo* in individual bowls over cooked beans or rice. To serve *fo* as they do in Africa, make a ring of cooked rice or beans on a large round platter and then pour the *fo* into the center. Eat with the fingers of your right hand.

Akara   *Black-eyed Pea Balls*

Yield: serves 4 to 6

2 cups cooked black-eyed peas, homemade or canned (drain liquid and save)
1 egg
1/2 onion, **finely chopped**
1/4 teaspoon ground red pepper
1 teaspoon salt
1 to 3 tablespoons flour
1 cup vegetable oil, more or less as needed

Equipment: Electric-food blender, rubber spatula, large-size mixing bowl, mixing spoon, large-size skillet, slotted spoon or pancake turner, paper towels

1. Using blender, grind peas into a smooth paste. Add a little drained liquid if they are too dry. To mash peas by hand, put in medium-size bowl and, using either a potato masher or back of a fork, mash to the consistency of mashed potatoes.
2. Use rubber spatula to transfer to a large bowl, add egg, onion, red pepper, salt, and 1 tablespoon flour, and mix well. The mixture should be very firm, not soupy. Add more flour if necessary.
3. Heat about 1 cup oil in skillet over medium-high heat. When hot, hold a spoonful of mixture close to the oil, and, using another spoon, carefully push mixture off into oil. Flatten slightly with back of spoon. Watch out for oil splattering and turn down the heat a bit if it splatters too much. Fry 3 or 4 at a time, in batches, turning to brown each side, about 5 minutes. Remove with slotted spoon or pancake turner and drain on paper towels.

Serve either warm or cold as a side dish with stews, in soup as dumplings, or serve as a midday snack.

Mali / Mauritania

Drought and spreading desert have affected agriculture and livestock raising in both Mali and Mauritania. This drought has forced Mauritanian nomads to become city dwellers.

Fishing along the coast is the major industry for Mauritania, although some raising of livestock, vegetable gardening, and grain growing goes on as well. Through Mali, a landlocked country, flows the Niger River, providing water to an otherwise arid land. Fish from the river provide excellent protein for the people. Fishing is so good along the river that the Malians salt and dry the excess to export. Around the fertile banks of the river, Malians grow food crops of rice, **millet**, sugar cane, corn, vegetables, and tree crops. Using the Niger River water, a massive irrigation project covering 40,000 hectares of land has increased rice production. In dryer areas **sorghum** is planted. Peanuts provide another source of protein for the Malians; this is a very important crop, grown all over the country, and a very popular flavoring in this part of the world.

Spinach and Peanut Stew

Fresh greens and peanuts are frequently eaten together. In this recipe they are combined into a special stew.

Yield: serves 4 to 6

2 to 4 tablespoons vegetable oil
1 onion, **finely chopped**
1/2 cup peanuts, chopped
2 tablespoons creamy peanut butter
1 tomato, chopped
1/4 cup tomato paste
3 cups, tightly packed, finely chopped spinach; fresh (**trimmed** and washed) or frozen (thawed)
1/4 teaspoon ground red pepper, more or less to taste
salt and pepper to taste

Equipment: Large-size skillet with cover, mixing spoon

1. Heat 2 tablespoons oil in skillet over medium-high heat, add onion and peanuts and fry until onion becomes soft, about 3 minutes; mix well. Reduce heat to medium, add peanut butter, tomato, tomato paste, spinach, red pepper, and salt and pepper to taste, and mix well. (Add more oil if necessary to prevent sticking.)
2. Cover and stir frequently; cook for 30 minutes.

Serve the stew hot, in individual bowls over rice or beans, as a side dish to fried fish.

Peanut and Meat Stew

This meal is regularly made on Sundays in Mali.

Yield: serves 6

2 to 4 tablespoons vegetable oil
1 1/2 pounds beef, **cubed** (use inexpensive stewing meat) or chicken, boned, cut into bite-size chunks
1 bell pepper, **coarsely chopped**
2 onions, coarsely chopped
2 tablespoons plain peanut butter
1/2 teaspoon *each* salt and thyme
1 to 2 cups water
1 beef or chicken **bouillon** cube
1 tablespoon tomato paste (optional)

Equipment: Medium-size saucepan with cover or **Dutch oven**, mixing spoon, medium-size mixing bowl

1. Heat 2 tablespoons oil in saucepan over medium-high heat. Add meat or chicken, and, mixing continually, brown well, about 5 minutes. Add more oil if necessary, reduce heat to medium, and add bell pepper and onions. Cook until vegetables are limp, about 4 minutes.
2. Put peanut butter, salt, thyme, 1 cup water, **bouillon,** and tomato paste in medium mixing bowl and mix well. Pour mixture over meat and mix well. Cover and cook for about 30 minutes at simmer, mixing frequently. Add more water if necessary to prevent sticking.

Serve with mounds of rice.

Morocco

Morocco is an Arab nation in northwest Africa, bordered by the Atlantic Ocean and the Mediterranean Sea. Moroccans enjoy a worldwide reputation for fine food and hospitality. The simplest meal is a ceremony in Morocco. The family and guests sit on floor cushions around a low table. Small hot damp towels are passed to each person before the food is served. The hands must be wiped clean since, in traditional households, hands are used to eat with, not flatware. Travelers to Morocco rave about exotic and delicious slow-cooked  stews called *tagines.* Meat, fragrant spices, and fruits are combined for a meal not soon forgotten. Moroccans are in a unique situation among Arab nations in that they are capable of self-sufficiency in food production. Indeed, they are self-sufficient in meeting the meat needs of the country. Livestock raised includes sheep, chickens, and cattle. Wheat, barley, corn, sugar cane, sugar beets, fruits, and vegetables are among Moroccan crops.

Zeilook   Eggplant Salad

In Morocco *zeilook* can be mashed to a smooth texture like mashed potatoes or left chunky as we suggest.

Yield: serves 4 to 6

1 1/2 pounds eggplant, peeled and **cubed**
4 to 6 tablespoons olive or vegetable oil
3 ripe tomatoes, **peeled** and chopped
3 garlic cloves, fresh **finely chopped** or 1 teaspoon garlic granules
1/2 teaspoon ground cumin
1 teaspoon paprika
1 tablespoon chopped fresh **coriander** or 1/2 teaspoon ground coriander
salt and pepper to taste
2 lemons cut in wedges for garnish

Equipment: Strainer, paper towels, large-size skillet, slotted spoon

1. Put eggplant in strainer, sprinkle it with salt, and set it aside for 30 minutes to drain over a plate or in sink.
2. Rinse eggplant in strainer under cold water, drain well, and pat dry with paper towels.
3. Heat 4 tablespoons oil in skillet over medium-high heat, add eggplant, and, stirring continually, fry until brown on all sides. Reduce heat to simmer, and add tomatoes, garlic, cumin, paprika, and coriander. Mix well and cook for 20 minutes or until most of the liquid has evaporated. Add more oil if necessary to prevent sticking. Add salt and pepper to taste.

Serve either hot or cold as a salad or as a side dish with meat or fish; garnish with lemon wedges.

Tagine de Poulet aux Pruneaux et Miel   Chicken with Prunes & Honey

Tagines can be very sweet or hot and spicy, varying from region to region or family to family. Quite often the seasonings overpower the natural flavor of the meat, poultry, or fish.

Yield: serves 4 to 6

2 1/2 to 3 pounds chicken, cut into serving-size pieces
6 cups water
1 teaspoon *each* salt and pepper
1/2 teaspoon ground turmeric
2 teaspoons ground cinnamon
1 onion, chopped
1 cup **pitted** prunes or other dried fruit; peaches, apricots, apples, or combination
1 cup honey
1 cup dark brown sugar
1 cup sliced almonds for garnish
1 tablespoon sesame seeds for garnish

Equipment: Large-size saucepan with cover or **Dutch oven**, slotted mixing spoon or tongs, heat-proof bowl or pan

1. Put chicken pieces in saucepan or Dutch oven and add water to cover chicken, about 6 cups. Add salt, pepper, turmeric, cinnamon, and onion. Bring to a boil over high heat, reduce heat to simmer, cover, and cook 1 hour, until chicken is tender. Using slotted spoon or tongs, transfer chicken pieces to bowl or pan, set aside, and keep warm in 150°F oven.
2. Add prunes or other dried fruit, honey, and brown sugar to the saucepan. Bring to a boil, mixing well to prevent sticking, and then reduce heat to simmer uncovered for 30 minutes, stirring frequently, until sauce thickens slightly.
3. Return chicken pieces to the pan and spoon sauce over them. Cover and simmer 10 minutes more to heat through.

To serve, transfer the chicken pieces to a large platter and cover with fruit sauce. Sprinkle with almonds and sesame seeds.

Quick Moroccan Bread

Yield: makes 2 loaves

1/4 cup lukewarm water (105°to 115°F)
1 envelope (1/4 ounce) active dry yeast
1/4 teaspoon sugar
3 1/2 cups all-purpose flour
1 cup whole wheat flour (coarse cracked grain, if available)
1 tablespoon *each* salt and anise seeds
1 1/2 cups cold water (more or less as needed)
1 teaspoon vegetable oil
1/2 cup white or yellow cornmeal

Equipment: Small-size bowl, large-size mixing bowl, mixing spoon, electric mixer with dough hook (optional), floured work surface, dry or nonstick cookie sheet, kitchen towel

1. Put warm water in small bowl and add yeast and sugar. Let stand 5 minutes or until foamy.
2. Put all-purpose and whole wheat flours, salt, and anise seeds in large mixing bowl. Add yeast mixture and water, a little at a time, and mix continually, using clean hands or electric mixer with dough hook, making a stiff dough. (It is better to add less rather than too much water.) Transfer to work surface and if **kneading** by hand, knead for about 10 minutes, or until smooth and elastic. (If using electric mixer with dough hook, knead at low speed for 5 minutes.)
3. Divide dough in 2 balls and let sit for 5 minutes. Lightly rub oil on each ball and flatten into a disk, 1-inch thick and about 6 inches in diameter.
4. Sprinkle the dry cookie sheet with 4 tablespoons cornmeal and put the rounds of dough on it, allowing room between them to rise. Cover with dampened kitchen towel and place in warm place for 2 hours to rise. Prick each loaf deeply 4 or 5 times to release the gas.
5. Preheat oven to 400°F.
6. Sprinkle tops of bread with remaining cornmeal. Bake for 10 minutes. Reduce heat to 300°F and bake 40 minutes longer, or until the bread sounds hollow when tapped.

Serve bread sliced in wedges, warm or cool.

Moroccan pastries are works of art. They have incorporated the flair of the French with the use of Middle East ingredients, such as honey, almonds, sesame seeds, and dried fruit. Here is a fun and easy recipe to get you started in the art of Moroccan pastry making.

Yield: 20 cookies

1 cup **blanched, finely ground** almonds
1/2 cup confectioners' sugar
1 to 1 1/4 cups all-purpose flour
1 teaspoon almond extract
1 egg, lightly beaten
1 teaspoon ground cinnamon
1/2 cup butter (at room temperature)
1/2 cup sesame seeds

Equipment: **mortar and pestle** or food processor to grind almonds, large-size mixing bowl, mixing spoon, pie pan, lightly greased or nonstick cookie sheet

Preheat oven to 350°F.

1. Put ground nuts, sugar, 1 cup flour, almond extract, egg, cinnamon, and butter in mixing bowl and mix well. Using clean hands, **knead** mixture into a dough (it will be slightly sticky).
2. Pour seeds into pie pan. Pinch off walnut-size pieces of dough (if too sticky [difficult to handle], add remaining flour). Roll dough pieces in seeds to coat, and then, between the palms of your hands, roll pieces into about 2-inch-long cylindrical shapes, thicker in the middle, tapering at the ends.
3. Place side-by-side on the cookie sheet, curving slightly into crescents. Bake in oven for about 30 minutes or until golden brown.

Serve *sesame cornes de gazelles* as a snack with milk or tea.

Algeria

Algeria, on the Mediterranean coast of North Africa, was invaded by France in 1830. It was a colony from 1848 until 1962, when the French finally consented to leave after much bloodshed. Some French influence still remains, including the language spoken and French foods, such as the crusty French bread that is commonly eaten. Algerians grow grains, olives, figs, grapes, dates, fruit trees, and vegetables along the fertile coastal areas. Livestock is raised in the interior of the country by the nomadic and semi-nomadic people to the south. Chickens, sheep, goats, cattle, and horses are the principal livestock. Algerians are Sunni Muslim; thus, no alcohol or pork are served. Sweet mint tea and black coffee are popular with the adults. Children like to drink apricot juice.

Couscous is popular in Algeria, Morocco, and Tunisia. It is made of **semolina**, the protein rich middling of grains of wheat. Excellent couscous is available already prepared at most supermarkets, so we are spared the long hours it takes to make it from scratch. There are many ways to serve this fine food, including the following recipe.

Algerian Couscous   Chicken Stew

Couscous refers both to the prepared grain itself and to stews made with couscous. The Mediterranean and Middle Eastern countries each have their own preferences and recipes for making *couscous*. In Algeria the meat is fried in olive oil first and tomatoes are rarely omitted. A fiery condiment made with hot **pimentos**, called *Harissais*, is always served with Algerian *couscous* and is enjoyed by those who are accustomed to hot foods. In Algeria stews are simmered slowly for several hours until everything in the pot is blended together and the chicken falls off the bones.

Yield: serves 6

2 to 4 tablespoons olive oil
2 to 3 pounds chicken, cut into serving-size pieces
3 cups chicken broth, homemade or canned
3 carrots, cut in about 2-inch chunks
2 onions, **coarsely chopped**
2 turnips, cut in about 2-inch chunks
3 cloves garlic, **finely chopped**, or 1 teaspoon garlic granules
2 teaspoons ground **coriander**
1/4 teaspoon *each* ground red pepper and ground **turmeric**
3 zucchini, cut into 1/4-inch slices
2 cups cooked garbanzo beans, canned or homemade
4 to 6 cups cooked *couscous* (cook according to directions on package and keep warm)

Equipment: Large-size saucepan with cover or **Dutch oven**, mixing spoon

1. Heat 2 tablespoons oil in saucepan or Dutch oven over medium-high heat. Add chicken pieces and fry until brown (add more oil if necessary to prevent sticking), about 6 to 10 minutes per side. Remove from pan and set aside. Fry in batches if necessary.
2. Add chicken broth, carrots, onions, turnips, garlic, **coriander**, red pepper, and turmeric in the same pan, mix well, and bring to a boil over high heat. Reduce heat to simmer and layer zucchini, beans, and chicken on top. Cover and cook very slowly for about 1 hour, until chicken is very tender.
3. Mound the *couscous* in the middle of a platter and place chicken pieces and vegetables around it.

To serve Algerian-style, place the platter in the middle of the table. The guests are given a damp towel to wipe their hands. The head of the house, and then special guests, are first to eat. They dip the fingers of the right hand in the platter of **couscous**. They then proceed to take a handful and roll it into a ball (using only the right hand). They then eat it off their fingers. The chicken and stew are eaten in the same fashion.

Different Ways to Serve and Eat Cooked Couscous as They Do in Algeria:

1. Make a salad of sliced ripe tomatoes topped with morsels of oil-packed canned tuna, chopped onion and anchovies; drizzle with olive oil and generously splash on lemon juice. Set in the middle of a large platter and spoon the *couscous* around it.
2. Make a salad of peeled, sliced oranges, thinly sliced radishes, and finely chopped mint leaves. Sprinkle with a dressing of orange juice sharpened by a dash of vinegar. Serve on the same platter with the *couscous*.
3. For dessert: pour the warm couscous in the center of a platter and sprinkle with chopped sticky dates, shelled almonds, and chopped fresh or dried figs. Serve dessert *couscous* by dipping the right-hand fingers into the mixture and make a small ball with dates, almonds, and figs. Then eat it off your fingers. (Always wash your hands before eating off them.)

Tunisia

Tunisia is 86 miles across the Mediterranean Sea from Sicily, Italy. Romans overran the city-state of Carthage (in Tunisia) in 146 B.C. and controlled the entire Tunisian area until the mid-seventh century. It provided wheat to the Romans and for centuries was known as the " breadbasket" of ancient Rome. Today Tunisia's food crops are cereals such as wheat and barley, olives, grapes, citrus fruits, dates, and vegetables. Some food is still exported to Europe, but Tunisians need to import food to meet their needs. Their livestock includes sheep, goats, cattle, camels, and donkeys.

Tunisian cooking reflects the many cultures that have touched Tunisian lives, including the French, Italian, and Spanish. Since most Tunisians are Muslims, Islamic dietary laws are followed, and pork and alcohol are excluded. The Tunisians eat with the fingers of the right hand and everyone eats directly from the same large platter; no forks, knives, or spoons are used.

Slata de Zaalouk   *Cooked Vegetable Salad*

Yield: serves 4 to 6

2 tablespoons olive or vegetable oil
1 eggplant (about 1/2 pound), skin-on, cut into 1/2-inch **cubes**
2 zucchini, cut in 1/2-inch-thick slices
3 cloves garlic, **finely chopped,** or 1 teaspoon garlic granules
3 cups water
1 *each* green bell pepper and red bell pepper; remove stem and seeds and cut into thin strips
2 tomatoes, **blanched, peeled** and chopped
1 teaspoon ground **coriander**
salt and pepper to taste

4 green onions, finely chopped, for serving
2 lemons, cut in wedges, for serving
24 black olives, Mediterranean-style, for serving
1/4 cup olive oil for serving, to drizzle as needed

Equipment: Large-size skillet with cover or **Dutch oven**, mixing spoon

1. Heat oil in skillet or Dutch oven over high heat. Add eggplant, zucchini, and garlic, fry for 3 minutes, and mix well. Add water, bring to a boil, cover, reduce heat to simmer, and cook for 10 minutes.
2. Add red and green peppers, **blanched** tomatoes, coriander, and salt and pepper to taste. Cook uncovered, stirring frequently, until almost all water evaporates, about 10 minutes. Remove from heat and cool to room temperature.

Serve in a bowl with little side dishes of green onions, lemons, black olives, and olive oil. Each person adds the condiments desired.

Salata Meshwiya   Tuna Fish Salad

A Tunisian specialty, this salad is popular all along the north African coast.

Yield: serves 2 to 4

2 *each* green bell peppers and red bell peppers, cut in half and **seeded**
4 tomatoes, **blanched, peeled**, and cut in 1/4-inch-thick slices
6 green onions, finely sliced
1 cup canned tuna fish (either oil or water pack—drain and discard juice)
3 tablespoons olive or vegetable oil
1 tablespoon lemon juice
salt and pepper to taste
2 hard-cooked eggs, thinly sliced for garnish
1 tablespoon **capers**, drained, for garnish
2 tablespoons chopped flat-leaf parsley, for garnish

Equipment: Salad bowl, mixing spoon, jar with tight fitting lid

1. Remove skin from peppers. To remove, place peppers, cut side down, in a hot broiler until the skin is soft, about 5 to 8 minutes. Remove and wrap in paper towel for 3 minutes. Rub the paper towel over the charred skin and the skin will rub off easily. Cut skinless pepper in thin strips.
2. Put green and red peppers, tomatoes, and onions in salad bowl. Crumble tuna, add it to vegetables, and toss gently.
3. In the jar combine oil, lemon juice, and salt and pepper. Tighten lid and shake well.

To serve, pour dressing over salad and toss gently. Garnish with egg slices, capers, and sprinkle of parsley.

Tunisian Tchat-tchouka   Baked Eggs Casserole

Yield: serves 4 to 6

2 tablespoons olive oil
4 onions, peeled and thinly sliced
4 tomatoes, **peeled** and cut each into 6 wedges

2 green bell peppers, **seeded** and cut into 1-inch chunks
1 cup red pimentos, canned, **cubed**
1 clove garlic, **finely chopped**, or 1/2 teaspoon garlic granules
6 eggs (1 per person)
1/4 teaspoon paprika

Equipment: Large-size skillet, mixing spoon, 9-inch shallow oven-proof baking dish or pan

Preheat oven to 300° F.
1. Heat oil in skillet over medium-high heat, add onions, and cook until brown, about 5 minutes. Add tomatoes, peppers, pimentos, and garlic, and mix well. Reduce heat to medium and cook until vegetables are a soft, pulpy mass, about 20 minutes.
2. Transfer mixture to baking pan. Using back of mixing spoon, smooth out top. Again using the spoon, make 6 slight indentations about the size of an egg yolk into the mixture at equal distances across the top.
3. Break an egg and set it in one of the indentations. Repeat using all eggs. Sprinkle eggs with paprika.
4. Bake in oven for about 15 minutes or until eggs are cooked through.

Serve as the main dish with a side dish of rice.

Ghoriba Sablee au Beurre   *Butter Cookies*

The Tunisian bakers are famous for melt-in-your-mouth, light-as-air cookies and cakes.

Yield: about 25

6 1/2 cups all-purpose flour, **sifted**
2 cups confectioner's sugar (powdered), reserve a little for garnish
2 cups melted butter or margarine

Equipment: Flour **sifter**, large-size mixing bowl, mixing spoon and clean hands, nonstick or lightly greased cookie sheet, floured work surface

1. Combine flour and sugar in mixing bowl and mix well. Make a well in the center of mixture and pour in melted butter or margarine. Gradually blend with dry ingredients to make a dough. Shape into ping-pong-size balls, place side-by-side on cookie sheet, and chill for about 2 hours.
2. Preheat oven to 350°F.
3. Flatten chilled balls between the palms of your hands. Place side-by-side on cookie sheet and bake for about 15 minutes, until golden brown. When cold, dust with confectioner's sugar.

Serve as a midday snack with a cool drink or tea.

Libya

Libyans import 75 percent of their food. The majority of their oil-rich land in North Africa is desert, with only 1 percent arable along the coast. On this small area more than 50 percent of the Libyan population grow wheat, barley, olives, dates, and citrus fruits. In the desert, sheep, goats, and camels are raised.

Before the discovery of oil in 1959, Libya was one of the poorest countries on the African continent. Consequently, beans were a favorite food; they are high in nutrition and low in cost. After the discovery of oil, and the sharing of the money the oil brought in, foods of the world began to be enjoyed by all Libyans. However, tradition still plays a strong role in this Sunni Islamic country, where pork and alcohol are not a part of the diet; old family recipes for bean dishes are still a source of pride to the Libyans. The recipe for *ful*, listed under Egypt (page 57), is also a popular Libyan bean dish. Most recipes listed in one Middle Eastern country are interchangeable with their neighbors. For example, Algerian *couscous* is enjoyed not only in the Middle East but throughout North Africa as well.

Al Batheeth   Date Candy

Libyan children, like children everywhere, love sweets. Dates have been cultivated for thousands of years in North Africa, where they are sometimes called the "candy that grows on trees." They are naturally sweet and have excellent nutritional value. Milk and dates create a sustaining diet. To cut dates easily, use kitchen scissors, dipping them in water frequently to prevent sticking. About 1/2 pound of **pitted** dates yields a little over 1 cup of chopped dates.

Yield: about 20 pieces

1 cup all-purpose flour
1/2 cup melted butter, margarine, or *ghee*
1 teaspoon ground **cardamom**
1/2 teaspoon ground ginger
1 cup finely chopped **pitted** dates (cut with scissors, see description above)
1/2 to 1 cup confectioners' sugar

Equipment: Nonstick or dry cookie sheet, medium-size mixing bowl, mixing spoon, clean hands, flat plate, pie pan

Preheat oven to 350° F.
1. Spread flour out on cookie sheet and set in oven for about 10 minutes, until flour turns golden brown. Pour flour into mixing bowl.
2. Add butter, cardamom, ginger, and dates and mix well. When cool enough to handle with clean hands, press rounded tablespoons of mixture into oval shapes and place side-by-side on flat plate.
3. Put 1/2 cup confectioners' sugar in pie pan or flat plate and roll each candy to coat, adding more sugar if necessary. Place on plate and chill.

Serve *al batheeth* as a candy treat. Store in covered bowl and refrigerate.

Middle East

The Middle East is also known as the Islamic Realm. Although less than one-half of all Muslims live in this vast realm, the prevalence of Islam is its chief cultural feature and suggests the name Islamic Realm. Some people extend the Middle East further west and east, but for this section of the book, it stretches from the eastern Mediterranean lands to Iran, and in the north from the Turkish border to the Indian Ocean in the south.

Middle Eastern cookery is distinctive, rich, and subtle in spicing. Some favorite spices include fennel, **cilantro**, mint, parsley, **cardamom**, ginger, nutmeg, and **turmeric** just to name a few. Favorite vegetables include cucumbers, eggplant, garlic, lettuce, onions, tomatoes, and zucchini. Almonds, **bulgur** wheat, chick-peas, **lentils**, pine nuts, rice, whole wheat flour, and broad beans called *ful medame*s are frequently used grains and nuts. Lamb is the most popular meat because pork is not allowed for either the Jews or the Arabs, and cows don't thrive well in the area. Chicken, however, is a favorite all over, and so several dishes are included here. Some popular drinks include fruit juices, tea, coffee, milk (camel's), sodas, and yogurt mixed with water.

Except for the more cosmopolitan city-dwellers of Cairo and Beirut and other major cities, most people retain the eating practices handed down for generations. The food is put on low tables and everyone sits around it on floor cushions. There are no eating utensils, soup is sipped from the bowl, and the food is eaten with the pre-washed fingers of the right hand.

Except for some of the recipes from Israel, many of the following recipes cross borders and are enjoyed in many Middle Eastern countries. (Check the recipe's notes to see if it crosses borders.)

One quick treat, not included as a recipe, are bow tie cookies made from puff pastry sheets, available in the freezer section of your supermarket. Cut the dough into 1-inch by 3-inch sections, twist in the middle, and bake according to directions on the box. Sprinkle each bow tie with confectioner's sugar and you have a standard Middle Eastern sweet.

Egypt

Egyptians have cultivated nature's bounty for thousands of years. Organized agriculture along the Nile in northern Africa began around 6000 B.C. Egyptians discovered the leavening process that makes bread rise and how to preserve fish through salting and drying. Ancient wall paintings in the pyramids depict these wonders in minute detail, and supplies of food have been found intact in these ancient pharaohs' tombs, adding a great deal to our knowledge of what was eaten.

Today, Egyptians live among sand dunes, awesome pyramids, camel caravans, and magnificent art and architecture. The foods rural Egyptians enjoy have changed little over the years. The growing season has become year-round because of the irrigation provided by the Aswan Dam, completed in 1971. Now Egyptians grow rice, sugar cane, and melons in the summer; corn in the fall; wheat in the winter; and a variation of these and other crops, such as onions and beans, during the spring. Throughout the rural areas, little kitchen gardens are found beside many homes, supplying a few fresh vegetables for daily use. Sustaining the Egyptian economy, however, are cash crops of sugar cane, wonderful cotton, wheat, and other grains.

Most people buy their groceries at the colorful open air markets selling everything imaginable. People live quite well, and city dwellers enjoy foods from around the world. The use of silverware, china dinner plates, and napkins is commonplace in city homes.

Ful Mesdames   Brown Fava Beans

The national dish of Egypt is *ful mesdames*, or brown fava beans. It is as old as the pyramids and is said to have been eaten by the pharaohs. Fava beans are eaten for breakfast, lunch, and supper by everyone from desert nomads to wealthy sheiks.

Yield: serves 2 to 4

2 to 4 tablespoons olive oil
2 cups cooked brown fava beans, dried (cooked according to directions on package) or canned (drained), available at most supermarkets and health food stores
3 cloves garlic, peeled and **finely chopped**, or 1 teaspoon garlic granules
salt and pepper to taste
2 to 4 **hard-cooked eggs**, peeled for garnish
1/2 cup chopped parsley, for garnish
1 lemon quartered, for garnish

Equipment: Medium-size saucepan, mixing spoon

Heat 2 tablespoons oil in saucepan over medium heat. Add beans, garlic, salt and pepper to taste, and mix well. Cook until heated through, about 8 minutes. If beans seem dry, add oil to prevent sticking.

Serve in individual bowls. Put a hard-cooked egg in each bowl, cover with hot beans, sprinkle with parsley, and serve lemon wedges on the side.

Eggeh Bi Betingan   Omelet with Eggplant

Egyptian omelets are cake-like. In this recipe any vegetable, noodles, chicken, or meat can be added in place of or in combination with eggplant. Eggplants are a favorite vegetable in the Middle East.

Yield: serves 4 to 6

2 cups peeled and **cubed** eggplant
2 to 6 tablespoons butter or margarine
1 onion, **finely chopped**
1 clove garlic, finely chopped, or 1/2 teaspoon garlic granules
8 eggs, lightly beaten
salt and pepper to taste

Equipment: **Colander** or strainer, large-size skillet with cover, mixing spoon, large heat-proof plate, paper towels

1. Put eggplant in colander or strainer, sprinkle with salt, and set aside in sink or over plate for 20 minutes.
2. Rinse eggplant under cold water to wash off salt, drain well, and pat dry with paper towels.
3. Melt 2 tablespoons butter or margarine in skillet over medium-high heat, add onions and garlic, mix well, and cook until onion is soft (about 3 minutes).
4. Reduce heat to medium, add eggplant, and cook until tender, about 6 minutes. Mix well and add more butter or margarine if necessary to prevent sticking. Pour in eggs, season with salt and pepper, and mix thoroughly.
5. Reduce heat to low, cover, and cook for 15 minutes or until bottom is set. When bottom is firm, remove from heat, flip omelet over onto the plate, and slide it back into pan. Cook for about 3 minutes to set.

Serve hot or cold and cut into wedges at mealtime or as a snack.

Bamia   Lamb and Okra Stew

Yield: serves 6

2 to 6 tablespoons vegetable oil
2 onions, **finely chopped**
6 cloves garlic, chopped, or 2 teaspoons garlic granules
2 pounds lean lamb or beef, cut into 1-inch **cubes**
4 cups chopped okra, fresh (trim ends) or frozen
3 tomatoes, **peeled** and cut in cubes, or 2 cups canned **stewed** tomatoes, drained and chopped
1/2 cup tomato sauce
1 teaspoon ground **cilantro**
1/2 teaspoon ground **cardamom**
salt and pepper to taste
4 to 6 cups water, more or less as needed
juice of 1 lemon

Equipment: Large saucepan with cover, mixing spoon

1. Heat 2 tablespoons oil in saucepan over medium heat. Add onions and garlic, fry until soft and golden (about 5 minutes), and mix well. Increase heat to medium high, add meat, and brown on all sides, stirring frequently; add more oil, if necessary, to prevent sticking.
2. Add okra, tomatoes, tomato sauce, cilantro, cardamom, and salt and pepper to taste. Add just enough water to cover meat and vegetables. Bring to a boil, reduce to simmer, cover, and cook for about 1 1/2 hours or until meat is tender and sauce is thick but not dry. If it is too dry, add a little more water and stir frequently. Remove from heat and stir in lemon juice.

Serve *bamia* in individual bowls. Plenty of flat bread is needed to sop the stew from the bowl to your mouth.

Kosheri   Lentils, Rice, and Macaroni Stew

Throughout Egyptian cities, *kosheri* street vendors ladle out portions of rice, lentils, and macaroni from huge vats. Customers help themselves to toppings of fried onions and spicy tomato sauce. This recipe is a popular, nourishing, and filling meal.

Yield: serves 4 to 6

1 cup *each* cooked brown **lentils**, elbow macaroni, and rice (each cooked separately according to directions on each package)
2 tablespoons vegetable oil
2 cups **coarsely chopped** onion
1 1/2 cups chunky-style spaghetti sauce, homemade or canned
2 tablespoons distilled white vinegar
1 teaspoon crushed red pepper, more or less to taste
1/2 cup water
salt and pepper to taste

Equipment: Large-size mixing bowl, medium-size skillet, mixing spoon, small-size and medium-size serving bowls

1. Drain cooked lentils and cooked macaroni in **colander** or strainer and put them in large mixing bowl. Add cooked rice, gently toss, and set aside in a warm place.
2. *Prepare fried onions:* heat oil in skillet over medium heat, add onion, mix well, and cook until tender and slightly brown (about 5 minutes). Remove from heat, transfer to small serving bowl, and set aside.
3. *Prepare tomato sauce:* using same skillet, combine spaghetti sauce, vinegar, red pepper, water, salt and pepper to taste. Mix well, bring to a boil over high heat, reduce to simmer, cook for 5 minutes, remove from heat, put in serving bowl, and keep warm.

To serve, ladle 1/2 cup, more or less, lentils, rice, and macaroni mixture into individual bowls. Let people add their own toppings of fried onions and tomato sauce.

Israel

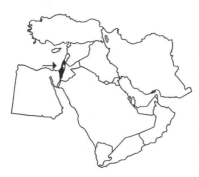

The foods of Israel are a blending of many cultures. Jewish people have immigrated from all around the world, even the Orient, making Israel the land of a thousand-and-one flavors. The Israeli people follow many of the ancient practices, rituals, and laws handed down from generation to generation. The "strictly Kosher" dietary laws concerning selection, preparation, and eating of food—even though delivered to Moses more than 3,000 years ago—are so deeply woven into Jewish religious and family life, they remain virtually unchanged today. The laws were established long before there were such things as ice and refrigeration and were created for health reasons. The ancient practice of not combining dairy with meat, and not eating shellfish and certain animals, is the way of life in many Israeli homes. Fresh fruit and vegetables are easily available in Israel because of successful agricultural techniques developed over the last 50 years.

In many cultures food plays an important part in celebrations, festivals, and special days of remembrance. Traditionally the flat unleavened bread called *matzo* is eaten during the Jewish Passover as a reminder of the Jews' hurried flight from Egypt, when there was not time for the bread to rise. Today matzo is eaten at any time and matzo meal flour is available at most supermarkets. The following recipe is made with matzo meal flour.

Chicken Soup with Knaidlach   Matzo Ball Dumplings in Chicken Soup

Yield: serves 6 or 8

1 chicken, cut into serving-size pieces
10 cups water
2 ribs celery, each cut into 4 pieces
2 onions, peeled
2 whole carrots, **trimmed** and scraped
2 tablespoons vegetable oil
2 eggs, slightly beaten
1/2 cup matzo meal, available at most supermarkets
2 tablespoons water
salt and pepper to taste

Equipment: Large-size saucepan with cover, slotted spoon, medium-size roasting pan with cover, medium-size mixing bowl, fork or **whisk**, ladle

1. *Prepare soup:* put chicken, water, celery, onion, and carrots in saucepan. Bring soup to a boil over high heat, cover, reduce heat, and simmer about 1 hour, until chicken is tender. Add salt and pepper to taste.
2. Remove chicken and vegetables from broth and transfer to roasting pan. Add 2 cups broth, cover, and place in warm oven, 150° F, until ready to serve.

3. Keep remaining soup broth hot over low heat until dumplings are ready.
4. *Prepare dumplings:* put oil and eggs in mixing bowl and mix well. Add matzo meal and water to egg mixture, and, stirring continually with fork or whisk, blend well. Add salt and pepper to taste. Refrigerate for about 15 minutes.
5. Increase heat under soup to medium-high. Using clean hands, make 6 or 8 balls, about 1 1/2-inch-size *matzo balls,* and drop them one by one into boiling soup. Continue until all mixture is used. Cover and reduce heat to simmer for about 30 minutes.

To serve *matzo balls,* put one in each soup bowl and ladle hot broth over it. Remove chicken with vegetables from the oven, transfer to a large platter, and serve after the soup, with side dishes of potatoes and additional vegetables.

Mandelbrot   Almond Cookies

In this *mandelbrot* recipe it is necessary to bake it twice in order to get a crisp, crunchy texture.

Yield: 18 slices

3 eggs, beaten
1/2 cup sugar
1 1/2 cups all-purpose flour
1 teaspoon baking powder
1/4 teaspoon salt
1/2 teaspoon ground ginger
1 teaspoon ground cinnamon
1/2 cup **finely chopped, blanched** almonds

Equipment: Large-size mixing bowl, **egg beater** or electric mixer, nonstick or greased 5- x 9-inch loaf pan, **serrated knife**, nonstick or plain cookie sheet

Preheat oven to 350°F.
1. Put eggs and sugar in large mixing bowl, and use egg beater or electric mixer to blend well. Add flour, baking powder, salt, ginger, cinnamon, and almonds and mix well to blend.
2. Pour into loaf pan and bake for about 45 minutes until golden. Remove from oven and cool before using serrated knife to slice into 1/2-inch-thick pieces.
3. Reduce oven heat to 200°F.
4. Place slices side-by-side on cookie sheet and return to oven to dry out. Bake for about 20 minutes on each side until very dry and lightly toasted.

Serve *mandelbrot* as a cookie snack. It keeps indefinitely when stored in an airtight container.

Lukshen Kugel   Noodle Pudding

Kugels are hot puddings made with noodles, potatoes, and some vegetables. They are staple side dishes in many Israeli homes, and every cook has a special way of making it.

Yield: served 6 to 8

3 eggs
1/2 cup sugar
1/4 teaspoon *each* salt and cinnamon
8 ounces cooked and drained medium noodles (cooked according to directions on package)
1/2 cup raisins
2 cups small curd cottage cheese
1/2 cup sour cream
1 apple, peeled and grated
1 teaspoon vanilla
3 tablespoons butter or margarine

Equipment: Grater, large-size mixing bowl, wooden mixing spoon, 2-quart baking pan or casserole

Preheat oven to 350° F.
1. Put eggs, sugar, salt, and cinnamon in mixing bowl and mix well. Add cooked noodles, raisins, cottage cheese, sour cream, grated apple, and vanilla. Mix well to blend.
2. To prepare baking pan or casserole grease bottom and sides generously with butter or margarine. Pour in noodle mixture and smooth top. Bake in oven for about 1 hour, or until top is nicely browned. Remove from oven and cool for about 20 minutes.

To serve *kugel* cut into squares and serve as a side dish with meat or chicken. *Kugel* is delicious when cooled to room temperature.

Kichels   Biscuits

Yield: about 18 pieces

1 cup butter or margarine, room temperature
1 cup sugar
2 eggs
2 cups self-rising flour

Equipment: Large-size mixing bowl, mixing spoon, clean hands, rolling pin, work surface, 2 nonstick or lightly greased cookie sheets, small-size bowl, fork, pastry brush

Preheat oven to 375°F.
1. Blend butter or margarine, sugar, and 1 egg in mixing bowl. Add flour and **knead** into stiff dough.
2. Using the rolling pin, roll dough about 1/4-inch thick on floured work surface. Cut into 2- x 4-inch pieces. Place pieces side-by-side on cookie sheet about 1-inch apart. Beat remaining egg in small bowl using a fork and lightly brush egg over tops of dough pieces. Bake for about 15 minutes until puffy and golden.

Serve *kichels* as a snack. They are great to dunk in milk or cocoa, and they keep well in a covered jar.

Tzimmes Fleishig   Stewed Carrots with Meat

There are many ways to prepare carrots, and there are popular recipes for either meat or vegetarian dishes in Israel. When meat is added, the dishes are called *fleishig,* and when they are made or served with milk or dairy, vegetarian dishes are *milchig.*

Yield: serves 4

1 pound lean brisket of beef, cut in chunks
4 cups sliced carrots, fresh, frozen or canned, drained
1/2 cup light brown sugar
2 to 3 cups water
1/2 cup all-purpose flour

Equipment: Medium-size saucepan with cover or **Dutch oven**, mixing spoon

1. Put beef, carrots, sugar, and 1 1/2 cups water in saucepan or Dutch oven. Bring mixture to a boil over high heat, reduce to simmer, cover, and cook until tender (about 1 hour). Add more water if necessary to prevent sticking.
2. Mix 1/2 cup of remaining water with flour making a smooth paste. Add to beef and carrots, mix well, and simmer for 15 minutes more. Season with salt and pepper to taste.

Serve *tzimmes* as the main dish with side dishes of potatoes or rice and bread.

Tzimmes Milchig   Stewed Carrots

Yield: serves 4 to 6

4 cups sliced carrots, fresh, frozen or canned, drained
1/2 cup *each* light brown sugar and orange juice
1 1/2 cups water
1/4 cup all-purpose flour
salt and pepper to taste

Equipment: Medium-size saucepan, mixing spoon

1. Put carrots, brown sugar, orange juice, and 1 cup of water in saucepan. Bring to a boil over high heat, reduce heat to simmer, and cook until tender (about 20 minutes—if using canned carrots cook only 10 minutes).
2. Mix remaining 1/2 cup water with flour and add to cooked carrots; stirring continually, simmer for about 4 minutes to cook flour. Remove from heat, add salt and pepper to taste, and mix well.

Serve *tzimmes* as a side dish with eggs, fish, or other vegetable dishes.

Lebanon and Syria

Lebanese and Syrian foods are world famous. Some of their excellent cooks have emigrated, spreading the fame of this wonderful food. Lebanon is a tiny fertile country nestled on the Mediterranean Sea on Syria's eastern shore. It is capable of producing

its own food. Syria is also a fertile area and produces most of its own food. Fresh fruits and vegetables are important in these peoples' diets. Salads accompany meals; fruits follow it. Here are dishes that both the Lebanese and Syrians love. *Kibby* is the national dish of both countries. It uses the most common of meats in these Islamic lands, lamb. Probably the most popular wheat product throughout the Middle East is a cracked wheat grain with a nutty texture and taste called **bulgur**. It is used in *kibby* and in a special salad built around this grain called *tabbouleh*. Another Middle Eastern favorite is the vegetable eggplant. Here we find it in a dip called *baba ghannooj*. Everyone loves sweets, and the recipe we have included for you has been a favorite for centuries!

Kibbeh Bil Sanieh   Stuffed Meat Loaf

Yield: serves 4 to 6

1 1/2 cups **bulgur wheat**, available at most supermarkets and health food stores
1 1/2 pounds chopped meat, either lamb or beef
2 onions, **peeled** and **finely chopped**
1 to 3 tablespoons olive or vegetable oil
1/2 cup pine nuts
1/2 teaspoon *each* ground cinnamon and ground nutmeg
salt and pepper to taste
1/2 cup melted butter

Equipment: Medium-size mixing bowl, strainer, large-size mixing bowl, clean hands, greased deep 9-inch square baking pan, medium-size skillet, mixing spoon

1. Put bulgur in small bowl and add enough cold water to just cover grains. Set aside for about 20 minutes, until water is absorbed and bulgur is tender. Drain in strainer and squeeze out excess water using back of spoon.
2. Put well-drained bulgur, 1 pound meat, 1 onion, and salt and pepper to taste in large bowl, and blend well, using clean hands. Rinse hands in water to prevent sticking and press half the mixture into bottom of baking pan. Leave other half of mixture in mixing bowl to be used later in recipe.
3. *Prepare stuffing*: heat 1 tablespoon oil in skillet over medium-high heat. Add remaining 1/2 pound meat and 1 onion, cook about 5 minutes, until meat is browned, and mix well. Add more oil if necessary to prevent sticking. Remove from heat, add pine nuts, cinnamon, nutmeg, and salt and pepper to taste; mix well.
4. Preheat oven to 350°F.
5. Spread stuffing evenly over mixture in loaf pan. Cover with remaining bulgur mixture and pour melted butter on top.
6. Bake in oven about 40 minutes, until the top is browned and crisp.

Serve either hot or cold, cut into squares or diamond shapes.

Baba Ghannooj   Eggplant Dip

Sometimes called "poor man's butter," *baba ghannooj* is a popular Mediterranean spread. It is a tasty dip to serve with raw vegetables, like carrot and celery sticks.

Yield: about 2 cups

1 eggplant (about 1 pound)
1 clove garlic, **finely chopped**, or 1/4 teaspoon garlic granules
juice from 2 lemons
2 to 4 tablespoons sesame oil
salt to taste
1 tablespoon **finely chopped** parsley, for garnish

Equipment: Fork, 9-inch baking pan, oven mitts, medium-size bowl with cover, potato masher or electric blender

Preheat oven to 450°F.
1. Poke eggplant skin with fork tines in about 8 places, put in baking pan, and cook in oven until soft and tender, about 30 to 40 minutes. Remove from oven and, when cool enough to handle, cut in half, scoop out meat, and discard skin.
2. Put eggplant meat, garlic, lemon juice, 2 tablespoons oil, and salt to taste in medium bowl or blender. Blend mixture to a smooth paste, either by hand using the potato masher, or in electric blender. If mixture is too dry add another tablespoon of oil. Transfer to a bowl with cover and refrigerate. When ready to serve, sprinkle with 1 tablespoon of remaining oil and parsley.

Serve in small bowl as a dip for vegetables, chips, crackers, or chunks of flat bread.

Fried Kibbeh   Hamburger

Kibbeh is the very popular hamburger of Syria and Lebanon made with ground meat, usually lamb, and a cracked wheat (**bulgur**). They are blended into a smooth lump-free mixture by either pounding in a **mortar** with a **pestle** or passing, several times, through the fine blade of a meat grinder. For the following recipe, ask the butcher to grind the meat extra fine for you. Fine grain bulgur (resembling grains of sand) is available at most health food and all Middle East stores.

Yield: serves 4

1/2 cup fine grain bulgur (cracked wheat)
1 pound finely ground meat (preferably lamb)
1 onion, **finely chopped**
2 tablespoons water
salt and pepper to taste
2 to 4 tablespoons olive oil, more or less as needed

Equipment: Strainer, medium-size mixing bowl, medium-size skillet, metal spatula

1. Put cracked wheat in strainer and rinse with cold running water. Drain well. Transfer to medium-size mixing bowl and add meat, onion, water, and salt and

pepper to taste. Using clean hands, mix well until blended and lump-free. Divide into 4 equal parts and, using wet hands, shape each into an oblong patty.

2. Heat 2 tablespoons oil in skillet over medium-high heat, add patties, and fry until browned and well done (about 5 minutes on each side). Add more oil, if necessary, to prevent sticking.

Serve each person a *kibbeh* with a side dish of beans and rice.

Tabbouleh   Cracked Wheat and Parsley Salad

Yield: serves 6

1 cup **bulgur**, available at some supermarkets and most health food stores
3/4 to 1 cup boiling hot water, more or less as needed
3 tomatoes, **peeled**, chopped
1 bunch green onions, chopped
1 1/2 cups **finely chopped** parsley
1/2 cup finely chopped fresh mint leaves or 3 tablespoons dried leaves
1/4 cup olive oil
1/2 cup lemon juice
salt and pepper to taste
leaf lettuce leaves, washed and patted dry, for garnish

Equipment: Small-size mixing bowl, mixing spoon, strainer, medium-size bowl

1. Put bulgur in small bowl and add enough boiling water to just cover grains. Set aside for about 20 minutes, until water is absorbed and bulgur is tender. Drain in strainer and squeeze out excess water using back of spoon. Put bulgur in medium bowl and add tomatoes, green onions, parsley, and mint.
2. Mix oil and lemon juice in small bowl and add salt and pepper to taste. Pour over salad and toss to mix well. Refrigerate until ready to serve.

Serve *tabbouleh* in a bowl surrounded with lettuce leaves. Each person spoons mixture onto a leaf and rolls it up, eating lettuce and all.

Ma'mounia   Dessert

This nourishing pudding, *ma'mounia*, dates back to the ninth century when camel caravans were the only means of travel between ancient cities. Traveling back through time and to other Mediterranean cities, one finds many variations and different names for this sweet dish, but they're all basically the same. In Syria *ma'mounia* is often served for breakfast. **Semolina**, an ingredient in this recipe, is a by-product of wheat flour. There are two kinds of semolina: one made from regular wheat used in puddings (the kind needed for this recipe), and **durum wheat** semolina, used in pasta making.

Yield: serves 4 to 6

3/4 cup sugar
2 cups water
1/2 cup butter or margarine
1 cup **semolina** (made from regular wheat, not durum wheat)
1/2 cup each raisins and slivered almonds

1/4 teaspoon salt
1 cup heavy cream, whipped, or yogurt for garnish

Equipment: Small-size saucepan, wooden mixing spoon, medium-size saucepan

1. Heat sugar and water in small saucepan. Bring to a boil, stirring frequently with wooden spoon, and then reduce to simmer for about 10 minutes until mixture thickens.
2. In medium saucepan melt butter or margarine. Add **semolina** and cook over low heat, stirring continually for about 3 minutes to heat through.
3. Pour sugar mixture, raisins, almonds, and salt into semolina, increase heat, and bring to a boil. Reduce heat to simmer and stir continually until thick (about 5 minutes). Remove at once from heat.

Serve either warm or cold in individual dessert bowls. Serve with side dishes of either whipped cream or yogurt to spoon over it.

Jordan

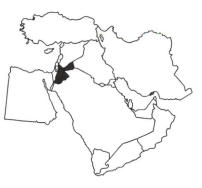

Jordan is a small, almost landlocked country in the Middle East. The only seaport is Aqaba on the Gulf of Aqaba. The economy is largely agricultural, despite the fact that only 10 percent of the land is usable for farming. Jordanians grow fruits and vegetables in their fertile mountainous areas to the west. Other principal crops include wheat, barley, and **lentils**. Nomadic Bedouins herd camels, goats, and sheep in the desert areas beyond the mountains to the east. More than half of the Jordanians live in the cities.

Jordanians' eating patterns differ somewhat from our own. Bread, white cheese, ripe olives, *hoomis*, and *ful*, a bean dish (see pages 72 and 57 for recipes to these last two), are an interesting breakfast combination. The adults top it all off with lots of coffee. Lunch is the main meal of the day. Meat, rice with nuts, and vegetable side dishes are commonly served. After the meal, diners go to the living room and end their meal with fruit, baklava, or little date sweets such as the following recipe.

Date and Nut Fingers

Yield: about 16 pieces

2 eggs, lightly beaten
1 cup sugar
2 cups chopped walnuts or pecans
1 cup chopped dates
1 cup chopped candied cherries
1 teaspoon vanilla
1/2 cup all-purpose flour
1 teaspoon baking powder

Equipment: Large-size mixing bowl, mixing spoon, sifter, nonstick or greased 8-inch-square baking pan

Preheat oven to 350°F.

1. Combine eggs and sugar in mixing bowl and mix until smooth. Add nuts, dates, cherries, and vanilla and mix until well blended.
2. **Sift** flour and baking powder into mixture and mix well. Pour into baking pan and spread evenly over the bottom. Bake for about 45 minutes or until lightly brown. Cut into finger-length strips while still warm.

Serve as a cookie or candy snack.

Saudi Arabia

Saudi Arabia is an oil-rich country that occupies most of the Arabian peninsula. It has at least one quarter of the world's oil reserves. Saudis are Sunni Muslim, and they are famous for their hospitality and generosity. Bedouin nomads, 30 percent of the population, traditionally live in the desert and raise livestock. This lifestyle is changing somewhat now because the Bedouins want their children to be educated; they are living closer to cities, forming semi-permanent dwellings. Desert nomadic Bedouins are generally poor and eat little meat. However, when guests arrive, an animal is killed, stuffed, and roasted for the occasion. Camels' milk is an important part of their diet. (Milk is always warmed, it is never served cold.) Sometimes all a Bedouin has to eat is dates, rice, and milk. The rice is a kind called *basmati*, which is imported from Pakistan. It is a hard grain that withstands long cooking periods and is aromatic. (Smells good!) The rice may have a little clarified butter and onion mixed in for flavor.

In the cities, the variety of foods available and the methods of cooking are very different. Wealthy city dwellers have the foods of the world at their fingertips. They use modern kitchen equipment and, of course, have ovens in which to bake foods. This first recipe uses an oven. Tomatoes are stuffed in this dish called *yalanchi*. It is a typical Middle Eastern stuffing used to fill all kinds of vegetables as well as grape and cabbage leaves. The second recipe listed, *blehat lahma*, could be made in a kitchen or over a fire in the desert. It uses the most common of meats in this part of the world, lamb.

Yalanchi   *Stuffed Tomatoes*

Yield: serves 6

6 medium-large, firm, ripe tomatoes
2 to 4 tablespoons olive or vegetable oil
1 onion, **finely chopped**
1/2 cup raisins, soaked in warm water 10 minutes, drained

1/2 cup pine nuts
1/2 teaspoon ground cinnamon
2 to 2 1/2 cups rice (cooked according to directions on package)
salt and pepper to taste

Equipment: Paper towels, large-size skillet, mixing spoon, teaspoon, nonstick or greased 9-inch baking pan

1. Cut a slice from the top of each tomato, about 1/4 to 1/2 inch down. **Core** and finely chop tops. Scoop out tomatoes and turn upside down on paper towels to drain. Refrigerate **pulp** to use at another time.
2. Heat 2 tablespoons oil in large skillet over medium-high heat. Add onion and cook until soft, about 3 minutes; stir frequently. Add chopped tomato tops, raisins, pine nuts, and cinnamon and mix well. Reduce heat to simmer for about 2 minutes. Remove from heat, and add cooked rice and salt and pepper to taste; mix gently until well blended.
3. Preheat oven to 350° F.
4. Fill tomatoes with mixture and set side-by-side in baking pan. Dab remaining oil on tomatoes so they are well greased. Bake in oven until tender but still firm (about 25 minutes).

Serve warm or at room temperature for best flavor.

Blehat Lahma — Lamb Loaves with Apricots and Egg

Yield: serves 6 to 8

2 pounds ground lamb shoulder
12 dried apricots, **coarsely chopped**, soaked in hot water for 5 minutes, drained
1 onion, **finely chopped**
1/4 cup pine nuts
1 teaspoon *each* ground cinnamon and ground allspice
salt and pepper to taste
2 **hard-cooked eggs**, with shells removed
1 cup tomato paste, canned
1 cup water

Equipment: Medium-size mixing bowl, clean hands or wooden mixing spoon, lightly greased or nonstick 9- x 13-inch baking pan

Preheat oven to 350° F.

1. Put lamb, apricots, onion, pine nuts, cinnamon, allspice, and salt and pepper to taste in mixing bowl. Mix well, using clean hand or wooden spoon.
2. Divide the mixture in half and shape each half into a loaf around an egg. Put the loaves side-by-side in the baking pan.
3. Mix tomato paste with water and pour over the loaves. Put loaves in oven and bake for about 45 minutes or until meat is cooked. **Baste** frequently with the tomato sauce to keep loaves moist.

To serve the loaves, cool to room temperature and cut into thick slices. *Blehat lahma* makes excellent filling for sandwiches.

Yemen, Oman, United Arab Emirates, Qatar, Bahrain, and Kuwait

The following countries are all on the Arabian peninsula, and all share borders with Saudi Arabia. Each is a separate political entity, but they share cultural heritage, including food habits. Each country will be described, but most of the recipes can be used as representative of any of the countries.

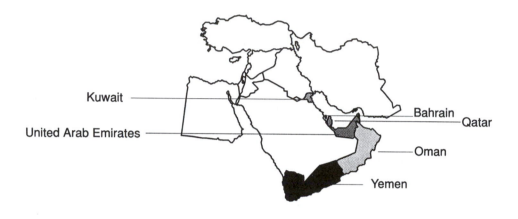

Yemen

Until May 23, 1990, Yemen was divided into two countries, North and South Yemen. Today, Yemen is one of the poorest nations in the world, with low per-capita income. The economy is primarily agricultural and food crops grown include **sorghum** and potatoes, dates, wheat, grapes, barley, corn, **millet**, and garden vegetables. Fishing is an important industry, as is raising livestock—mostly sheep, goats, and cattle. Yemeni food can be hot and spicy. Poorer Yemenis eat meat perhaps once a week, but soup bones are customarily used for flavoring all the time, such as in the lentil soup dish on page 72.

Oman

Oman's economy is based on oil, but most Omanis are involved with either fishing or farming. Fish, both fresh and dried, is a major source of protein. Fishing is done in the Gulf of Oman and the Arabian Sea. Omani agriculture is very limited. Rice is the staple food, but it must be imported. Dates, limes, mangos, melons, wheat, bananas, and onions are grown in irrigated fields. Livestock raised include sheep, chickens, and goats. Most of the people live in rural areas.

United Arab Emirates

Oil exports have made this nation one of the wealthiest in the world. Most of the people live in the coastal cities. Grains have to be imported, but by using pumping irrigation systems, the country is almost self-sufficient in fruit and vegetables. Dates are a primary crop. Poultry and dairy farming provide eggs and milk products for the people.

Qatar

Qatar is another of the oil-rich nations on the eastern coast of the Arabian peninsula. Qataris are city dwellers. Food has to be imported because of the lack of water and fertile soil. Rice and dates are staples in their diets. Qataris can afford to import their food because of the money made from oil exports, which accounts for 99 percent of Qatar's exports.

Bahrain

Bahrain is made up of a group of tiny islands off the Arabian Peninsula in the Persian (Arabian) Gulf. The people of Bahrain are city dwellers for the most part. The north and northwestern coasts have lovely date groves and vegetable gardens, which are possible because of springs and wells that provide artesian water. Bananas, citrus fruits, pomegranates, and mangos are the main foods grown here. Livestock raised include chickens, goats, sheep, and cattle for dairy farming. These food sources help the country but are not enough to sustain it, and so food must be imported. In recent years, Bahrain has attempted to diversify its nonagricultural industrial sector because its oil reserves will soon be depleted.

Kuwait

Kuwait has about one-fifth of the world's oil reserves. In addition to the oil production, there are a few fertile bits of land in Kuwait where, using irrigation techniques, garden produce and livestock feeds are grown. The fishing industry is being revitalized, having been neglected after the discovery of oil. Shrimp is the main catch in Kuwaiti waters in the Persian Gulf. Most of the land is desert, however, and oil money is what allows Kuwait to import its food. Kuwaitis enjoy travel and sample new foods abroad. Because they are relatively wealthy, many foods of the world are imported, but because they are Muslim, they observe traditional food restrictions.

Shourba Bilsen   Thick Lentil Soup

This dish is particularly popular in Yemen.

Yield: serves 6

1 pound soup bones, beef or lamb
8 cups water
2 cups brown **lentils**
2 onions, **finely chopped**
3 cloves garlic, finely chopped, or 1 teaspoon garlic granules
2 cups **stewed** tomatoes, homemade or canned
1/4 cup finely chopped **cilantro** leaves or 3 tablespoons dried cilantro
salt and pepper to taste

Equipment: Large-size saucepan with cover or **Dutch oven**, mixing spoon

1. Rinse soup bones and put in saucepan with water, bring to a boil over high heat, and reduce heat to simmer.
2. Add lentils, onions, garlic, tomatoes, cilantro, and salt and pepper to taste, cover, and cook for 1 1/2 hours, stirring frequently to prevent sticking.

Serve hot in individual soup bowls. If there is meat on the bones eat it and also the rich and nutritious bone marrow. Your dog will love you forever if you feed it the bones.

Hoomis   Chickpea Spread

Hoomis, also spelled *hummus*, *homus*, and *humus* refers both to **chickpeas** (also known as garbanzo beans) and to the following spread. Chickpeas are an important food throughout the Middle East.

Yield: 2 1/2 cups

2 cups cooked chickpeas, homemade or canned, with liquid
2 tablespoons lemon juice
4 tablespoons *tahineh*, homemade (recipe page 74) or bottled
1 teaspoon salt
3 cloves garlic, **finely chopped** or 1 teaspoon garlic granules
1/4 teaspoon liquid hot red pepper sauce
1 teaspoon olive oil or sesame oil for garnish
1 teaspoon finely chopped fresh parsley for garnish

Equipment: Electric blender, spoon or spatula, small-size bowl

1. Using blender, blend chickpeas, lemon juice, *tahineh*, salt, garlic, and red pepper sauce until mixture is lump-free and resembles a smooth paste.
2. Transfer to small bowl, drizzle with oil, and sprinkle with parsley.

Serve *hoomis* as a spread on pita bread, crackers, or as a dip with raw vegetables such as carrot and celery strips, cut-up broccoli or cauliflower, cherry tomatoes, etc.

Limonada   Lemonade

Lemon and lime are popular drink flavorings in the Middle East. Here is a favorite recipe, nice and cold for a hot day.

Yield: 10 servings

1 1/2 cups lemon or lime juice with seeds removed (soak fruit in hot water first before squeezing fruit for greatest yield)
1/2 cup corn syrup, or to taste
2 teaspoons orange blossom water (optional), available at Middle East food stores
8 12-oz bottles of clear carbonated water
10 glasses with crushed ice
10 mint sprigs

Equipment: Pitcher, long stirring spoon

1. Put lemon or lime juice in pitcher, add syrup and orange blossom water, and mix well.
2. Pour about 1/4 cup mixture into each glass filled with crushed ice and fill to the top with carbonated water. Garnish each glass with a mint sprig.

Date Bars

Dates are popular all over the Middle East. This date recipe is simple and fun to make. Sweets are served in the evening following dinner with coffee, tea, or, milk and good conversation.

Yield: 16 pieces

1 cup rolled oats, plain or instant
1/2 cup all-purpose flour
1/2 teaspoon baking powder
1/2 cup dark brown sugar
1/2 teaspoon salt
1 teaspoon cinnamon
1 cup melted butter or margarine
2 eggs, well beaten
1 cup **finely chopped pitted** dates (cut with scissors, see page 53)
1 cup chopped nuts, walnuts, peanuts, or pecans (optional)
1/2 cup confectioners' sugar for garnish

Equipment: Large-size mixing bowl, mixing spoon, clean hands, greased 8-inch-square baking pan

1. Put oats, flour, baking powder, brown sugar, salt, and cinnamon in mixing bowl and mix well. Add butter or margarine, eggs, dates, and nuts, and mix well using clean hands.
2. Preheat oven to 350° F.
3. Put mixture into baking pan and bake in oven for about 35 minutes, until firm. Remove from oven and cut while warm into 1 1/2-inch squares. Sprinkle with confectioners' sugar.

Serve as cookie or candy treat. Store in covered bowl and refrigerate. Date bars make excellent holiday food gifts.

Tahineh (also Tahini) — Sesame Seed Paste

Among the most popular dishes in Middle East cooking are *tahineh* and *mjeddrah*. In a land where food and eating habits have evolved for thousands of years, both hold a place in the history of Arabic cooking.

Yield: about 2 cups

1 cup sesame seeds
1 to 1 1/2 cups water, more or less as needed
3 cloves garlic, **finely chopped,** or 1 teaspoon garlic granules
juice of 2 lemons
salt to taste
1/4 teaspoon ground red pepper, more or less to taste
1 teaspoon white vinegar

Equipment: **Mortar and pestle,** electric food processor, or blender; spatula; small-size bowl; mixing spoon

1. Put sesame seeds, 1 cup water, garlic, and lemon juice in mortar, processor, or blender and grind mixture to smooth consistency of mayonnaise. Add a little more water if necessary.
2. Transfer mixture to bowl, add vinegar, red pepper, and salt to taste and mix well.

Serve *tahineh* as a spread on bread, or as a sauce on vegetables or meat. *Tahineh* keeps up to 3 weeks refrigerated.

Mjeddrah — Rice with Lentils

Yield: serves 6 to 8

1 cup brown **lentils**
4 to 6 cups water
2 to 4 tablespoons olive oil or vegetable oil
3 onions, **coarsely chopped**
1 cup rice
salt and pepper to taste
1/2 cup *each* slivered almonds and raisins (optional)

Equipment: Large-size saucepan with cover, mixing spoon, medium-size skillet

1. Put lentils and 4 cups water in saucepan. Bring to a boil over high heat, reduce heat to simmer, mix well, cover, and cook for 25 minutes.
2. Heat 2 tablespoons oil in skillet over medium-high heat, add onions, and fry until soft and golden, about 5 minutes. Add rice, mix well to coat grains, reduce heat to medium, and cook for about 3 minutes. Add more oil if necessary.
3. Add onions and rice to lentils and mix well. Increase heat to boil for 1 minute, reduce to simmer, cover, and cook until rice and lentils are tender but not soft, about 20 minutes. Stir frequently to prevent sticking. If mixture is too dry, add just enough hot water to moisten, but not to make it soupy. Add salt and pepper to taste, nuts, and raisins and mix well.

Serve *mjeddrah* as a side dish with meat, fish, or poultry.

Stuffed Dates, Figs, and Prunes

Stuffed dried fruit are popular sweet treats throughout the Middle East. They are tasty and wonderfully colorful when set in individual, mini-size paper cups or each wrapped in colored waxed tissue. Colored waxed tissue is available at most craft stores.

Yield: 30 pieces

10 *each* **pitted** large-size whole dates, figs, and prunes
2 cups confectioners' sugar
1 teaspoon almond extract
1 egg white (refrigerate yolk to use at another time)
30 whole pecans or walnuts or combination, more or less
1/2 cup sugar

Equipment: **Steamer pan,** large-size mixing bowl, mixing spoon

1. Steam figs and prunes until soft (about 5 minutes) over boiling water. Drain on paper towels to cool.
2. Put confectioners' sugar, extract, and egg white in bowl and blend well.
3. Fill each fruit cavity with about 1/4 teaspoonful of mixture then press whole pecan or walnut-half onto the filling so top side of nut shows.
4. Put sugar in a flat dish and roll each filled fruit in it. Place side-by-side on wax paper and refrigerate until set (about 2 hours).

Serve as sweet snacks or box assortments of stuffed fruit to give as gifts. They will keep refrigerated in covered containers for about 3 months; they can also be frozen.

Almond Biscuits

Yield: makes about 21

1/2 cup butter, margarine, or **ghee**
1/2 cup sugar
1 egg
1 teaspoon almond extract
1 cup all-purpose flour
1/2 cup **crushed or finely ground** almonds
1/2 cup sugar
21 whole almonds

Equipment: Large-size mixing bowl, mixing spoon, clean hands, flat dish, nonstick or greased cookie sheet

Preheat oven to 400°F.
1. Blend butter, margarine, or **ghee** with sugar in mixing bowl. Add egg and almond extract and mix well. Add flour and ground almonds and **knead** into stiff dough. Pinch off pieces and roll into ping-pong-size balls between the palms of your hands.
2. Put sugar into flat dish and roll balls in sugar to coat. Press balls flat between your hands, place on cookie sheet and put an almond on top of each.
3. Bake in oven for about 10 minutes, until edges are browned.

Serve almond biscuits as a cookie treat with tea or milk.

Fruit Balls

Yield: about 24

1/2 cup **finely chopped pitted** dates
1 cup finely chopped seedless raisins
1/2 cup finely chopped prunes
1/2 cup finely chopped dried apricots
1 cup finely chopped almonds
1/2 teaspoon ground cinnamon
2 tablespoons lemon juice
1/2 cup grated coconut, homemade (see recipe page 208), frozen, or canned

Equipment: Medium-size mixing bowl, clean hands, flat dish

1. Mix dates, raisins, prunes, apricots, and almonds in medium-size bowl. Add cinnamon, lemon juice, and mix well. Roll into ping-pong-size balls using clean hands.
2. Pour coconut in a flat dish, roll the fruit balls in the coconut, and press well between your hands. Set the finished balls on flat plate or pan and refrigerate.

Serve as a midday snack.

Iraq

Iraq is an oil-rich nation with an ancient past. In northeastern Iraq in the Kurdistan area, archaeologists have uncovered 12 levels of a town called Jarmo. It is thought to be one of the first agriculturally based societies. Milling stones for wheat, and fire-blackened stones where bread was baked, have been found at even the lowest levels of the dig and date back 9,000 years. To this day, Kurdish women bake bread over fires in a 9,000-year-old, time-honored way.

From Jarmo similar agricultural practices radiated out to the better soils between the Tigris and Euphrates rivers, the site of ancient Mesopotamia. The soils between these two rivers are still the best agricultural area for Iraq. Iraqis grow wheat and vegetables there now as before. To the south, dates are grown and are found in many Iraqi desserts. In fact, Iraq is the leading exporter of dates in the world. Many Iraqi foods are fried in lard, making them different from other Middle Eastern recipes, which use olive oil. Another difference is that soups are seldom served in Iraq, and sweet pastries follow meals instead of fruit. One thing is the same, however—strong hot coffee for the adults is a favorite drink.

Nan-e Lavash   Flat Bread

Yield: about 15 pieces

1/2 package dry activated yeast granules
1 1/2 cups lukewarm water
2 1/2 cups all-purpose flour
1 teaspoon salt
2 teaspoons vegetable oil
1 cup yellow cornmeal

Equipment: Cup, large-size mixing bowl, mixing spoon, floured work surface, kitchen towel, rolling pin, wax paper, 3 or 4 nonstick or greased baking sheets, small-size bowl

1. In cup, dissolve yeast in 1/2 cup of lukewarm water.
2. Combine 2 cups flour, salt, and oil in mixing bowl. Make a well in center; add yeast mixture, remaining 1 cup water, and mix well. Transfer to work surface and **knead** dough until smooth and elastic (about 5 minutes).
3. Put dough in lightly greased mixing bowl, cover with towel, and set in warm place to double in bulk (about 1 1/2 hours).
4. Pinch off tennis-ball-size pieces of dough and roll into balls. Repeat, using all the dough. Set 2 inches apart on baking sheets, cover with towel, and set again in warm place to double in bulk (about 30 minutes).
5. Preheat oven broiler to very hot.
6. Combine the cornmeal with 1/2 cup of flour in a small bowl. Roll each doughball in cornmeal mixture until coated. Sprinkle a little of the mixture on work surface and, using rolling pin, flatten each ball paper-thin. Stack flat breads, separating each with wax paper.
7. Preheat oven broiler to very hot.
8. To bake, place flattened breads side-by-side on baking sheets and put under broiler heat for 15 to 20 seconds or until breads are crisp and brown.

Serve bread with Middle Eastern dishes. It keeps well wrapped in plastic.

Compot-e Aloo   Prune Compote

Yield: serves 4 to 6

1 cup **pitted** prunes, soaked in 1 cup water for 1 hour
1/2 cup sugar
1 teaspoon ground cinnamon
2 cups whipped cream or prepared frozen whipped topping, thawed
1 teaspoon vanilla extract

Equipment: Small-size saucepan, mixing spoon, medium-size mixing bowl

1. Combine prunes with water and sugar in saucepan, bring to a boil over high heat, and mix well. Reduce heat to simmer and cook until prunes are tender, about 20 minutes. Remove from heat, add ground cinnamon, and mix well. Cool to room temperature and refrigerate.
2. Put prunes in medium bowl and add whipped cream or topping and vanilla. Mix well to make **marble** effect. Refrigerate until ready to serve.

Serve *compot-e aloo* in small individual dishes or cups as a dessert.

Iran

Iran is another of the oil-rich nations of this region. More than 80 percent of Iran's revenue is derived from oil exports. The land Iran occupies has historically been known as Persia. That is why the people, foods, and language of Iran are called Persian. The ancient Persian kingdom was vast, encompassing countries as distant as India. Trading merchants, statesmen, and travelers brought back to Persia exciting new foods and spices. Most are still important ingredients in Iranian cooking today. The Indian influence on Iranian cooking is especially showcased in the use of spices. Rice is eaten at almost every meal in both India and Iran.

Iranians love their yogurt and eat it in some form at every meal, including yogurt cheese (see recipe page 84); dugh, a drink made with water-diluted yogurt, salt, and mint; plain yogurt spooned over other foods; and yogurt in desserts. *Cheo kebab* is the national dish. It consists of rice, well-**marinated** meat, yogurt, raw egg, and a spice called sumak. Sumak is sour tasting, a common taste in Iranian cooking. Another ingredient that produces a sour taste is pomegranate juice, used in the chicken dish that follows.

Khoresht-e Fesenjan   *Chicken in Pomegranate Sauce*

The queen of all stews is called *fesenjan.* It is prepared with great care for special occasions, made with syrupy sauces from juices of fruits such as pomegranates. Pomegranates are found throughout the Middle East; they are not only used in cooking but the juice is also as popular as orange juice is with Americans. Persians have used the wood of the pomegranate tree for fuel, the bark for tannic acid, and the roots for medicine; the juice is used for dyes; the silhouette of the fruit is used for carpet and fabric designs; and the pomegranate is a symbol used in poetry. The following recipe combines **stewed** chicken with syrupy pomegranate juice.

Yield: serves 6

5 tablespoons butter, margarine, or **ghee**
6 boneless and skinless chicken breasts
2 onions, **finely chopped**
1 cup *each* chicken broth and water
2 cups **finely ground** walnuts
1 cup pomegranate syrup, or genuine grenadine syrup
1/2 cup sugar, more or less to taste
1/2 teaspoon *each* salt and **turmeric**
1/4 teaspoon *each* cinnamon, nutmeg, black pepper
2 tablespoons lemon juice, more or less to taste

Equipment: Large-size saucepan with cover or **Dutch oven**, mixing spoon, small-size saucepan

1. Melt butter, margarine, or ghee in saucepan or Dutch oven over medium-high heat. Add chicken breasts and cook until light brown on both sides, about 4 minutes per side. Add onions, chicken broth, and water and bring to a boil. Reduce heat to simmer, cover, and cook for 30 minutes.
2. *Prepare sauce:* put nuts, syrup, sugar to taste, salt, turmeric, cinnamon, nutmeg, black pepper, and lemon juice in small saucepan and mix well. Cook for about 3 minutes, until heated through. Pour mixture over chicken breasts and continue cooking chicken uncovered for about 30 minutes more until sauce thickens.

Khoresht, **stewed** meat or fowl served with rice, is the mainstay of Middle Eastern cooking. Made with a variety of meats and vegetables, a hostess often serves platters of several different *khoreshts* at a single feast. To serve, arrange chicken breasts on platter over a mound of cooked white rice and top with sauce.

Coucou-ye Sabzi   Omelet of Greens and Herbs

A most popular Persian dish is *coucou,* similar to a fritter or omelet. There are endless ways to make *coucou.* All kinds of vegetables, fish, chicken, and meat can be added. The most popular *coucou* is inexpensive to prepare since it is made only with eggs, greens, and herbs.

Yield: serves 4 to 6

2 cups **finely chopped** spinach, fresh, or frozen, thawed and drained
2 cups finely chopped green onions, including tops
1/2 cup *each* finely chopped parsley, **cilantro**, and dill weed, fresh, or 1/4 cup *each* dried flakes
1 clove garlic, finely chopped
8 eggs, beat until **frothy**
1/2 teaspoon *each* baking soda and cinnamon
salt and pepper to taste

Equipment: Large-size mixing bowl, mixing spoon, greased 2-quart baking dish

Preheat oven to 350° F.
1. Put spinach, green onions, parsley, cilantro, dill, garlic, eggs, baking soda, cinnamon, and salt and pepper to taste in mixing bowl and mix well.
2. Pour mixture into baking dish and bake in oven for 45 minutes or until crisp on the bottom and light brown on top.

Serve hot or cold, cut in squares. Serve with yogurt to spoon over top.

Sharbat-e Toot-farangi   Strawberry Syrup

If you were to visit an Iranian home on a hot day they would serve a cool, homemade, fruit-flavored drink called "sherbet." It has been an Iranian thirst-quencher for hundreds of years. The drink is fruit syrup made from oranges, lemons, sour cherries, crab apples, raspberries, and strawberries or other combinations of fruits. First a "simple syrup" is made by boiling equal amounts of sugar and water until thick and syrupy; then the fruit of your choice is added to the syrup. If making syrup with orange or lemon juice, boil the juice with sugar instead of adding water. This syrup is poured over crushed ice to make snow cones, and it is a delicious topping for ice cream.

Yield: serves 8 to 10

1 cup sugar
1 cup water
1 cup **finely chopped** fresh strawberries, washed, and stems removed or frozen, thawed
1/2 teaspoon vanilla extract

Equipment: Medium-size saucepan, mixing spoon, fine strainer, jar with lid

1. Put sugar and water in saucepan, bring to a boil over high heat, and mix well. Reduce heat to simmer and cook for about 5 minutes, until thick.
2. Add strawberries and vanilla extract, and, mixing continually, increase heat to medium-high. Bring to a boil, reduce heat to simmer, and cook for 5 to 10 minutes, until syrup thickens, and then remove from heat.
3. **Strain** and pour into a jar with lid and refrigerate.

To make drink, add about 2 tablespoons syrup to 1/2 glass of water, mix well, and add ice to fill glass and serve.

Nan-e Shirini   Persian Cookies

Yield: makes about 20

5 egg whites (refrigerate yolks to use at another time)
1 cup sugar
2 tablespoons lemon juice
1 tablespoon grated orange rind
1 cup chopped walnuts

Equipment: Large-size mixing bowl, **egg beater** or electric mixer, **whisk** or mixing spoon, nonstick or greased cookie sheet

Preheat oven to 350°F.

1. Beat egg whites in bowl with egg beater or mixer until **frothy**. Slowly add sugar, mixing continually until whites are stiff. Add lemon juice and orange rind and mix well. Gently blend in the chopped nuts using whisk or mixing spoon.
2. Drop heaping teaspoonfuls of mixture onto cookie sheet, about 1 inch apart. Bake in oven for 30 minutes or until edges are golden.

Khorak-e Mahi Sefid   Pan-fried Fish

In many cultures holiday traditions require the eating of special foods. (For example, eating turkey on Thanksgiving is an American tradition.) An important Iranian holiday is the New Year (*no ruz*), celebrated with the arrival of spring. The combination of pan-fried fish **fillets**, *khorak-e mahi sefid* with green herb rice, *sabzi pollo*, is traditionally eaten on the New Year.

Yield: serves 4 to 6

1 cup all-purpose flour
salt and pepper to taste
4 or 6 fish **fillets**, about 8 ounces each, rinse and pat dry
4 to 6 tablespoons butter, margarine, or **ghee**
lemon wedges for garnish

Equipment: Plate, large-size skillet, pancake turner or metal spatula

1. Combine flour and salt and pepper together on the plate.
2. Coat each fillet with the seasoned flour and shake off excess.
3. Heat 4 tablespoons butter, margarine, or ghee in skillet over medium-high heat, swirling pan to coat bottom. Pan-fry fillets on both sides until golden brown, about 6 minutes per side. Add more butter, margarine, or ghee and reduce heat to medium if necessary.

Serve with wedges of lemon and *sabzi pollo* (green herb rice). (See recipe below.)

Sabzi Pollo   Green Herb Rice

Adding fresh herbs to rice gives it a wonderful fragrant flavor.

Yield: serves 4 to 6

1/2 cup **finely chopped** green onions
1/4 cup finely chopped fresh dill weed or 2 tablespoons dried dill
1/2 cup finely chopped fresh parsley or 1/4 cup dried flakes
1/2 cup finely chopped fresh **cilantro** or 1/4 cup dried cilantro
1/2 cup butter, margarine, or **ghee**
4 to 5 cups cooked rice (cooked according to directions on package)

Equipment: Medium-size bowl, mixing spoon, large-size skillet with cover

1. Combine onions, dill weed, parsley, and cilantro in a bowl and mix well.
2. Heat butter, margarine, or ghee in skillet over medium heat. Swirl pan to coat bottom. Pour in 1/2 the cooked rice and sprinkle with 1/2 herb mixture. Add remaining rice and sprinkle with remaining herb mixture. Do not mix. Cover, and steam over low heat for 30 minutes.

Serve hot, right from the skillet as a side dish with the pan-fried fish.

Koofteh Tabrizi   The City of Tabriz Meatballs

According to Iranian legend, the finest meatball-makers are in Tabriz, in northwestern Iraq, where all kinds of surprises are stuffed into apple-size meatballs. It's not unusual to find a filling of prunes, walnuts, or **hard-cooked** eggs. Highly accomplished Tabriz cooks have been known to make giant-size meatballs stuffed with whole chickens.

Yield: serves 4 to 6

2 pounds ground lean beef
4 onions, **finely chopped**
2 eggs, lightly beaten
2 cups cooked rice (cooked according to directions on package)
1/2 teaspoon *each* salt and pepper
1/4 teaspoon *each* nutmeg and cinnamon
Fillings:
   2 dried apricots or **pitted** prunes, soaked 1 hour in warm water
   2 walnut halves
   1 egg, hard-cooked and shelled
   1 tablespoon raisins, soaked in warm water for 1 hour
   2 cups *each* water and tomato paste

Equipment: Large-size mixing bowl, mixing spoon, greased 9- x 13-inch baking pan

1. Put beef, one-half of the chopped onions, eggs, rice, salt, pepper, nutmeg, and cinnamon in mixing bowl. Mix well with clean hands and shape into balls, about apple-size. Press one of the fillings into each meatball, seal, and shape the meatball again. (You'll have 2 meatballs with apricots or prunes, 2 with walnuts, one with egg, and one with raisins.) Place meatballs side-by-side in baking pan.
2. Preheat oven to 350°F.
3. Combine remaining onions, water, and tomato paste and mix well. Pour over meatballs and bake for 1 hour; turn at least once and **baste** with sauce.

Serve meatballs with side dishes of cooked rice or vegetables.

Cyprus

Cyprus is an island nation in the eastern Mediterranean Sea. Many of the Cypriots are involved in agriculture. In the fertile plains between their mountain ranges potatoes, wheat, barley, vines, vegetables, grapes, and citrus fruits are grown. Sheep, goats, donkeys, and cattle are raised. Dairy farming is important here because of the demand for yogurt and cheeses. The cooking habits of Cyprus are similar to its neighbors, Greece and Turkey, yet Cypriots have added some foods and a cooking style definitely their own.

For example, corn oil and lard are the preferred cooking oils instead of olive oil, which is more commonly used in the Mediterranean countries.

In this recipe, potatoes, a main crop in Cyprus, are used along with other fresh vegetables and bread.

Polypikilo   *Mixed Vegetables*

Yield: serves 6

1 eggplant, with stem cut off, cut in 1/2-inch thick slices
salt and pepper to taste
1/4 cup corn or vegetable oil
2 cups **finely chopped**, soft white bread
3 cloves garlic, finely chopped, or 1 teaspoon garlic granules
2 cups thinly sliced new potatoes
2 cups 1/4-inch slices zucchini
2 tomatoes, thinly sliced
1/2 to 1 cup water

Equipment: **Colander** or strainer, paper towels, 2 1/2-quart baking dish

1. Put slices of eggplant in colander, sprinkle with salt, and set aside in sink or over plate for about 30 minutes. Rinse well and pat dry with paper towels.
2. Preheat oven to 350° F.

3. Pour 1/8 cup oil in baking dish and swirl to coat bottom and sides. Add 1 cup chopped bread and half of the garlic. Cover with eggplant slices, add layers of potatoes, zucchini, and tomatoes, and season with salt to taste. Repeat layering, ending with tomatoes. Sprinkle remaining bread, garlic, 1/2 cup water, remaining oil, and salt and pepper to taste over tomatoes.

3. Bake in oven for about 1 1/2 hours, until vegetables are tender. Add more water if necessary. The dish should be fairly moist but not soupy.

Serve hot or at room temperature, as a vegetarian main dish, or with meat, fish, or poultry.

Turkey

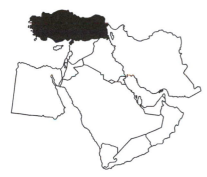

Turkey is in both Europe and Asia, and it has been influenced by both regions. Turkish food, in particular its sweets and coffee, is world famous. Turkey gave us *shish kabobs*, *pilaf* (rice dish), and Turkish coffee (very strong!). Olive oil or butter are the preferred cooking oils. Commonly used seasonings include garlic, parsley, dill, mint, bay leaves, oregano, pepper, allspice, cinnamon, and paprika. Fresh vegetables are preferred. Some favorites are eggplant, tomatoes, cucumbers, green peppers, and okra. Drying and pickling of fruits and vegetables are done to preserve summer's bounty. Agriculture is an important part of the Turkish economy. In some areas up to three growing seasons are possible, producing a wide variety of fruits, grains, and vegetables. Most of the world's supply of hazelnuts comes from Turkey. Interestingly, world famous Turkish coffee is only served at special times. Coffee is too expensive to drink daily, and so tea is the national beverage of Turks.

Imam Bayildi   *Vegetarian Stuffed Eggplant*

This dish, *Imam bayildi*, literally means, "the Imam fainted." As the legend goes, a certain Imam (Muslim religious leader), after observing a holy day and ending a long fast, was so taken with the delicious aroma of this dish, he fainted dead away. The dish was named in his honor.

Yield: serves 4

4 small eggplants, washed and dried
1/8 cup olive oil or vegetable oil
2 onions, **coarsely chopped**
3 cloves garlic or 1 teaspoon garlic granules
2 *each* green peppers, **seeded** and chopped, and tomatoes, **peeled** and chopped
1/2 cup tomato paste
1/2 cup **finely chopped** parsley

salt to taste

2 cups water, more or less as needed

Equipment: Potato peeler, large-size skillet, mixing spoon, 9- x 13-inch baking pan (large enough to hold 4 eggplants and water)

Preheat oven to 375° F.

1. Cut 1-inch-deep slice from stem end down the length of each eggplant. With small spoon, scoop out **pulp**, leaving about 1/4-inch wall around sides. Set scooped-out pulp aside. Sprinkle inside of shell with salt, and turn upside down on work surface for about 1 hour to drain.
2. Heat oil in skillet over medium-high heat. Add eggplant pulp, onions, garlic, and peppers, mix well, and fry until onions are soft. Reduce heat to simmer, stir in tomatoes, tomato paste, and parsley. Add salt to taste, mix well, simmer for 5 minutes longer, and remove from heat.
3. Rinse eggplants to remove salt, pat dry, and place side-by-side in baking pan. Fill each with eggplant mixture. Pour about 1 inch of water in baking pan with eggplants and bake in oven for 45 minutes or until eggplants are tender when poked with fork.

Serve hot or cold as a main dish. Each person is served a whole eggplant.

Thick Yogurt

The following recipe calls for thick yogurt (also called yogurt cheese), which is very easy to make. Thick yogurt is a standard food in almost all Islamic countries including those in the Middle East. It graces the table as a side dish in many homes at almost all meals.

Yield: Depends on amount used

Plain yogurt

Equipment: Mesh filter—**colander** or strainer, cheese cloth; *or* clean nylon stocking

Pour plain yogurt (as much as you need) into a mesh filter and let it drain for about 8 hours at room temperature.

The following are two easy ways to make a mesh filter:

1. Line a strainer or colander with cheese cloth about the size of a handerkerchief. (Surgical gauze can also be used.) Set the strainer or colander on top of a slightly smaller pan, allow the yogurt to drain free of the liquid. Discard liquid.
2. A clean nylon stocking with the reinforced top cut off makes a great filter. (You might need help holding the stocking top open while you fill it with yogurt.) Only the foot part of the stocking will be filled with yogurt. Tie the leg part over the kitchen sink faucet, allowing the yogurt-filled bottom part to hang freely and drain.

Cacik   Cucumber and Yogurt Salad

Yield: serves 4 to 6

2 cups thick yogurt (see recipe above)

3 cloves garlic, peeled and **finely chopped** or 1 teaspoon garlic granules

1 large cucumber, finely chopped
1/2 teaspoon salt
1 cup black olives, for serving
crusty bread, for serving

Equipment: Medium-size mixing bowl, mixing spoon, strainer or **colander**

1. In medium-size bowl mix thick yogurt with garlic.
2. Put chopped cucumber in strainer or colander and sprinkle with salt; let drain for about 20 minutes. Rinse with water and drain well. Add cucumbers to yogurt, mix well, and refrigerate

Serve salad cold with side dish of black olives and plenty of crusty bread.

Shish Kabob   Meat Grilled on a Skewer

Turkish soldiers invented the *shish kabob*. As the legend goes, the soldiers speared chunks of lamb with their swords and cooked the meat to perfection over open fires. Today, *shish kabobs* are **marinated**, threaded on skewers, and then grilled or broiled. It is best to cook meat and vegetables on separate skewers, as the meat takes longer to cook.

Yield: serves 4

1 pound lamb, boneless shoulder, cut into 1-inch chunks
1/4 cup lemon juice
2 tablespoons olive or vegetable oil
1/2 teaspoon *each* salt, pepper, and dried oregano flakes
2 green bell peppers, cut into 1-inch chunks
2 onions, peeled and each cut into 4 wedges
1 cup 1-inch chunks eggplant

Equipment: Medium-size mixing bowl, mixing spoon, 8 metal 10- to 12-inch skewers, broiler pan, oven mitts

1. Put lemon juice, oil, salt, pepper, and oregano in medium-size bowl. Mix well and add meat chunks. With clean hands make sure meat is well coated. Cover and refrigerate for about 4 hours, stirring frequently. Remove meat from **marinade** and set both aside.
2. Preheat broiler or grill to hot.
3. Alternate chunks of green pepper, onion, and eggplant on 4 skewers.
4. Thread meat on 4 remaining skewers.
5. Place meat kabobs on broiler pan, broil in oven about 3 inches under heat for about 5 minutes. Put on oven mitts and turn kabobs and **baste** with marinade; broil for about 5 minutes more. Carefully place vegetable kabobs on broiler pan with meat kabobs. Brush all sides with marinade. Broil vegetables for about 5 minutes until golden brown.

Serve one meat and one vegetable kabob to each person and eat right off the skewer.

Simple Halva

This dessert is a favorite among Turkish women. It is often given as a gift to friends for special favors and is symbolically offered as a gift of devotion.

Yield: serves 6 to 8

4 tablespoons butter
1 cup cream of wheat
2 cups warm water
1/2 cup seedless raisins
1 cup **finely chopped** nuts: pecans, almonds, or walnuts

Equipment: Medium-size skillet, wooden mixing spoon, 9-inch square baking pan

1. Melt butter in skillet over medium heat; add cream of wheat, stirring continually, until it is golden brown (about 5 minutes).
2. Add water and sugar, mixing continually, bring to a simmer, and cook until mixture thickens (about 10 minutes). It will turn quite thick. Remove from heat, add raisins and 1/2 cup nuts, and mix well. Pour mixture into baking pan and using back of spoon, spread evenly.

Halva is like a thick pudding. Sprinkle the remaining 1/2 cup nuts on the top. It is served and eaten with a spoon.

Europe

Europe is a cornucopia of cooking pleasures. From the northern Scandinavian countries to the Mediterranean Sea and from the Asian border on the east to the Atlantic Ocean, the variety of foods and cooking styles is immense. Europe is made up of a diverse group of societies, nations, and people. Each country has a unique makeup and proud traditions of cooking and food. Much interchanging of people, foods, and customs has taken place because of invasion, colonization, immigration, and travel, but strong differences remain. In this section we will concentrate on the foods that people eat every day, from the Mediterranean Sea to Scandinavia.

Greece

Greek cooking is renowned for its simplicity and distinctive rich tastes. Greece takes full advantage of the bounty of the Mediterranean Sea that surrounds it, and fish, squid, octopus, and mussels are important foods. Fish are cooked with olive oil, tomatoes, and garlic. Lamb is the primary meat eaten, not beef. The hilly countryside is perfect for raising sheep, and lamb is very inexpensive in Greece. Feta cheese is a farmer's cheese in Greece, white and crumbly with a distinctive salty taste. It is often put on Greek salads in the United States. In Greece, feta cheese is served with the meals or spread on bread. It is also served along with tomatoes, olives, and pickled peppers as an appetizer to accompany the anise liqueur, ouzo. The hills of Greece are covered with sweet-smelling lemon trees and ancient, gnarled olive trees, and so among the most important ingredients in traditional Greek cooking are the lemons, olives, and olive oil from these trees. For example, lemon juice and olive oil are used to make salad dressing in place of vinegar and oil. About half of all Greeks live in cities, with the other half residing either in small rural villages or out in the country, tending to the agriculture of the land. They grow wheat, lemons, olives, and raisins, and raise chickens, sheep, goats, pigs, and some cattle. Greece is almost self-sufficient in providing its own food.

Soupa Avgolemono   *Lemon Soup*

Lemons are used in many dishes, and the national soup of Greece is *soupa avgolemono*, lemon soup. In the following recipe, the lemony broth is basic, and it is used for many different soups. Adding noodles, vegetables, **lentils**, or beans instead of rice creates an entirely new flavor and type of soup.

Yield: serves 4 to 6

8 cups chicken broth, homemade or canned
1/2 cup uncooked rice
1 tablespoon cornstarch
1 cup milk
2 egg yolks (refrigerate whites to use at another time)
1/2 cup lemon juice
1 tablespoon butter or margarine
2 teaspoons **finely chopped** flat leaf parsley
salt and pepper to taste

Equipment: Medium-size saucepan, mixing spoon, small-size bowl

1. Bring chicken broth to a boil in saucepan over high heat. Add rice, reduce to simmer, cover, and cook for 20 minutes, until rice is fully cooked.

2. Combine cornstarch, milk, and egg yolks in small bowl and mix well. Pour mixture into soup, mix well, and remove from heat. Stirring continually, add lemon juice slowly to prevent soup from curdling. Add butter or margarine, parsley, and salt and pepper to taste, and mix well. Return to low heat and heat through.

Serve soup warm in individual bowls.

Patate Moussaka   Potato Casserole

What Americans call chopped, ground, or hamburger meat is called **minced** meat in Greece. It can be lamb, pork, beef, goat, or any combination. A small piece of meat goes a long way to feed a hungry family when it is minced and other grains, such as rice, are added. It stretches even further and becomes more nutritious when stuffed in vegetables, such as green bell peppers, eggplant, squash, tomatoes, cabbage, and even grape leaves. Stuffed vegetables are as popular in Greece as hotdogs are in the United States. The most popular Greek dish is a casserole called *moussaka*. This is baked ground meat with sliced eggplant, squash, or potatoes. It is best served at room temperature, making it an excellent dish to take on picnics.

Yield: serves 6 to 8

4 half-cooked white boiling potatoes (boil with skins on for about 15 minutes)
2 to 4 tablespoons olive oil
1 pound chopped lean meat: lamb, beef, pork, or combination
2 onions, chopped
1 cup tomato sauce, canned
1/2 cup chopped flat leaf parsley
1 cup *each* dry bread crumbs and grated Parmesan cheese
2 egg whites (set aside yolks for sauce, recipe follows)
salt and pepper to taste
white sauce (recipe follows)

Equipment: Knife, large-size saucepan, mixing spoon, greased 2 1/2-quart casserole

1. When potatoes are cool enough to handle, peel and slice into 1/8-inch slices. Set aside.
2. Heat 2 tablespoons oil in large saucepan over medium-high heat. Add meat and onions, reduce heat to low for 15 minutes, until meat is browned; stir frequently to prevent sticking. Remove from heat, add tomato sauce, parsley, 2 tablespoons bread crumbs, 2 tablespoons grated cheese, and egg whites, and mix well.
3. Preheat oven to 350°F.
4. Sprinkle bottom and sides of baking pan with 2 tablespoons bread crumbs. Cover bottom of casserole with slightly overlapping potato slices. Spread meat mixture over potatoes. Cover meat with white sauce (recipe follows) and sprinkle with remaining cheese and bread crumbs to form top crust. Sprinkle top with remaining 2 tablespoons oil.
4. Bake for 40 minutes or until golden brown. Cool before cutting into squares. (If cut when hot, the pieces will fall apart.)

Serve *moussaka* warm or at room temperature with salad and plenty of bread.

Moussaka Sauce   White Sauce for Casserole

Yield: about 5 cups

1 cup all-purpose flour
4 cups milk
2 egg yolks, slightly beaten
1/2 teaspoon ground or grated nutmeg

Equipment: Small-size bowl, medium-size saucepan, mixing spoon or **whisk**

1. Add flour to 1 cup milk in small bowl, mix well to blend, and set aside.
2. Put remaining 3 cups milk in saucepan and bring to a boil over high heat. Add flour mixture, stirring continually, and reduce heat to simmer, cooking until mixture thickens. (When sauce coats spoon, it is thick enough.) Remove from heat, and, stirring continually, slowly add egg yolks a little at a time and nutmeg. Pour sauce over *moussaka* (see step 4 in previous *moussaka* recipe).

Salata   Greek Salad with Dressing

The true flavors of Greece—lemon juice, olives, olive oil, and feta cheese—are all combined in the following salad.

Yield: serves 6

6 tablespoons olive oil
juice of 1 lemon
3 cloves garlic or 1 teaspoon garlic granules
1 Romaine lettuce, torn into bite-size pieces
3 tomatoes, cut in wedges
12 Greek black olives, in oil
1 onion, thinly sliced
1/4 cup chopped flat leaf parsley
1/2 cup crumbled feta cheese, available at most supermarkets
salt and pepper to taste

Equipment: Pint-size jar with tight-fitting lid, salad bowl, salad tools

1. Put oil, lemon juice, and garlic in jar, tighten lid and shake well.
2. Put lettuce, tomatoes, olives, onion, parsley, and feta cheese in salad bowl. Pour on dressing from jar, add salt and pepper to taste, and toss gently, using salad tools.

Serve Greek salad at room temperature for best flavor.

Melomacrons   Honey Cake

Greece has been known for its fine honey and the art of beekeeping since the second century B.C. Honey is an important sweetener for desserts, cakes, and pastries. Every New Year is ushered in with the eating of honey cakes, a symbol of good luck, wealth, and health for the coming year. In a household with children, it is customary to insert one or two new drachmas (Greek coins) into the cake just before it's baked. The cake is not cut until midnight, when the New Year starts. Children finding the coins will have extra good luck, unless by mistake they should swallow one; then they're not so lucky.

Yield: makes 8 to 10 pieces

3 eggs
1 cup sugar
1 cup warm honey
1/4 cup vegetable oil
2 teaspoons baking powder
1 teaspoon baking soda
3 cups flour
1/4 teaspoon *each* ground ginger, cinnamon, and cloves
1 cup strong brewed tea, cold

Equipment: Large-size mixing bowl, mixing spoon or electric mixer, medium-size mixing bowl, **whisk**, flour **sifter**, nonstick or greased 9 x 5-inch loaf pan or nonstick or greased 9-inch **bundt pan**

Preheat oven to 350°F and place oven shelf on lowest brackets.
1. Put eggs, sugar, honey, and oil in large mixing bowl, and, using spoon or electric mixer, mix until well blended.
2. **Sift** baking powder, baking soda, flour, ginger, cinnamon, and cloves into medium mixing bowl.
3. Mixing egg mixture continually, add flour mixture alternately with tea until batter is lump-free and smooth.
4. Pour batter into prepared loaf or bundt pan. Bake on bottom shelf in oven for 50 to 60 minutes, until toothpick inserted into center of cake comes out clean.

Serve honey cake with jam or fruit; it is never frosted.

Albania

Albania is a small country located on the Balkan Peninsula across the Adriatic Sea from Italy. Albanians are Muslim, although until recently the state was an official atheist state. Albania is primarily an agricultural society, growing food with fairly primitive methods. For example, although some farm machines have been introduced in the country, Albanians use horse-drawn plows. Farming is hard in this mountainous region, and only a tenth of the land is cultivated. Livestock such as sheep, goats, cattle, and pigs are kept, although meat is generally scarce. The majority of the livestock are grazed in the mountains. Albanians grow wheat, barley, corn, vegetables, olives, fruit, and sugar beets. Their best fields lay along the coastal plains to the west. Dairy products are a daily part of Albanians' diet, and they especially like yogurt and sour milk. Mint is a popular flavoring used in meat dishes, salads, and cold drinks.

Tanabour   Barley Yogurt Soup

Yield: serves 4 to 6

1/2 cup precooked pearl barley (available at most supermarkets)
4 cups beef broth, homemade or canned
2 cups yogurt
1 cup sour cream
1 egg
4 tablespoons butter or margarine
2 tablespoons chopped parsley
salt and pepper to taste

Equipment: Large-size saucepan, mixing spoon, large-size mixing bowl

1. Put barley and beef broth in saucepan and bring to a boil over high heat. Reduce heat to simmer and cook for about 2 hours or until barley is soft; stir frequently to prevent sticking.
2. Mix yogurt, sour cream, and egg in mixing bowl. Remove 1 cup of hot broth from saucepan, and, stirring continually, slowly pour it into yogurt mixture.
3. Remove saucepan of barley broth from heat. Stirring continually, slowly add yogurt mixture. Add butter or margarine, parsley, and salt and pepper to taste. Mix well and heat through over low heat. Do not allow to boil.

Serve *tanabour* in individual soup bowls, with crusty bread and butter.

Emator   Puff Pastry with Nuts

Yield: makes 8 to 10 puffs

1/2 cup butter or margarine
1 cup water
1/2 cup sugar
1/2 teaspoon salt
1 cup all-purpose flour
4 eggs
1 teaspoon almond extract
1/2 cup **crushed** or chopped nuts: **blanched** almonds, pecans, or walnuts

Equipment: Medium-size saucepan, wooden mixing spoon, nonstick or greased cookie sheet, metal spatula or pancake turner

Preheat oven to 450°F.

1. Put butter or margarine, water, sugar, and salt in saucepan and bring to a boil over medium-high heat. Add flour all at once, stirring vigorously with wooden spoon until mixture pulls away from sides of pan, about 2 minutes. Remove from heat and cool about 5 minutes. Add eggs, one at a time, beating after each, and mix in extract and nuts.
2. Drop by heaping tablespoonfuls onto cookie sheet, about 2 inches apart, and bake for 10 minutes. Reduce heat to 325°F and continue baking for 10 minutes more or until golden brown. Remove from baking sheet and set on platter to cool.

Serve *emator* as a snack with a glass of milk or tea.

Bulgaria

Bulgarians are famous for their yogurt, which is made from the milk of their sheep. Almost everyone agrees that yogurt was first made in Bulgaria. The Turks, whose country borders Bulgaria to the south and the east, conquered and occupied Bulgaria for 500 years. The dietary habits of the Muslim Turkish people were enforced; thus Bulgarian foods reflect this influence. Dairy products are emphasized more than other foods. Lamb is the main meat, and potatoes are the main vegetable in their recipes. Wheat, corn, barley, rye, oats, and rice are the principal crops. Breakfast is large, but as in many countries, the main meal of the day is lunch. Supper is generally lighter, sometimes consisting of reheated leftovers, cheered by a glass of wine for the adults.

Kisselo Mleka   *Homemade Yogurt*

Throughout many East European and Middle Eastern countries yogurt is an important part of the daily diet. It is used in and on everything from soups, to desserts, to cooling drinks. Yogurt is very easy to make, needing no complicated equipment. A **candy thermometer** (available at most supermarkets), is helpful for checking the warmth of the milk. If the milk is too hot the culture will die, and if it is too cold nothing will happen. It takes a spoon of "starter" yogurt for each pint of milk. The spoon of starter must come from fresh live yogurt culture called **acidophilus**. Acidophilus is available at most supermarkets and all health food stores. Once the fresh warm milk begins to ferment, with the help of the starter, it becomes the "culture." Each time a fresh batch of yogurt is made, set aside a spoonful to become the starter for the following batch, and so on. This recipe would be fun to do at home or as a class project.

Yield: about 2 cups

2 cups whole milk
2 tablespoons fresh commercial live yogurt starter

Equipment: Medium-size heavy bottomed saucepan, mixing spoon, **candy thermometer,** large-size heat-proof glass or enamel bowl with cover, bath towel with heating pad.

1. Put milk in saucepan and bring to a boil over high heat. (For smooth yogurt the milk must come to a boil.) When milk froths and starts to boil over, quickly remove pan from heat. Reduce heat to medium and return pan to heat for 2 minutes more. Remove from heat and set pan on heat-proof work surface.
2. The milk must cool down to between 95°F and 110° F. This cooling takes about 1 hour at room temperature; use the candy thermometer to check. With a spoon, carefully skim off any skin that forms on milk.

3. Transfer 1 cup of warm milk to bowl, add 1 tablespoon yogurt starter, and mix to blend. Add remaining milk and mix well. Cover and wrap bowl in bath towel, put it on heating pad, and set pad on low. Leave undisturbed for about 10 hours. When set, refrigerate for 4 hours before using.

Serve yogurt on salads, in recipes, or on desserts.

Lassi   Iced Yogurt Beverage

Yield: 2 drinks

1 cup plain yogurt
1 cup water
2 cups crushed ice
1 1/2 tablespoons sugar or honey
1/4 teaspoon **rose water** (optional)
sprig of mint for garnish

Equipment: Small-size bowl, mixing spoon, tall glass for serving

1. Put yogurt and water in small bowl and mix well.
2. Fill each glass with about 1 cup ice.
3. Add yogurt, sugar or honey, and rosewater and mix well. Garnish each glass with sprig of mint.

Serve *lassi* as a refreshing and nourishing drink on a hot day. This same drink, made with bananas, is popular in India.

Walnut Tarator Soup   Walnut Yogurt Soup

Yield: serves 6

1/2 cup **finely chopped** walnuts
6 cloves finely chopped garlic or 2 teaspoons garlic granules
5 teaspoons olive oil
5 cups yogurt
1 medium-size cucumber, peeled and chopped
salt and pepper to taste
1/2 cup finely chopped fresh mint or fresh parsley for garnish

Equipment: Electric blender, large-size bowl with cover, rubber spatula, mixing spoon

1. Using blender, mix walnuts with garlic. Add olive oil, a little at a time, making a smooth paste.
2. Transfer to large bowl, using spatula to scrape out mixture. Add yogurt, cucumber, and salt and pepper to taste and mix well. Cover and refrigerate.

Serve cold; mix well and then ladle into individual bowls; sprinkle each with mint or parsley.

Romania

Romanian food has been influenced by the Italians and the Turks who at various times controlled this Eastern European country. Cornmeal mush, called *mamaliga* here and *polenta* in Italy, is a traditional staple of Romanian diet.

Main meals include tangy soups, sausage, and vegetables. Their sausage has black pepper in it, and indeed, pepper is an important seasoning in Romania. Cabbage is a popular vegetable. People like to roll meat stuffings into a pickled cabbage dish called *sarmale*.

Food crops include corn, wheat, vegetables, and fruit. Farmers raise cattle, sheep, pigs, and horses.

Mamaliga   Cornmeal Porridge Bread

Romanian porridge, *mamaliga*, is eaten at nearly every meal. When *mamaliga* cools, it becomes firm and is sliced like bread. The slices are sometimes fried in a skillet or dipped in egg, then fried, something like French toast. *Mamaliga* can be eaten with cheese, spread with yogurt, or dipped in a spice mixture and eaten as a snack. As a sweet dish, *mamaliga* can be topped with cinnamon, sugar, and cream. Another popular Romanian way of eating *mamaliga* is topped with **stewed** apples, poppy seeds, and honey.

Yield: serves 4 to 6

3 1/2 cups water
1 teaspoon salt
1 cup yellow cornmeal
2 tablespoons butter or margarine
1 cup sour cream

Equipment: Medium-size saucepan with cover, **whisk** or mixing spoon, greased 9-inch oven-proof baking dish.

Preheat oven to 450°F.
1. Put water in saucepan, add salt, and bring to a boil over high heat. Stirring continually, slowly add cornmeal and reduce to simmer. Add butter or margarine, mix well, cover, and cook for about 15 minutes or until all water is absorbed and mixture is thick; stir frequently to prevent sticking. Remove from heat.
2. Pour mixture into baking dish and spread top with sour cream. Put in oven for about 8 minutes, until top is golden. Remove from oven.

Serve *mamaliga* hot from the baking dish. It is eaten at any meal, day or night. It is also eaten cold, cut into squares, or sliced and fried.

The rugged Romanian mountains have been home to generations of shepherds, tending their flocks. Day and night these hard-working shepherds and their trusty dogs watch over their wooly flock. At nightfall, around the blazing campfire, the shepherds prepare their supper, a thick soup-stew, *tokana*.

Yield: serves 6 to 8

2 pounds lamb meat, **cubed** (any meat can be substituted), trim and save fat
4 onions, **coarsely chopped**
3 cups water
2 bay leaves
4 large potatoes, coarsely chopped
1/2 cup sour cream
1 tablespoon vinegar
salt and pepper to taste

Equipment: Heavy-bottomed large-size saucepan with cover, mixing spoon

1. Heat fat trimmings in large saucepan over medium-high heat. When bottom of pan has a thin coating of grease, remove fat trimmings with mixing spoon and discard. Add meat and onions, and fry, stirring frequently, until well browned (about 8 minutes).
2. Add water and bay leaves and bring to a boil. Reduce to simmer, cover, and cook for 1 hour. Add potatoes, cover, and simmer for 30 minutes more. Remove the cover for about the last 15 minutes to allow gravy to thicken by evaporation. Remove from heat and discard bay leaves.
3. Stirring continually, add sour cream, vinegar, and salt and pepper to taste.

Serve *tokana* hot, with a side dish of *mamaliga* or crusty bread.

Yugoslavia

Yugoslavia no longer exists in the form it had held since World War I. A number of ethnic groups in this diverse Balkan area have formed their own independent countries, but, unfortunately, this breakup has been marred by violence and war. The recipes listed in this section are for traditional Balkan foods, and so they are still appropriate despite the break-up of the country. A small area of the former nation still retains the name Yugoslavia, but this section refers to the whole region.

For centuries, wine has been produced in this region, not only from grapes but plums as well. Plums grow well and are not only fermented for wine but eaten fresh, canned, and cooked in stews, breads, pastries, and desserts. They are also made into jams and marmalades. A spoonful of plum preserve in a glass of water is a popular hot weather drink, and in the winter a touch of plum preserves is added to hot tea.

Corn, wheat, sugar beets, and sunflowers (for oil) are the crops grown in this region. Farmers raise goats, cattle, sheep, horses, barnyard fowl, and pigs. A common way to preserve food in this area is by pickling, and pickled pigs' knuckles and pigs feet are very popular.

Kisel Zelje   *Pickled or Fresh Cabbage Salad*

In this region, cabbage is an important staple, and often several dishes made with cabbage will be served at the same meal. During the summer months fresh cabbage salad is on every dinner table, and pickled cabbage salad is eaten all winter long. When the following recipe is made with sauerkraut it becomes the winter cabbage salad recipe. When made with fresh cabbage, it is the summer salad.

Yield: serves 6 to 8

2 cups canned sauerkraut, rinsed to remove brine, drain well
OR 2 cups finely **shredded** fresh green cabbage
2 cups shredded carrots
1 green pepper, **cored, seeded,** and **finely chopped**
1 onion, finely chopped
6 tablespoons sunflower or olive oil
salt and pepper to taste

Equipment: Salad bowl, salad tools

Put washed sauerkraut *or* fresh cabbage, carrots, green pepper, and onion in salad bowl. Add oil, and toss with salad tools to mix well. Add salt and pepper to taste. (Salt is probably not needed with sauerkraut.)

Serve cabbage salad as a perfect starter to a Balkan meal. Always serve with lots of crusty bread.

Creveni Kupus   *Stewed Red Cabbage*

Yield: serves 4 to 6

4 tablespoons vegetable oil
1 pound red cabbage, **finely chopped**
1 cup water
1/2 cup apple cider vinegar
1 tablespoon sugar, more or less to taste
salt and pepper to taste

Equipment: Large-size saucepan with cover or **Dutch oven**, mixing spoon

1. Heat oil in saucepan or Dutch oven over medium-high heat, add cabbage, and mix well to coat with oil. Cook for 3 minutes.
2. Add water, vinegar, 1 tablespoon sugar, and salt and pepper to taste. Reduce to simmer, cover, and cook for 30 minutes, stirring frequently. Add more sugar to taste if necessary.

Serve the cabbage warm, as a side dish with meat or poultry.

Yield: serves 6 to 8

4 cups self-rising flour
1/2 cup plus 2 tablespoons olive oil
1/2 teaspoon salt
1 cup plain carbonated water (club soda)

Equipment: Large-size mixing bowl, floured work surface, rolling pin, sharp knife, nonstick or greased baking sheet

Preheat oven to 375°F.

1. Put flour, 1/2 cup oil, and salt in mixing bowl, and mix well to blend. Add carbonated water and mix to form a soft dough. Transfer to floured work surface and **knead** for about 5 minutes, adding more flour if necessary.
2. Using the floured rolling pin, flatten dough into a 9-inch circle, about 1/2 inch thick. Sprinkle remaining oil on both sides of dough circles and place on baking sheet. Using a sharp knife, make 3 1/4-inch-deep cuts, about 4 inches long, across top of each bread. Bake for about 45 minutes, or until golden brown.

Serve bread warm with plenty of yogurt cheese or butter.

Hungary

The Hungarian people are great *gourmands* (people who love good food and drink). They have had an ongoing love affair with food for centuries. They love everything about food, from raising exceptional fruits and vegetables to enjoying some of the best and plumpest chickens, geese, and ducks. Their beef and pork are of the finest quality. They have some of the best fresh-water fish in Europe, including carp, crayfish, and fogos, the pike-perch of Lake Balston. Hungarians are originally Magyars who arrived in Hungary in about A.D. 896 and settled in after being nomadic, invading tribes. They absorbed other cultures of the area into their own. For example, Austrian influence can be seen in the pastries, dumplings, and noodles that are conjured up in many different ways. The pastries are complicated and difficult to master. Noodles are sometimes served with melted butter and poppy seeds.

Hungary was one of the first nations in the old Soviet Bloc to break away to a less rigid system of economics after the failed revolution of 1956. This development influenced food in Hungary. Fine foods had been a part of Hungarian culture before World War II, and the relaxation of the economic policies rewarded successful chefs. For example, pastry chefs were able to make and sell their elegant goods, encouraging the production of quality food. This phenomenom was something not seen in other Soviet Bloc countries at the time. Agriculture has been restored to individual farmers for the most part. They grow food crops of corn, wheat, potatoes, sugar beets, and barley and raise chickens, pigs, sheep, ducks, and cattle.

Bogracs Gulyas   Hungarian Goulash

Goulash is Hungary's most famous national dish; it can be either a stew or a soup. Originally cooked in large iron caldrons, called *bogracs*, over the open fire by shepherds, known as *gulya*, it came to be known as *bogracs gulyas*. There are as many different ways to make goulash as there are sheep roaming the vast Hungarian plains. One ingredient, **Hungarian paprika**, must always be added for the authentic flavor. Also called rose paprika, it has a vibrant red color and sweet taste. According to spice experts it is the world's finest paprika.

Yield: serves 6

2 tablespoons vegetable oil
1 1/2 pounds beef, round steak or boneless chuck, cut into 1-inch **cubes**
2 onions, **coarsely chopped**
3 cloves garlic, chopped, or 1 teaspoon garlic granules
2 cups water
2 cups beef broth, homemade or canned
1 cup canned **stewed** tomatoes
2 teaspoons Hungarian paprika
2 bay leaves
2 potatoes, cut into 1-inch cubes
2 carrots, cut into 1/2-inch slices
2 green peppers, cut into 1-inch pieces
salt and pepper to taste

Equipment: Large-size saucepan with cover or **Dutch oven**, mixing spoon

1. Heat oil in skillet or Dutch oven over medium-high heat, add beef, and cook, stirring continually, until brown (about 5 minutes). Reduce heat to medium, add onions and garlic, and cook for 5 minutes more until onions are soft. Mix well. Add water, beef broth, tomatoes, paprika, caraway seeds, and bay leaves, reduce to simmer, cover, and cook for 1 hour.
2. Add potatoes, carrots, green peppers, and salt and pepper to taste. Mix well, cover, and simmer for about 20 minutes more or until vegetables are tender. Before serving, remove bay leaves and discard.

Serve in individual bowls with chunks of crusty bread for dunking. Both a fork and spoon are needed to eat goulash.

Chicken Paprikash   Chicken Paprika

Paprika is the national seasoning of Hungary. It has a mildly pungent sweet flavor. In the original recipe for chicken paprika sour cream was not added. In recent years it is added by most Hungarian cooks to give the gravy a smoother, more pleasing taste.

Yield: serves 4 to 6

2 1/2 to 3 pounds chicken, cut into serving-size pieces
2 tablespoons **Hungarian paprika**

salt and pepper to taste
2 to 6 tablespoons vegetable oil
2 onions, **finely chopped**
2 1/2 cups water or chicken broth, homemade or canned, more or less as needed
1 tablespoon all-purpose flour
1 cup sour cream

Equipment: Wax-paper-covered work surface, large-size skillet with cover or **Dutch oven**, spatula or tongs, mixing spoon or **whisk**, cup, heat-proof serving platter

1. Put chicken pieces side-by-side on wax paper and sprinkle generously with 1 tablespoon paprika and salt and pepper to taste, turning them to coat on all sides.
2. Heat 2 tablespoons oil in skillet or Dutch oven over medium-high heat, add chicken, in batches, and brown on all sides (about 8 to 10 minutes per side), adding more oil if necessary. Use spatula or tongs to handle chicken and when browned, set aside, and keep warm.
3. Add onions to the same pan, reduce heat to medium, and fry until soft, mixing continually (about 3 minutes). Return browned chicken pieces to the pan on top of the onions.
4. Pour 2 cups water or broth, not over the chicken, but around the inside edges of pan so it will run under the chicken. Bring to a boil and then reduce heat to simmer, cover, and cook until tender (about 35 minutes). Add more liquid if necessary to prevent sticking. When done, remove chicken and place on serving platter. Set in warm place.
5. If there is very little liquid remaining in the pan add more broth or water. (You need about 1 1/2 cups liquid in the skillet for the gravy.)
6. *Prepare gravy:* In a cup, mix flour with 1/2 cup broth or water into a smooth paste. Add to simmering liquid, mixing continually, with whisk or mixing spoon, until mixture is smooth and begins to thicken (about 2 minutes). It should be a rich red-gold color. Add salt and pepper to taste and mix well. Remove from heat and set aside for about 5 minutes. Add sour cream, mixing continually until well blended. Return to low heat for about 3 minutes to heat through.

To serve, pour gravy over chicken and call everyone to dinner. Serve with cooked noodles or rice and buttered green beans.

Czechoslovakia

Czechoslovakia is in the midst of changes that will break up this country made up of people called the Czechs and Slovaks. In a recent election, the Slovaks voted to form a separate country. Despite the political differences between Czechs and Slovaks, there are little, if any differences in their cooking and eating habits. Czechs and Slovaks love meat, dumplings, and pastries, among them, their famous *kolaches.* For generations mothers have passed their cooking se-crets on to daughters. Czech and Slovak women are generally excellent cooks and share in kitchen duties at an early age. In fact, prior to Communist rule, Czechs and Slovaks were known as some of the finest cooks in the world. Czech and Slovak cooks were so good that they frequently were hired to manage the kitchens in many wealthy homes in surrounding countries prior to World War II. Sausages and streudal cakes made by Czechs and Slovaks are still among the world's best. One pastry that has been exported by emmigrating Czechs and Slovaks are *kolaches*. Many Czech and Slovak communities in the United States have *kolache* festivals and contests to find the best *kolache* makers. Popular fillings are meat, cheese, vegetables, and sweetmeats, and some are made with open tops and others are folded over and sealed.

Snadne Kolaches   Easy Kolaches

The following recipe is for quick and easy *kolaches*. We suggest using canned pie fillings, available at most supermarkets.

Yield: makes about 12 pastries

1/4 cup lukewarm water
1 package active dry yeast
3/4 cup plus 1 tablespoon sugar
1 cup boiling hot milk
1/2 cup butter or margarine
1 teaspoon salt
2 eggs, beaten
4 cups all-purpose flour
2 cups apple, peach, blueberry or strawberry (canned prepared pie filling)

Equipment: Cup, large-size mixing bowl, mixing spoon or electric mixer, kitchen towel, floured work surface, floured rolling pin, nonstick or lightly greased cookie sheet

1. Put warm water in cup. Add and dissolve yeast, sprinkle with 1 tablespoon sugar, and set aside. Put hot milk in large bowl, add butter or margarine, 3/4 cup sugar, and salt. Mix well. Cool to room temperature, add yeast mixture, and mix well.
2. Stirring continually, add egg to mixture and slowly add flour to form a semi-firm dough, using spoon or mixer. Cover bowl with towel and set in warm place until double in bulk (about 45 minutes).
3. Transfer dough to work surface and, using floured rolling pin, roll out about 1/2 inch thick. Cut into 3-inch squares, place side-by-side on cookie sheet, allowing space between, cover with towel, and set in warm place to double in bulk, about 40 minutes.
4. Preheat oven to 375° F.
5. Using a teaspoon, make a small dent in top of each piece and fill with about 1 teaspoon filling of your choice. Pull dough corners up slightly to keep filling in place. (Should resemble an open pouch.) Bake in oven for about 15 minutes or until golden brown.

Serve *kolaches* as a sweet treat or for dessert.

Zemakove Placky   Potato Pancakes

Yield: serves 4 to 6

4 cups peeled, raw, grated potatoes, well drained
2 eggs, well beaten

1 tablespoon flour
1/4 teaspoon baking powder
salt and pepper to taste
2 to 4 tablespoons butter or margarine

Equipment: Medium-size mixing bowl, mixing spoon, large-size skillet or griddle, pancake turner or metal spatula, baking sheet

1. Put drained potatoes and eggs in mixing bowl and blend well. Add flour, baking powder, and salt and pepper to taste.
2. Preheat oven to 150° F.
3. Melt 2 tablespoons butter or margarine in skillet or on griddle over medium-high heat. Drop mixture by tablespoonfuls onto skillet and spread with back of spoon, making each pancake about 4 inches across. Brown on both sides. Transfer fried pancakes to baking sheet and keep in warm oven until ready to serve. Repeat using all the mixture.

Serve pancakes as main dish or as side dish with meat. Serve with applesauce and sour cream to spoon over the pancakes for added flavor.

Austria

Austria is a Central European nation, which was once the seat of the Holy Roman Empire and the long-lived Hapsburg Empire. But since that time, it has had more than its share of conquerors, oppression, and suffering. It is now located on only a sliver of the land that it once occupied. Through it all, it has had a history of storybook kings and queens, beautiful music, the romantic Blue Danube River, and the waltz. According to many leading food experts, it is the land of exceptional cooks and

pastry bakers. When its empire was spread throughout Europe, Austria shared its cooking and recipes for special dishes. Likewise, Austrians took with them their favorites and incorporated those recipes into the menus at home. For example, they enjoy Czech dumplings and streusel, German roasts and sausages, and Venetian fish.

Austrians like three meals a day, plus a midmorning snack of sandwiches or pastries and a midafternoon coffee break with little sandwiches and cakes. Lunch is the big meal of the day. It starts with soup and includes salad, meat and potatoes, and a vegetable as well as hot rolls with plenty of butter and, perhaps, a dessert such as cake. Dinner is likely to be cold meat, sausage, cheese, eggs, a vegetable casserole, and a salad.

Sachertorte   *Chocolate Cake*

Over 150 years ago, a very unusual war broke out in Austria that lasted nearly 7 years. It was the war of the *sachertorte*, a chocolate cake that became world famous. Two pastry chefs claimed to have created the original recipe, and the battle was taken to court. The case ended in a draw, and both parties were permitted to bake and serve the cake. To this day, the cake is one of Austria's national treasures. The following recipe is one version of this delicious cake.

A good quality chocolate sauce to pour over the cake for frosting can be purchased at most supermarkets; however, if you'd like to make your own, the recipe follows.

Yield: serves 12 to 14

1/2 cup butter or margarine
1/2 cup sugar
6 eggs, **separated**
1 cup melted semi-sweet chocolate squares or chips, warm
1 cup all-purpose flour, **sifted**
1/2 cup strained apricot jam, warm, for frosting
1/2 cup semi-sweet chocolate sauce, for frosting, canned or homemade (recipe follows)

Equipment: Large-size mixing bowl, mixing spoon or electric mixer, medium-size mixing bowl, rubber spatula, buttered 9-inch **springform pan**, wax paper, wire rack

Preheat oven to 350° F.

1. Put butter or margarine and sugar in large mixing bowl and, using mixer or mixing spoon, blend until light and fluffy. Add egg yolks, one at a time, and beat well after each addition. Slowly add chocolate and blend well.
2. Using clean and dry mixer, beat egg whites until they are stiff and form peaks. With spatula, gently **fold** half of egg whites into chocolate mixture, and then fold in half of flour. Slowly add remaining whites and flour and blend well.
3. Lay springform pan on wax paper and, with a pencil, trace a circle around the bottom of the pan. Cut out the circle and butter the top side of it. Line bottom of buttered springform pan with buttered wax paper. Sprinkle the paper lightly with flour, and tip pan to pour out extra flour. Pour mixture into springform and bake in oven for about 35 minutes or until toothpick inserted in center of cake comes out clean. Remove from oven and cool on wire rack. Transfer to platter.
4. Spread apricot jam over top of cake. Pour chocolate sauce (see below) over top of cake and let it drip down and cover sides. Refrigerate to set.

Serve *sachertorte* cut in wedges with a **dollop** of whipped cream.

Chocolate Sauce

Yield: about 2 cups

1/4 cup butter
1/2 cup semi-sweet chocolate chips
1/2 cup sugar, more or less as needed
1/2 cup cream
pinch of salt
1 teaspoon vanilla

Equipment: Small-size saucepan, mixing spoon

Melt butter and chips in saucepan over low heat, mixing frequently. Add sugar, more or less to taste, cream, and salt. Mixing continually, increase heat to boil, mix, and remove from heat. Mix in vanilla. Cool to room temperature and pour over *Sachertorte* (see recipe above).

The sauce holds well refrigerated and can be reheated over a pan of hot water if necessary.

Switzerland

The Swiss speak German, French, Italian, and Romansch, a language that descends directly from Latin. This diversity tells us something about their food habits, which reflect German, French, and Italian traits. Their land, which is mostly mountainous, also tells us something about their cooking traditions. Livestock graze in the Alpine region, but wide-scale planting is impossible. Thus products from their animals, such as milk and cheese, are very important to the Swiss. Most Swiss people do not live in the mountains. They live on a stretch of land between the Alps and the Jura ranges in cities and towns. Banking and tourism are big industries. It is a highly industrialized country, famous for its craftspeople and precision products such as clocks. Thus, the Swiss can afford to import food instead of trying to raise it in a relatively inhospitable environment.

The Swiss are most famous for their cheese and their chocolates, which are among the best in the world. Wines, brandies, and liqueurs of Switzerland are world famous, too.

Fondue

The cheeses of Switzerland are legendary, and every village seems to have a cheese maker. For centuries, long before the Romans invaded the tiny country, the process of making cheese was already well established. Fondue, the national dish of Switzerland, shows off the excellent Swiss cheeses. Fondue, which means "to melt," is easy and fun to make and heavenly to eat. Do not use American processed cheeses, as they do not melt properly.

Yield: serves 6 to 8

2 cups *each* **finely chopped** Gruyere and Swiss cheeses
1/2 cup all-purpose flour
3 cloves garlic, finely chopped, or 1 teaspoon garlic granules
2 cups pure apple juice
1 tablespoon lemon juice
1/2 teaspoon ground nutmeg
salt to taste
1 loaf Italian or French bread, crust-on, cut into bite-size chunks

Equipment: Medium-size bowl; medium-size saucepan with electric hot plate, or electric fondue pot; wooden mixing spoon; long-handled fondue forks, or 12-inch skewers

1. Put Gruyere and Swiss cheeses in bowl, add flour, and toss to coat.
2. Put garlic, apple juice, and lemon juice in saucepan or fondue pot and heat to simmer. Add cheese, a handful at a time, and stir continually until melted. Add nutmeg and salt to taste.

To serve, the cheeses must be kept hot over either electric or canned heat, such as sterno. Each person has a plate of bread **cubes** and a long-handled fork or skewers. The cubes are put securely on the fork tines and dipped into the pot to coat with melted cheese. Serve an assortment of fresh fruit to eat with *fondue*.

Bundner Gerstensuppe   Grison Barley Soup

In this recipe *grison* is a special **marinated**, dried beef, made in Switzerland. Any dried chipped beef can be substituted.

Yield: serves 4 to 6

4 tablespoons butter or margarine
1 onion, chopped
1 *each* carrot, **diced**; leek, washed and diced; celery stalk, sliced
1/2 cup *each* chopped dried beef and chopped smoked ham
1/2 cup barley
8 cups chicken broth, homemade or canned
1/4 teaspoon ground nutmeg
1/2 cup heavy cream
1/2 cup cooked Great Northern beans, homemade or canned
salt and pepper to taste

Equipment: Large-size saucepan with cover or **Dutch oven**, mixing spoon

1. Melt butter or margarine in saucepan over medium heat. Add onion, carrot, leek, and celery and cook until soft, stirring occasionally (about 10 minutes). Add beef, ham, barley, and chicken broth, and mix well. Increase heat to boil, reduce to simmer, cover, and cook for 1 hour, stirring occasionally.
2. Add nutmeg, cream, cooked beans, and salt and pepper to taste. Heat through (about 3 minutes), and remove from heat.

Serve this hearty soup as a one-dish supper with crusty bread and cheese as they would in the Alps after skiing the slopes.

Double Chocolate Cake

Swiss chocolates are world famous, and Swiss chefs can be justly proud of the wonderful pastries and candies that have found their way around the world. The following cake recipe is very unusual; it uses identical ingredients and procedures for both cake and icing, but the cake is cooked and the icing is not.

Yield: serves 10 to 16

2 cups semisweet chocolate: bar, chopped, or chips
1/2 cup butter or margarine, softened at room temperature
4 eggs, **separated**
1/2 cup sugar

Equipment: Small-size saucepan, wooden mixing spoon, large-size mixing bowl, **egg beater** or electric beater, medium-size mixing bowl, **whisk,** buttered 9-inch **springform pan**, wire rack

Preheat oven to 325° F.

1. **Melt chocolate** and butter in saucepan over low heat, stirring frequently until melted and blended. Remove from heat.
2. Put egg yolks and sugar in large mixing bowl and beat with egg beater or electric beater until light and lemon colored, about 5 minutes. Add chocolate mixture and mix well.
3. Beat egg whites in medium-size bowl with electric mixer or egg beater until stiff but not dry. Add half the whites to chocolate mixture and mix well. Using spoon or whisk, gently **fold** in remaining whites.
4. Pour batter into springform pan and bake in oven for about 45 minutes, until cake pulls away from sides of pan. Remove from oven and place cake pan on wire rack to cool for about 30 minutes. Release from pan and cool completely before icing (recipe follows).

Serve cake cut in small wedges; it is very rich.

Chocolate Icing

Yield: icing for one 9-inch cake

1 cup semisweet chocolate: bar, chopped, or chips
1/4 cup butter or margarine, softened at room temperature
2 eggs, **separated**
1/4 cup sugar
1 teaspoon confectioners' sugar for garnish

Equipment: Small-size saucepan, wooden mixing spoon, large-size mixing bowl, **egg beater** or electric beater, medium-size mixing bowl, **whisk** or mixing spoon, knife or metal spatula, small strainer

1. Follow steps 1 through 3 for the double chocolate cake recipe.
2. Cake must be completely cool before icing. Using knife or spatula, cover cake top and sides with icing. Put confectioners' sugar in strainer and lightly shake over icing.

Serve cake covered with chocolate icing.

Italy

Italy's culinary history can be traced back more than 2,000 years to the ancient civilization of Rome. With the fall of the Roman Empire came the decline of fancy cooking and feasting. But the interest in cooking revived in Italy during the Renaissance along with art, literature, and music. Italy consists of 20 regions, and for centuries did not exist as the nation we now know. After hundreds of years of regional differences, even erupting into vio-

lent wars, in 1861 Italy became a united country. Strong regional pride still exists, however, and Italians have one word for it, "campanilismo," meaning "my region is the best." Even today each region jealously clings to its own culinary heritage, believing it is the best. In the north, butter and rice are common ingredients. To the south, olive oil and tomatoes are the common ingredients.

Agriculture is still an important part of Italy's economy, but in recent years industry has become predominant. Produce from Italy makes its way to the rest of Europe, especially during the winter when fresh produce is not available in the colder countries. In addition to vegetables, rice, wheat, potatoes, and olives are grown. Some livestock—including sheep, cattle, pigs, goats, water buffalo, and horses are raised—but the Italians have to import a portion of their meat and eggs.

Cheeses are a very important part of Italian life and are a national product. There are hundreds of wonderful cheeses made not only from cows' milk but also from the milk of goats, ewes, and water buffalo. Some of the most popular are shipped all over the world: ricotta, provolone, mozzarella, and pecoriano made from the milk of ewes. The most highly prized cheese is made from the milk of water buffalo, called "mozzarella di bufalo." The full name is stamped on the rind, and its production and distribution are tightly controlled by the government. Usually an Italian meal ends with an assortment of fresh fruit and a cheese or two.

Antipasto   "Before the Food"

Antipasto means "before the food." It designates the time that *antipasti*, which refers to an assortment of "little dishes," are eaten. *Antipasti* can simply be raw vegetable sticks, cheese cubes, pickles, sliced cold cuts, or cubes of melon. They can each be served in a different "little dish" or separated in a decorative way on one platter. A variety of colors, textures, and flavors is important.

Frittata   Omelet

A *frittata* is often served as an *antipasto*. It can be made with any cooked or chopped meat and is a good way of using leftovers.

Yield: serves 2 to 4

2 eggs
1 teaspoon **finely chopped** flat leaf parsley
1/2 cup finely chopped pepperoni
1 tablespoon olive oil
salt and pepper to taste

Equipment: Small-size bowl, mixing spoon, small-size skillet, 9-inch plate

1. Put eggs, parsley, and pepperoni into bowl and mix well.
2. Heat oil in skillet over medium heat. Swirl oil to coat pan bottom. When hot, add mixture. Cook for 3 to 4 minutes, slide onto plate, invert back into skillet, and cook other side until firm, about 1 minute. Add salt and pepper to taste.

Serve either warm or cold; cut into 4 or 6 wedges.

If Italy has a national soup it would be a tie between *minestrone* and *pasta e fagioli* made with noodles and beans.

Yield: serves 6 to 8

5 cups water
1 1/2 cups dried white beans: navy, baby lima, or northern
1 onion, **coarsely chopped**
2 cups canned Italian-style tomatoes, with juice
1 cup *each* **finely chopped** celery and sliced carrots
3 cloves garlic, coarsely chopped, or 1 teaspoon garlic granules
1/2 pound cooked smoked ham, chopped
3 bay leaves
1/2 cup uncooked macaroni (shells, bows, or elbow shapes)
salt and pepper to taste
1/2 cup grated Parmesan cheese for garnish

Equipment: Large-size saucepan with cover or **Dutch oven**, mixing spoon

1. Put water and beans in saucepan or Dutch oven. Bring to a boil over high heat, boil for 3 minutes, and remove from heat. Cover and set aside for 1 hour.
2. Add onion, tomatoes, celery, carrots, garlic, smoked ham, and bay leaves; mix well; and bring to a boil over high heat. Reduce to simmer, cover, and cook until beans, are tender (about 1 1/2 hours); stir frequently.
3. Add macaroni and mix well. Cover and continue simmering until macaroni is tender (about 12 minutes). Remove and discard bay leaves before serving.

Serve hot soup in individual bowls with a side dish of Parmesan cheese for the guests to sprinkle into their soup. Serve crusty bread for sopping.

Pastas and Sauces

When people think of Italian cooking, they think of pastas and sauces. All pastas regardless of shape or name, are basically the same; they're simply made from a dough flour and water; sometimes eggs are added. It's the sauces that give different flavors. There are many kinds of pastas all named after what they look like, such as ribbons, thimbles, butterflies, bows, angels hair, etc. There are over 200 different noodle shapes and each with a different name. **Semolina**, a flour made from **durum wheat,** is the very best flour for pasta making. It's a high-protein, hard-wheat grain. Noodles made from semolina flour hold their shape, staying **al dente** longer when properly cooked. Cooked pasta should be firm when you bite into it, not soft and mushy. If you're an inexperienced pasta cook it is best to taste a strand of pasta from time to time, near the end of cooking time, to make sure it's just right. Remove from heat and drain at once, don't run cold water over it; instead, have the sauce ready and serve immediately. Remember, cooking time will vary according to pasta thickness and whether it is dry, frozen, or freshly made. Freshly made pastas require less cooking time than dried pastas.

Sauces get their names from a variety of sources: a town, a region, a chef who first created it, from a certain food in the recipe, a fantasy, or a historical legend, and sauces distinguish dishes one region from another. For instance, in the Emilia-Romagna region the local sauce is ragu, a sauce made with meat. In the Rome-Latium region, it is tomatoes and basil; in Lombardy, it is butter and the herb sage. The following are recipes for sauces to pour over pastas.

Primavera Sauce   Fresh Vegetable Pasta Sauce

Primavera means "spring style" and is a sauce made with any combination of vegetables.

Yield: serves 4 to 6

3 tablespoons olive oil
3 cloves fresh garlic, **finely chopped,** or 1 teaspoon garlic granules
3 tablespoons butter or margarine
1 cup thinly sliced zucchini, fresh or frozen, thawed
1 cup **coarsely chopped** broccoli, fresh or frozen, thawed
1 cup coarsely chopped onions
2 green peppers, **cored, seeded,** cut into strips
2 cups tomato sauce, homemade or canned
1/2 cup tomato paste
salt, pepper, and red pepper flakes to taste
one pound (before cooking) cooked pasta, for serving (cooked according to directions on package, kept warm); a few drops of oil tossed with the pasta keep it from sticking together
grated Parmesan cheese, for garnish

Equipment: Large-size skillet, wooden mixing spoon, 2 forks

1. Heat oil in skillet over medium heat, add garlic, and cook for about 2 minutes. Increase heat to medium high. Add butter or margarine, zucchini, broccoli, onions, and green peppers, and stir frequently, cooking for 6 minutes, until vegetables are cooked through but still crisp.
2. Add tomato sauce and paste, mix well, heat through (about 3 minutes), and add salt, pepper, and red pepper to taste.

To serve, put warm pasta in large serving bowl and pour hot sauce over it. With a fork in each hand, toss pasta to coat with sauce, sprinkle with Parmesan cheese, and serve with extra cheese, extra red pepper flakes, green salad, and warm garlic bread.

Salsa al Limone   Lemon Cream Sauce for Pasta

Italian sauces are very easy to make and uncomplicated. This cream sauce is from the Amalfi coastal region of Italy.

Yield: serves 4

1 cup heavy cream
1/2 cup half-and-half

2 teaspoons dried red pepper flakes, more or less to taste

2 tablespoons freshly grated lemon rind

one pound (before cooking) cooked pasta, such as rigatoni, for serving (cooked according to directions on package), kept warm; a few drops of oil tossed with pasta keep it from sticking together

1 cup grated Parmesan Cheese

1/2 cup **finely chopped** fresh basil

salt and pepper to taste

Equipment: Medium-size saucepan, mixing spoon, large-size bowl, 2 forks

1. Put cream, half-and-half, 1 teaspoon red pepper flakes, and lemon rind in medium saucepan and cook over medium-low heat for about 20 minutes, stirring frequently until liquid is slightly thick and reduced to about 1 cup.
2. Put the warm cooked pasta in large bowl and add sauce. With a fork in each hand, toss pasta with an up and down rotating motion over the bowl, until pasta is completely covered with sauce. Sprinkle in 1/2 cup Parmesan cheese, basil, and salt and pepper to taste and continue to toss and coat pasta. Sprinkle top with remaining cheese, remaining red pepper flakes, more or less to taste, basil, and salt and pepper to taste.

Serve with extra cheese, red pepper flakes, green salad, and warm garlic bread.

Fettucine Alfredo   Parmesan Sauce with Pasta

The following sauce is exactly the same as that used in the world-famous dish known as *Fettucine Alfredo*. The pasta is fettucine and the sauce is named for the chef/restaurant owner in Rome who made it famous.

Yield: serves 4

1 cup butter or margarine at room temperature

1/2 cup heavy cream

1/2 cup grated Parmesan cheese

1 pound cooked pasta, such as fettucini, for serving (cook according to directions on package); time the cooking so it can be drained and mixed with the sauce while still very hot

salt, pepper, and ground nutmeg to taste

Equipment: Large-size heat-proof serving bowl, medium-size mixing bowl, wooden mixing spoon, oven mitts, heat-proof work surface, 2 forks

1. Warm the heat-proof serving bowl in the oven until ready to use.
2. Put butter or margarine in mixing bowl, and, using wooden spoon, beat until light and fluffy. Add cream, a little at a time, and mix until well blended. Add cheese by tablespoon, beating well after each addition.
3. Using oven mitts, remove heated serving bowl from oven and place on heat-proof work surface. Put drained cooked pasta in warm bowl and add cheese mixture. With a fork in each hand, toss pasta in an up and down rotating motion over the bowl until pasta is well-coated with sauce. Add salt, pepper, and nutmeg to taste and continue to toss and coat pasta.

Serve at once while very hot, on individual plates, with a side dish of extra grated cheese. Adding green salad with Italian dressing and warm garlic bread makes a wonderful meal.

Pane Untata

Garlic Bread

Yield: serves 6 to 8

1 loaf French or Italian bread, split in half lengthwise.
1/2 to 1 cup olive oil, melted butter, or melted margarine
3 cloves garlic, **finely chopped**, or 1 teaspoon garlic granules
salt and pepper to taste
1/2 cup grated Parmesan cheese

Equipment: Bread knife, nonstick or greased baking sheet, small-size bowl, pastry brush or spoon

1. Place both halves of bread on a baking sheet with cut sides up.
2. Put oil, butter, or margarine in a bowl, add garlic, and mix well. Using either pastry brush or spoon, spread mixture over cut side of bread. Sprinkle with salt, pepper, and cheese.
3. Preheat oven to 375°F.
4. Just before serving put in oven for 15 minutes or until top is golden and bread is heated through.

To serve bread hot, wrap in napkin or towel to keep warm, and place in basket or on a platter.

Portugal

Portugal is surrounded by Spain to the east and the Atlantic Ocean on the west coast. It is one of the poorest of the European nations, with an underdeveloped industrial and agricultural base. With 32 percent of their land potential farm land, the Portuguese people are in a position to improve agricultural yields, but right now they import about half of their food. The primary food crops grown are wine grapes, grains, potatoes, and olives. The Portuguese also raise sheep, pigs, cattle, goats, and donkeys. One of the most important food industries is fishing, most notably for oysters, crabs, cod, and sardines. Portuguese like sardines dried or fresh, not out of the can as we are accustomed to eating them.

Portugal is a country of hearty soups, stews, and casseroles that vary from region to region, day to day, and cook to cook. What the fishers catch; what is at the market, in the garden, or on the pantry shelf; or how the cook is feeling (as everywhere) can determine what will be tossed in the pot. Combining fish and meat in the same casserole or stew is unique to Portuguese and Spanish cooking. Garlic is added with a "heavy hand," and no dish is complete without it. Other basic ingredients are tomatoes, olive oil, and onions.

Sopa De Pedra   Stone Soup

Sopa de pedra is a thick country soup from northern Portugal; there it is served with big chunks of *pao*, bread. The bread is used for sopping every last drop of broth. Any combination of beans and vegetables can be used, but you can skip the stones.

Yield: serves 6 to 8

2 tablespoons vegetable oil
1 onion, **coarsely chopped**
1 leek, coarsely chopped (rinse in strainer and drain well)
1 *each* potato, carrot, and white turnip, all chopped
1 cup **cored** and thinly sliced green cabbage
2 cups cooked kidney beans, dried (cooked according to directions on package), or canned
6 cups chicken broth, homemade or canned
1 bay leaf
1 cup coarsely chopped smoked ham, pepperoni, or sausage
1/2 cup 1-inch cut green beans, fresh or frozen, thawed
1 cup **stewed** Italian tomatoes, with liquid, canned
2 tablespoons Italian parsley, chopped
1/2 cup cooked elbow macaroni (cooked according to directions on package and well-drained)
salt and pepper to taste

Equipment: Large-size saucepan with cover or **Dutch oven**, mixing spoon

1. Heat oil in large saucepan or Dutch oven over medium-high heat. Add onion and leek, mix well, and fry about 5 minutes, until golden. Reduce heat to low and add potato, carrot, turnip, and cabbage. Mix well, cover, and cook about 10 minutes, until vegetables begin to soften.
2. Add kidney beans with liquid, chicken broth, bay leaf, meat, green beans, and tomatoes. Simmer for 30 minutes more or until vegetables are tender. Remove bay leaf and discard.
3. Just before serving, add parsley, macaroni, and salt and pepper to taste. Cover and heat through over medium heat (about 5 minutes).

To serve, ladle as a meal-in-a-bowl with plenty of freshly baked bread.

Pao   Country Bread

No Portuguese meal is complete unless it is served with bread. In most Portuguese villages housewives bring their freshly shaped loaves of bread to communal brick ovens to be baked. The bread they are most likely to make contains only four ingredients. It is chewy and thick crusted because of vigorous hand **kneading** and brick-oven baking with intense steam heat. Not having a brick oven, the following cooking tip for crusty bread works very well in any household oven. Before preheating the oven, place an oven-safe pan of water (about 2 quarts) on the bottom shelf.

Yield: 2 round (8-inch) loaves

3 packages active dry yeast (each envelope 1/4 oz)
1 1/2 cups lukewarm water (105°-115°F)

7 cups **sifted** all-purpose flour
2 teaspoons salt

Equipment: Large-size mixing bowl, wooden spoon, kitchen towel, floured work surface, 2 oiled 9-inch round cake pans, roasting pan with 2 quarts water for steaming

1. Combine yeast with 1/2 cup warm water and 1 cup flour in large bowl and beat with wooden spoon until smooth. Cover bowl with towel and set in warm place. Let dough rise until spongy and double in bulk, about 25 minutes.
2. Stir yeast mixture down and add remaining 1 cup water, salt, and remaining 6 cups flour, 1 cup at a time, making a stiff but workable dough. Transfer to floured work surface and **knead** vigorously for 5 minutes until smooth and elastic. Shape dough into ball and place in warm, lightly greased bowl. Cover with towel, set in warm place, and let rise until double in bulk, about 1 hour.
3. Put dough on floured work surface and **punch down.** Knead for 5 minutes. Divide dough into 2 pieces, knead each for about 3 minutes, and shape into balls. Place each ball in a cake pan and dust top lightly with flour. Cover with towel and set in warm place to rise until double in size (about 45 minutes).
4. Have 2 quarts of water in roasting pan already in the oven for steaming.
5. Preheat oven to 450°F.
6. When the oven is hot and steamy, place pans of bread on middle shelf, using oven-mitts to protect your hands. Bake for 15 minutes at 450°F, and then lower heat to 400°F. Bake bread about 20 to 30 minutes until browned and hollow sounding when tapped.

Serve the *pao* warm with butter as an accompaniment to any meal.

Spain

In a country where being thin was once a sign of poverty, every meal except breakfast is robust and filling. Spanish food is colorful but not too spicy hot. Main flavorings include garlic, paprika, olives, and olive oil. Favorite main course foods are seafood, in particular salted cod, smoked sausages, and **stewed** meat. Rice, beans, and fresh produce are also served in abundance. Spanish wine is well received around the world, and wine grapes are an important crop. Other important crops include grains, citrus fruits, and vegetables. Livestock include pigs, sheep, cattle, horses, and mules.

History has played an important role in the development of food in Spain. The occupation of the country from 711 A.D. to 1492 by the Moors, who were Muslims from northwestern Africa, brought great agricultural treasures and methods to the Iberian Peninsula. For example, the Moors introduced advanced irrigation techniques, which made increased agricultural production possible. They also brought rice, figs, almonds, citrus fruits, peaches, and bananas and planted them in Spain. The Muslim Moors introduced the spices of the East, including cumin and aniseed, which are still used extensively. In turn, the Spanish Conquistadors introduced these things to the areas that they conquered and brought back peppers, tomatoes, and chocolate from the Americas, along with many other indigenous plants and animals.

Tortilla a la Espanola — Spanish Omelet

Omelets are a Spanish favorite, eaten hot or cold, and at any time of day or night. All kinds of vegetables, meats, and fish are added for variety. A Spanish omelet is cakelike, with a crusty brown outside and soft creamy center.

Yield: serves 4 to 6

2 to 4 tablespoons olive oil
2 *each* potatoes and onions, peeled and **coarsely chopped**
3 cloves garlic, peeled and chopped, or 1 teaspoon garlic granules
6 eggs, lightly beaten
salt and pepper to taste

Equipment: Large-size skillet with cover, mixing spoon, pancake turner or metal spatula, heat-proof plate or flat pan larger than skillet

1. Heat 2 tablespoons oil in skillet over medium-high heat. Add potatoes, onions, and garlic and mix well. Cover, reduce heat to low, and cook for 15 minutes without browning, stirring frequently. Add more oil if necessary to prevent sticking.
2. When vegetables are tender, but still firm, add eggs. After edges start to cook, using pancake turner or spatula, raise edges of omelet so uncooked eggs can flow under it. Cook for about 5 minutes more over medium heat, and add salt and pepper to taste.
3. To turn omelet over, remove from heat, invert skillet over plate or flat pan, and slide omelet back into skillet with browned-side up. Cook for 2 minutes more, until set.

Serve omelet either hot or cold on a large platter; cut in wedges.

Gazpacho — Chilled Tomato Soup with Vegetables

For centuries, only the very poorest Spanish peasants ate a lowly "bread and water" soup called *gazpacho*. Today it's world famous and considered very classy, eaten by rich and poor alike. The old, traditional *gazpacho* is made with stale bread soaked in olive oil and tomato juice. Over the years the recipe has changed somewhat, with the same delicious results.

Yield: about 1 1/2 quarts

1/2 cup **peeled, finely chopped** fresh tomato
1/2 cup peeled and finely chopped cucumber
1/2 cup **cored, seeded,** finely chopped green pepper
1/2 cup finely chopped celery
2 cloves garlic, peeled, finely chopped or 1/2 teaspoon garlic granules
1 tablespoon apple cider vinegar
1 tablespoon olive oil
4 cups tomato juice

salt and pepper to taste

4 green onions, finely chopped, for garnish

Equipment: 1/2-gallon jar or container with tight-fitting cover

1. Put tomato, cucumber, green pepper, celery, garlic, vinegar, oil, tomato juice, and salt and pepper to taste in jar. Cover tightly and shake well. Refrigerate until ready to serve.
2. When ready to serve, shake well and pour into individual bowls, making sure some chopped vegetables are in each bowl. Sprinkle each serving with green onions.

Serve gazpacho very cold. Small dishes of chopped **hard-cooked eggs** and croutons can be served and sprinkled in the soup for added flavor.

France

France is a country with a long history of talented and creative cooks. When Catherine de Medici left Italy for France to marry Henry II in 1533, she brought her personal chefs. They introduced "grand" cooking to the French court. The French developed and perfected techniques and cooking skills still revered and practiced today. By the time of the French Revolution, many skilled chefs were working for the aristocracy, but most people did not eat the "fancy foods," and in fact a lack of food among the poor played a crucial role in the Revolution. At the end of the French Revolution a new kind of revolution emerged, with classical French cooking available to everyone, as the chefs opened restaurants and went to work for the French elite. French chefs are held in the highest esteem by professional chefs and *gourmands* (people who love good cooking), the world over.

New developments in French cooking occurred during the 1970s when a new kind of cooking (*nouvelle cuisine*) caught on. It emphasized cooking food in its own juices, less heavy sauces, and using food combinations in new ways; for example, chicken in raspberry vinegar, or oysters on a bed of leeks. Most of the fervor of *nouvelle cuisine* has died down, but the philosophy of enjoying natural flavors instead of heavy, rich sauces is stronger than ever.

Agriculturally, France has both managed to have a highly industrialized farm sector (nearly 60 percent of the land), and yet maintain some hand farming, which is not totally a thing of the past. Grapes are the most important crop, with the government encouraging the planting of the best grapes for the highest quality wines possible. Other food crops include cereals, sugar beets, potatoes, and garden vegetables. Livestock include cattle, pigs, sheep, and goats.

Soupe a l'Oignon   Onion Soup

Yield: serves 4

3 tablespoons butter or margarine
2 cups peeled and thinly sliced onions
4 cups beef broth
4 slices French bread cut 1/4 inch thick, crust on
1 cup **shredded** Gruyere or Swiss cheese
1/2 cup grated Parmesan cheese

Equipment: Large-size saucepan with cover or **Dutch oven**, mixing spoon, toaster, ladle, individual oven-proof soup bowls, baking sheet, oven mitts

1. Melt butter or margarine in saucepan or Dutch oven over medium heat. Add onions, cover, and cook, stirring frequently, until limp (5 minutes). Add beef broth, cover, and simmer for 10 minutes more.
2. Toast the bread and set aside.
3. Set oven shelf 8 inches under broiler and heat.
4. Ladle soup into 4 individual oven-proof bowls and sprinkle half the shredded cheese equally among the bowls. Cut toasted bread to fit into each bowl and place a slice on top of each. Cover toast with equal amounts of remaining shredded cheese and equal amounts of Parmesan cheese. Place bowls on baking sheet, and, using oven mitts, set under broiler for about 5 minutes, until cheese is bubbly and light brown. Using oven mitts, remove bowls from oven and set on heat-proof surface. **Be careful,** bowls are very hot.

To serve, place bowls on individual serving plates and serve immediately.

Ratatouille a la Nicoise   Vegetarian Stew

Every province and peasant has a different way of making *ratatouille,* a popular French vegetable casserole. Using the freshest vegetables from garden or market is all that really matters. The dish is a blending of cooked vegetables and should not be overcooked and mushy. In this recipe, vegetables grown locally around the Mediterranean port city of Nice are used. Cooking them with olive oil and garlic is typical French Mediterranean cooking.

Yield: serves 6

1/2 cup olive oil
2 onions, chopped
3 cloves garlic, **finely chopped**, or 1 teaspoon garlic granules
4 cups eggplant, peeled and cut into 1/2-inch chunks
2 green bell peppers, **cored**, **seeded**, cut into thin strips
2 zucchinis, cut into 1/4-inch rounds
1/2 teaspoon *each* ground oregano and ground thyme
3 bay leaves
4 tomatoes, **peeled**, cut into chunks or 2 cups canned whole tomatoes
salt and pepper to taste

Equipment: Large-size saucepan with cover, mixing spoon, **colander** or strainer, oven-proof 2 1/2 quart casserole

Preheat oven to 350° F.

1. Sprinkle eggplant with 1 teaspoon salt and set aside in colander or strainer in sink or over plate for 30 minutes.
2. Heat 2 tablespoons olive oil in saucepan over medium heat. Add onion and garlic, mix well, and cook until onions are soft, about 5 minutes. Transfer to casserole.
3. Rinse eggplant in a colander or strainer under cold water and drain well. Return skillet to medium heat and add 2 tablespoons oil, eggplant, bell peppers, zucchinis, oregano, thyme, and bay leaves. Stirring frequently, reduce heat to simmer, cover, and cook for about 5 minutes. (Add more oil if necessary to prevent sticking.)
4. Remove bay leaves and discard. Transfer mixture to casserole and mix with onions. Cover top with tomatoes and add salt and pepper to taste. Drizzle with remaining oil and bake in oven for about 45 minutes or until top is browned.

Serve hot as the main dish with plenty of crusty French bread and butter.

Truffles au Chocolat   Chocolate Candy

Giving a gift of homemade truffles to friends and family is a wonderful treat; they are inexpensive and easy to make. Homemade truffles are far superior to the very expensive store-bought truffles. Chopped nuts, dates, grated coconut, chocolate, butterscotch, white chocolate mini-chips, or candied cherries can be added to this recipe for a variety of textures and flavors.

Yield: makes about 12 pieces

4 ounces semisweet chocolate chips or bar
2 tablespoons water
3 egg yolks (refrigerate whites to use at another time)
4 tablespoons butter or margarine
3/4 cup confectioners' sugar
5 tablespoons cocoa

Equipment: Small-size saucepan, rubber spatula, mixing spoon, medium-size mixing bowl, wax paper, cookie sheet, small-size bowl, aluminum foil

1. **Melt chocolate** in saucepan over low heat. Add water and mix to blend. Remove from heat and pour chocolate into mixing bowl. Scrape out the pan with rubber spatula. Add egg yolks, butter, and sugar and mix until well blended. Refrigerate until firm, about 2 hours.
2. Remove mixture from refrigerator, and using clean hands, shape into ping-pong-size balls. Place balls side-by-side on wax paper covered cookie sheet.
3. Put cocoa in small bowl and roll balls, one at a time, in cocoa until coated. Return balls to cookie sheet, cover with foil, and refrigerate until ready to serve.

Serve *truffles* as a candy treat. Wrap each in plastic wrap and store in covered container, refrigerated.

Clafouti   Cherry Pudding Cake

The following dessert is originally from the Limousin region of central France where the hillsides are covered with cherry trees. This recipe is a typical peasant dessert especially popular among the workers during cherry-picking season.

Yield: serves 6 to 8

2 cups stemmed, **pitted**, dark sweet cherries, fresh, or frozen and thawed, or canned and drained
1/2 cup sugar
1 cup milk
1 cup heavy cream
4 eggs
1 teaspoon vanilla
1 cup all-purpose flour
1/4 teaspoon salt
1/2 cup confectioners' sugar

Equipment: Small-size bowl, large-size mixing bowl, spoon or electric mixer, buttered 10-inch cake pan, wire rack

Preheat oven to 350° F.
1. Put cherries in small bowl and sprinkle with 1 tablespoon sugar.
2. Put milk, cream, eggs, and vanilla in large mixing bowl and mix with spoon or electric mixer until well blended. Mixing continually, add remaining sugar, flour, and salt.
3. Pour one quarter of the batter into buttered cake pan. Place pan in oven for about 5 minutes, until set, and then remove from oven. Place cherries on top of batter, cover with remaining batter, return to oven, and continue baking for about 60 minutes, until top is puffed and golden brown. Remove from oven, set on wire rack to cool, and sprinkle with confectioners' sugar. The cake will sink somewhat as it cools.

Serve the pudding-like cake while still warm, cut into squares. It can be served with a **dollop** of sour cream, whipped cream, or yogurt.

Belgium

The Belgians love good food and have many excellent vegetable gardeners, cooks, and pastry chefs. This tiny, fertile country north of France is known for outstanding meats and fresh vegetables. It's such a small country that it only takes about four hours at most to get food from the farm to the market. Livestock include pigs, cattle, sheep, goats, and horses. Belgians are known for growing vegetables such as Brussels sprouts and their famous Belgian endive. Belgian
endive is not considered just a salad green; it is, however, a lovely looking and tasting light green vegetable, eaten raw in salads or cooked in soups and stews. It is only available fresh and is rather expensive in U.S. markets. Brussels sprouts look like miniature cabbages and are readily available in the U.S., where they are also grown. They are very easy to cook.

Choux de Bruxelles   Brussels Sprouts

Yield: serves 4 to 6

1/2 cup butter or margarine
1 pound Brussels sprouts, fresh, **trimmed**, or frozen, thawed
1/2 teaspoon ground nutmeg
salt and pepper to taste

Equipment: Medium-size skillet with cover, mixing spoon

Melt butter or margarine in skillet over medium-high heat. Add Brussels sprouts and mix to coat. Reduce heat to medium, cover, and cook for about 8 minutes, until tender but firm. Remove from heat and season with nutmeg and salt and pepper to taste.

Serve *choux de bruxelles* warm as a side dish with meat, chicken, or fish.

Waterzooi de Poularde   Flemish Chicken and Vegetable Stew

A Belgian specialty is the *waterzooi*, originally made with fish and shellfish, and now also made with chicken. There are many different ways of making *waterzooi*, and this recipe is but one example.

Yield: serves 6 to 8

2 to 3 pounds chicken, cut into serving-size pieces
salt and pepper to taste
6 tablespoons butter or margarine
2 *each* onions, chopped; carrots, thinly sliced; and celery stalks, thinly sliced
10 fresh mushrooms, chopped
6 cups chicken broth, homemade or canned
2 tablespoons bread crumbs
2 eggs, lightly beaten
1/2 cup chopped parsley, for garnish

Equipment: Work surface, large-size saucepan with cover or **Dutch oven**, mixing spoon

1. Put chicken pieces on work surface and add salt and pepper to taste.
2. Melt butter or margarine in saucepan or Dutch oven over medium heat. Add onions, carrots, celery, and mushrooms and cook for about 5 minutes, until vegetables are softened and well coated. Add chicken pieces and broth and increase heat to boil. Reduce heat to simmer, cover, and cook for about 1 hour, until chicken is tender. Remove chicken pieces and set aside. Add breadcrumbs and eggs, mix well, and continue cooking on low heat.
3. When chicken cools, remove meat from bones and return meat to soup. Mix well and heat through.

Serve *waterzooi* in soup bowls as a meal-in-a-bowl. In Belgium it is traditionally served with plain boiled potatoes, bread, and butter.

United Kingdom

The United Kingdom (UK) of Great Britain and Northern Ireland, which includes England, Northern Ireland, Scotland, and Wales, was once a major colonial empire and imported foods and spices from all over the world. Today, though it still has some of its colonial holdings, the UK is pretty much reduced to the islands that it inhabits. Agriculture is dominated by livestock raising, especially cattle and sheep. Much of the finer meats are exported to France and beyond.  Dairy products such as cheese are also an important part of the agricultural system. Major food crops include wheat, barley, potatoes, and sugar beets, but the UK still has to import about half of its food supplies.

In Northern Ireland, Scotland, Wales, and England the cooking is wholesome, nourishing, and robust, which goes well with the damp and foggy weather hovering over the UK a great deal of the time. There are many British foods and beverages that have traveled the Atlantic and crossed cultures quite well: dark fruit cakes, plum puddings at Christmas time, tea drinking, and Scotch whiskey are just a few.

Tea drinking became a part of English culture about 1600. It came from China by way of Holland. Tea was expensive and heavily taxed, keeping it a luxury available only for the privileged few. Today, tea drinking is a national pleasure, and "taking afternoon tea" usually happens about 4 pm, and everyone, from the palace drawing room to the back rooms of factories and shops, stops for tea. There are regional tea drinking practices, such as "cream tea" served in Devonshire, England, named after the clotted cream spread on the biscuits served with tea. In the industrial regions of northern England a more hearty repast called "high tea" came about. When factory workers returned home they wanted a light supper to tide them over until a full meal was eaten. "High tea" is also called "meat or ham tea," where, as the name suggests, little meat pies are served with tea.

Cucumber Tea Sandwiches

Served along with afternoon tea are traditional little cakes, bite-size bits of fruit, pastries, and sandwiches. Cucumber tea sandwiches are a classic, even served at teatime by the Queen in her palace. The secret to making perfect sandwiches is to slice the cucumbers paper thin.

Yield: 16 sandwiches

8 slices thinly sliced white bread
8 teaspoons butter or margarine, more or less, at room temperature
1 cucumber, peeled, thinly sliced
salt and white pepper to taste

Equipment: Sharp knife, work surface, butter spreader

1. Cut crusts off bread slices and spread one side of each piece with thin layer of butter or margarine. Place on work surface, buttered-side up.
2. Arrange cucumber slices, slightly overlapping, on 4 bread slices, and sprinkle each with salt and white pepper to taste. Place remaining bread slices on top and gently press down with the heel of your hand. Holding the sandwich securely together, cut each one into 4 triangle-shaped pieces. Place sandwiches on a serving platter, standing on end with the point up. Cover with slightly damp cloth and refrigerate until ready to serve.

Serve *cucumber sandwiches* at tea time, or any time; they're delicious.

Scones   English Baking Powder Biscuits

Scones and *crumpets* are traditionally served with afternoon tea. Scones are basically baking-powder biscuits, usually served warm with a drizzle of jam.

Yield: about 12

2 cups cake all-purpose flour
2 teaspoons double-action baking powder
1 tablespoon sugar
1/2 teaspoon salt
1/4 cup butter or margarine
2 eggs
1/3 cup half-and-half

Equipment: Flour **sifter**, large-size mixing bowl, wooden mixing spoon, small-size bowl, **whisk**, floured work surface, cookie cutter or firm water glass, nonstick or lightly greased baking sheet, pastry brush

Preheat oven to 450° F.
1. **Sift** flour, baking powder, sugar, and salt into mixing bowl. Using clean hands, blend in butter or margarine until mixture is crumb-like.
2. With whisk, beat eggs in small bowl and set aside 2 tablespoons. Add half-and-half to remaining eggs and mix well.
3. Make a well in center of flour mixture, pour in egg mixture, and blend together, making an elastic dough just firm enough to handle, working it as little as possible. Transfer to work surface and pat flat to about 3/4-inch thick. Cut into rounds with a cookie cutter or top rim of a water glass. Lightly flour greased baking sheet and place *scones* side-by-side, spaced at least 1 inch apart. Brush tops with remaining egg. Bake in oven for about 15 minutes, until golden brown.

Serve *scones* while still warm with plenty of jam and butter. They are delicious to eat at any time.

Bubble and Squeak

Bubble and squeak got its name from the noise it makes while cooking. There is no standard or basic recipe to follow, and quantities can vary according to whatever is on hand. You may do this or just follow the recipe as given.

Yield: serves 4 to 6

4 to 6 tablespoons vegetable oil

3 cups cooked mashed potatoes, freshly made or instant potato flakes (prepare according to directions on package)

3 cups cooked, **finely chopped** cabbage (boil in water for 5 minutes, drain, and discard water)

salt and pepper to taste

Equipment: Large-size skillet, mixing spoon, pancake turner or metal spatula, large-size plate

1. Heat 4 tablespoons oil in skillet over high heat. Add potatoes, cabbage, and salt and pepper to taste and mix well. Reduce heat to medium and cook until bottom is brown. Press down on the mixture with pancake turner or metal spatula so that it forms the shape of a flat cake.

2. Remove from heat, invert on a plate, and slide back into skillet to brown the other side. Add more oil along the sides of the skillet, if necessary, to prevent sticking. When brown on both sides, transfer to flat serving plate and cut into wedges.

Serve *bubble and squeak* hot, as either a main dish or as a side dish.

Shepherd's Pie   Meat and Vegetable Casserole

Traditionally, *shepherd's pie* was made with mutton or lamb. If the pie was made with beef, it was called *cottage pie.* Today any meat or poultry can be used, and the recipe is still called *shepherd's pie.*

Yield: serves 6 to 8

2 tablespoons vegetable oil

2 *each* onions, chopped, and carrots, peeled, sliced in thin rounds

1/2 cup chopped celery

2 pounds ground beef

2 tablespoons all-purpose flour

1 cup beef broth

salt and pepper to taste

4 cups cooked mashed potatoes, freshly made or instant potato flakes (prepare according to directions on package)

1/2 cup *each* melted butter or margarine and shredded Cheddar cheese

Equipment: Large-size saucepan, mixing spoon, small-size bowl, greased, shallow 2 1/2-quart baking pan

Preheat oven to 350° F.

1. Heat oil in skillet over medium-high heat. Add onions, carrots, and celery and cook until onions are tender, about 3 minutes. Add meat, reduce heat to medium, and stirring continually, cook until meat looses its pink color (about 8 minutes).

2. Add flour to beef broth in small bowl and mix to blend. Add to meat mixture, mix well, season with salt and pepper to taste, and remove from heat. Transfer mixture to baking pan and smooth top.

3. Combine mashed potatoes with 1/4 cup melted butter, add salt and pepper to taste, and mix well. Spoon potatoes on top of meat mixture. Drizzle with remaining butter and cheese. Bake in oven for about 10 minutes, until potatoes begin to brown and cheese is melted.

Serve *shepherd's pie* as a one-dish meal with plenty of bread for sopping.

Queen of Puddings

An English dinner is incomplete unless ending with dessert pudding. It is typically a dish that includes jam and is often baked, making it more like a cake than the puddings Americans are accustomed to. The following recipe is very light and is a favorite with English children. Despite its simplicity, it has a very regal air and can be served at the most elegant dinner party.

Yield: serves 4 to 6

2 cups milk
grated rind of 1 lemon
pinch of salt
2 cups unseasoned bread crumbs
1/2 cup butter or margarine (at room temperature)
3/4 cup sugar, more or less
4 eggs, **separated**
3 tablespoons strawberry jam, more or less to taste

Equipment: Small-size saucepan, mixing spoon, large-size mixing bowl, strainer, buttered 2 1/2-quart oven-proof casserole, **egg beater** or electric mixer, oven mitts

1. Put milk in saucepan and bring to a boil over medium-high heat. Add lemon rind and salt, remove from heat, and set aside.
2. Put crumbs, butter, and 1/2 cup sugar in mixing bowl. Pour milk and lemon rind into strainer to remove rind, and then pour over the crumb mixture and mix well. Set aside to cool for about 15 minutes.
3. Preheat oven to 350° F.
4. Add yolks to mixture and mix well. Pour into casserole and bake in oven for about 20 minutes or until firm. Remove from oven with oven mitts and spread top with jam.
5. Using egg beater or electric mixer, beat egg whites until they are firm and form stiff peaks. Slowly add remaining 1/4 cup sugar, beating continually until well blended. Cover the pudding with whites and return to oven and bake until whites are golden brown (about 5 minutes).

Serve *queen of puddings* as dessert, either hot or cold, with cream.

Feather Fowlie   Scottish Chicken Soup

This recipe is an old Scottish chicken soup. The original recipe calls for *pot-posy* which refers to the herbs and spices.

Yield: serves 6 to 8

2 1/2 to 3 pound chicken, cut in serving-size pieces
6 cups water
1/4 cup **finely chopped** parsley, fresh or dried
3 tablespoons thyme, fresh or dried flakes
1 onion, finely chopped
2 celery ribs, finely chopped
3 egg yolks (refrigerate whites to use at another time)
1/4 cup half-and-half
1 teaspoon ground **mace**
salt and pepper to taste

Equipment: Large-size saucepan with cover, mixing spoon, small-size bowl, fork or whisk

1. Put chicken pieces, water, parsley, thyme, onion, and celery in saucepan. Bring to a boil over high heat, reduce to simmer, and cook for about 1 1/2 hours, until chicken is tender.
2. Put egg yolks, half-and-half, and mace in small bowl and whisk until blended. Remove soup from heat. Transfer cooked chicken pieces to serving platter. To the soup, add egg mixture, and salt and pepper to taste, stirring continually until well blended.

Serve the soup in individual bowls first and the chicken as the next course.

Scotch Eggs   Sausage Covered Eggs

Scotch eggs are **hard-cooked eggs** encased in sausage meat; dipped in egg, flour, and bread crumbs; and fried. They have become very popular as an appetizer or snack treat.

Yield: serves 6

1 pound bulk seasoned pork breakfast sausage
6 hard-cooked eggs, peeled
1 egg, beaten
1 cup *each* all-purpose flour and bread crumbs
4 to 6 cups vegetable oil

Equipment: Work surface, small-size bowl, 2 small-size low dishes, flat pan, medium-size skillet, slotted spoon, paper towels

1. On work surface, divide sausage into 6 equal portions. Flatten each piece between the palms of your hands. Take hard-cooked eggs, one at a time, and cover completely with meat.
2. Put raw egg in small bowl and beat well. Put flour in one low dish and bread crumbs in another. One at a time, dust sausage-covered eggs lightly with flour, dip in beaten egg, and roll each one in crumbs. Place coated eggs side-by-side on flat pan and refrigerate until ready to fry.
3. Put about 1 inch of oil into skillet, heat over medium-high heat, and add coated eggs, 2 or 3 at a time. Using slotted spoon, roll eggs around in oil to brown on all sides. When golden brown, about 5 minutes, remove eggs with slotted spoon and drain well on paper towels.

Serve eggs at room temperature or cold, as a snack.

Scots Shortbread

The Scots are not big dessert eaters. Shortbreads are quick and easy to make and are as sweet as anything gets in Scotland except for the smiles on young faces when they see someone has made shortbread. The following recipe is so easy it's goof-proof.

Yield: serves 6 or 8

1/2 cup butter or margarine, at room temperature
1/4 cup sugar

pinch of salt
1 cup flour
1/2 cup strawberry, raspberry, plum, or pineapple jam

Equipment: Mixing spoon or electric mixer, medium-size mixing bowl, mixing spoon, buttered 9-inch-square baking pan

Preheat oven to 350° F.
1. Using mixing spoon or electric mixer on medium, mix butter and sugar until light and fluffy. Add pinch of salt and flour a little at a time, with spoon or mixer, until mixture is crumb-like. Don't overmix.
2. Pat dough into baking pan using back of spoon or your clean hand. Prick surface about 10 times with fork tines, and cut into 1 1/2-inch squares. Bake in oven until light brown (about 25 minutes).
3. While still warm, spread the top with jam of your choice.

Serve *shortbread* warm or cold as a cookie treat.

Sticky Welsh Gingerbread

Nothing smells better than gingerbread baking in the oven, and most of the time the end result is as delicious as it smells. The following recipe has a shiny, sticky top and a spicy molasses taste, just as old fashioned traditional gingerbread should.

Yield: serves 8 to 12

1/2 cup butter or margarine
1 1/2 cups dark brown sugar
1 1/4 cups dark molasses
2 1/2 cups all-purpose flour
2 eggs, beaten
2 teaspoons ground ginger
1 tablespoon ground cinnamon
3 tablespoons warm milk
1 teaspoon baking soda
1/2 cup raisins

Equipment: Small-size saucepan, **whisk** or mixing spoon, large-size mixing bowl, electric mixer, greased 9-inch baking pan, rubber spatula

Preheat oven to 325° F.
1. Melt butter or margarine, sugar, and molasses in saucepan over low heat. Heat until sugar is dissolved and mix well. Remove from heat.
2. Put flour, eggs, ginger, cinnamon, milk, baking soda, and raisins in mixing bowl. Add butter mixture and mix with spoon or electric mixer until well blended.
3. Pour mixture into baking pan and bake in oven until toothpick inserted in center of cake comes out clean (about 45 minutes).

To serve, allow to cool to room temperature before cutting into squares.

Caws pobi   Welsh Rabbit or Rarebit

There are legends about almost everything one eats in the British Isles, and the stories about *Welsh rabbit* or *rarebit* are no exception. One story says that an imaginative monk in a Welsh abbey created the dish by placing some stale bread and hard crumbly cheese near a blazing fire. The cheese melted over the bread and that was the beginning of Welsh rarebit. Another tale says that when a Welshman returned home from a hunting trip with nothing, his wife invented a dish with melted cheese and called it "Welsh rabbit."

Yield: serves 4 to 6

4 tablespoons butter or margarine
2 1/2 cups grated Cheddar cheese, mild or sharp (do not use American processed cheese)
1/2 cup apple cider
2 egg yolks, beaten (refrigerate whites to use at another time)
2 teaspoons **prepared mustard**
salt and pepper to taste
6 to 8 slices white bread, toasted
sprinkle of paprika, for garnish

Equipment: Medium-size saucepan, mixing spoon

1. Melt butter or margarine in saucepan over medium-low heat. Add cheese, apple cider, egg yolks, mustard, and salt and pepper to taste, stirring continually until mixture is well blended and smooth. Do not let the mixture boil or bubble or it will become stringy and lumpy.
2. Arrange toast slices on individual plates and spoon cheese mixture equally over them. Sprinkle with paprika and serve at once.

Serve *Welsh rarebit* hot, as the main dish for lunch or supper; it is eaten with a knife and fork.

Ireland

Ireland is known as a potato-eating country, and indeed this is true, but the Irish diet does not consist solely of potatoes. Oatmeal porridge is a perennial favorite for breakfast, and all types of breads, especially "soda bread," are enjoyed. Agriculturally, the Irish have diversified their crops now and grow wheat, barley, and sugar beets in addition to potatoes. Oats are still grown, but in lesser amounts because fewer horses are needed for farm labor.  Household gardens in the country often provide vegetables for the Irish. The fine grazing land available to herds contributes to the successful raising of livestock, including cattle, sheep, and pigs. Many vegetables, grains, and fruits must be imported, however. Although many people have left farming, production is up because of the increased use of fertilizers and modern equipment and methods. The fish industry is important, too, and the Irish eat herring, halibut, cod, trout, salmon, and haddock. Fish soups are popular and well made. Some other favorite dishes are bacon and cabbage casserole, ham and french fries, and bacon, eggs, and potato cakes. Although Irish food is simple, it is nourishing and plentiful.

In the sixteenth century the potato made its way to Europe from Peru where Spanish conquistadors had found it cultivated. Proof of who brought potatoes to Europe is not available, but by 1688 they had become a staple in the Irish diet. Absentee landlord practices led to the Irish peasants subsisting on potatoes, which proved devastating when the potato famines of the nineteenth century struck. An estimated one million people starved to death, and 1.5 million emigrated, mostly to the United States, to escape starvation. Finally, potato farming came back stronger than ever, and without question, they are the favorite food of the Irish. A meal isn't complete unless praties, as the Irish call them, are on the table.

Yield: serves 4 to 6

3 cups finely **shredded** green cabbage
1 onion, **finely chopped**
1/4 cup water
6 cooked potatoes, mashed or 4 cups prepared instant mashed potatoes (prepare according to directions on package)
1/4 cup milk
1/4 cup butter or margarine
salt and pepper to taste

Equipment: Medium-size saucepan with cover, mixing spoon

1. Put cabbage, onion, and water in saucepan, and bring to a boil over high heat. Reduce heat to simmer, cover, and cook for about 8 minutes or until tender, not mushy.
2. Add mashed potatoes, milk, butter or margarine, and salt and pepper to taste. Mix well to blend and heat through.

Serve *colcannon* warm, as a side dish with meat, chicken, or fish.

Irish Stew

Irish stew is the national dish of Ireland. To be authentic, it must be made with mutton or lamb, but other than that, there are as many ways to make *Irish stew* as there are Irish kitchens to cook it in. It is not necessary to use expensive cuts of meat for this recipe.

Yield: serves 4 to 6

2 pounds lamb, lean boneless neck or shoulder, cut into bite-size chunks
6 potatoes, peeled and thinly sliced
3 onions, peeled and thinly sliced
salt and pepper to taste
1/2 cup chopped parsley
2 cups water

Equipment: Medium-size saucepan with cover or **Dutch oven**

1. Layer potatoes, lamb, and onions in saucepan or Dutch oven, beginning with potatoes and ending with onions on the top. Repeat several times. Sprinkle each layer with salt and pepper to taste and parsley.

2. Add water and bring to a boil over high heat. Reduce heat to simmer, cover, and cook until lamb is tender (about 1 1/2 hours). Remove from heat and skim off any fat on top.

Serve *Irish stew* as a one-pot meal, with plenty of oatmeal bread for sopping (see following recipe).

Oatmeal Bread

There is nothing more wonderful than the smell of homemade bread baking in the oven. Try our hearty oatmeal bread, which is easy and fun to make.

Yield: 1 loaf

2 cups old-fashioned oatmeal
1 1/2 cups buttermilk
1 to 1 1/2 cups flour
1 teaspoon baking soda
1/2 teaspoon salt
1 tablespoon cream

Equipment: Large-size mixing bowl, aluminum foil, flour **sifter**, medium-size mixing bowl, floured work surface, greased baking sheet, pastry brush

1. Put oatmeal and buttermilk in large bowl, mix well, and cover tightly with foil. Set aside for about 2 hours.
2. Preheat oven to 350° F.
3. **Sift** flour, baking soda, and salt into medium-size bowl, add to oatmeal mixture, and, placing on floured work surface, **knead** to a smooth stiff dough. Shape dough into round loaf, about 6 inches in diameter and about 2 inches thick.
4. Place on baking sheet and, using a floured knife, make 2 deep slashes, crisscrossing the top and dividing dough into 4 wedges. Bake in oven for about 45 minutes or until bread is golden brown. Remove from oven, allow to cool for 20 minutes, and brush top with cream.

Serve *oatmeal bread* while still warm for the best flavor and with plenty of butter.

Bread and Butter Pudding

Bread puddings are favorite desserts in most Irish homes. They are usually simple to make and require only simple ingredients. The following recipe is a favorite of Irish children.

Yield: serves 4 to 6

1 teaspoon ground cinnamon
1/4 cup sugar
4 tablespoons butter or margarine, more or less as needed, at room temperature
5 slices crust-on white bread
1/2 cup golden raisins
2 cups milk
2 eggs

Equipment: Cup, nonstick or greased 8-inch baking pan, small-size mixing bowl, **whisk** or fork

Preheat oven to 350° F.
1. Add cinnamon to sugar in cup and mix well. Set aside.
2. Generously spread one side of each piece of bread with butter or margarine. Cutting diagonally, slice each in half. Arrange triangle slices in pan, slightly overlapping, with butter-side up and cut edges facing the same direction, making a spiral. As you add the bread, sprinkle with sugar, cinnamon, and raisins.
3. Put milk in small bowl, add eggs, and using whisk or fork, mix to blend well. Pour milk mixture over bread and raisins in baking pan. Set aside for about 15 minutes for bread to absorb liquid. Bake in oven for about 30 minutes, or until top is golden brown.

Serve the pudding while still warm in individual dessert bowls. It is eaten plain or with cream poured over it.

Netherlands

The land of tulips, windmills, canals, and wooden shoes is the Netherlands, also known as Holland. The Hollanders, also referred to as the Dutch, live in a fish-lovers paradise. The Netherlands (which means "low-land") is built on land reclaimed from the sea. With miles of coastline fishing is a very important industry.

The Dutch are very proud of the tulips they grow and ship all over the world. They love their flowers, and in the cities, on every street corner, push carts overflow with a mosaic of fresh cut blossoms. They are sold next to street vendors peddling their daily catch of herring, still glistening from the cold waters of the North Sea.

Fruits and vegetables are primarily grown under hothouse conditions. (They are grown in large glass buildings, where they are sheltered from the cold.) Thus fresh produce is available year round. Grains, potatoes, and sugar beets are main crops. Livestock include chickens, pigs, cattle, sheep, horses, and ponies.

The cheeses, Dutch chocolates, and pastries of the Netherlands are some of the world's best. Edam and Gouda are two of the most well-known Dutch cheeses, which the Dutch like to nibble on at the conclusion of their meals.

Dutch cooking is similar in many ways to that of its neighboring countries in Europe, yet it has an international flavor, combining foods native to northern Europe with the exotic spices and rice that were introduced from its former tropical colonies, such as Indonesia.

Hutspot Met Klapstuck   *Meat and Vegetable Stew*

The tradition of eating a special dish or food to commemorate a historical date is common practice in many countries of the world. The *hutspot* became a national dish of the Dutch, honoring their victory in 1574 against Spain, who had ruled the area for over a century. In Holland, before serving the *hutspot*, the vegetables are mashed to a pulp with the back of a spoon or potato masher.

Yield: **serves** 6

2 pounds brisket of beef
2 to 4 cups water
3 bay leaves
4 carrots, finely sliced
4 potatoes, peeled and **cubed**
2 onions, **finely chopped**
salt and pepper to taste

Equipment: Large-size saucepan with cover or **Dutch oven**, mixing spoon

1. Put meat in saucepan or Dutch oven and add 2 cups water and bay leaves. Bring to a boil over high heat, reduce heat to simmer, cover, and cook for about 1 1/2 hours or until meat is tender. Add more water if necessary to prevent sticking.
2. Add carrots, potatoes, onions, and salt and pepper to taste. Stirring frequently, cook uncovered until vegetables are tender (about 30 minutes). Remove bay leaves and discard before serving.

To **serve** *hutspot*, remove and slice the meat. Put the vegetables in the middle of the platter with the meat slices around it. Serve with **prepared mustard**.

Curried Kool Sla Au Gratin

Curried Cabbage Cheese Casserole

Yield: serves 6

3 pounds cabbage, finely **shredded**
2 cups water
1 bay leaf
3 cloves garlic, **finely chopped**, or 1 tablespoon garlic granules
1 onion, finely chopped
8 tablespoons butter or margarine
1/4 cup all-purpose flour
1 cup milk
1 teaspoon curry powder
1 cup shredded mild cheddar cheese
salt and white pepper to taste
1/2 cup bread crumbs

Equipment: Large-size saucepan with cover, mixing spoon, **colander** or strainer, medium-size saucepan, fork or **whisk**, large-size mixing bowl, nonstick or buttered 9-inch oven-proof casserole

1. Put cabbage, water, bay leaf, garlic, and onion in the large saucepan. Bring to a boil over high heat, reduce heat to simmer, cover, and cook for about 10 minutes or until cabbage is tender. Remove from heat, drain well in colander or strainer, and discard liquid and bay leaf.
2. *Prepare sauce:* melt 4 tablespoons butter in medium saucepan over low heat, add flour, and mix until well blended. Increase heat to medium, and, stirring continu-

ally, slowly add milk. Cook until mixture thickens. Do not boil. Remove from heat, add curry, cheese, and salt and pepper to taste, and mix well.
3. Preheat oven to 400° F.
4. Transfer cabbage to large mixing bowl and **fold** in sauce. Pour mixture into casserole. Sprinkle with breadcrumbs and dot with remaining butter or margarine. Bake for 15 minutes or until top is golden brown.

Serve casserole as a side dish with meat, poultry, or fish.

Speculaas   *Dutch Christmas Cookies*

Cookies of every shape and flavor are popular with Dutch children of all ages, all year long. *Speculaas* are easy to make and keep well in the cookie jar.

Yield: about 24 cookies

1/2 cup butter or margarine, at room temperature
1/2 cup light brown sugar, firmly packed
1 egg
2 cups all-purpose flour
2 teaspoons baking powder
1/2 teaspoon *each* ground nutmeg, ground cinnamon, ground cloves, and salt

Equipment: Large-size mixing bowl, mixing spoon or electric mixer, medium-size mixing bowl, aluminum foil, nonstick or lightly greased cookie sheet

1. Combine butter or margarine and sugar in large mixing bowl, with mixing spoon or electric mixer, and blend until smooth. Add egg and mix well.
2. Put flour, baking powder, nutmeg, cinnamon, cloves, and salt in medium mixing bowl and mix well. Slowly add to butter mixture, mixing continually until soft dough is formed. Remove from mixer and transfer dough to work surface. Using clean hands, shape into a cylinder, or log shape, about 2 inches thick, wrap in foil, and chill for about 1 hour, until firm.
3. Preheat oven to 350° F.
4. Unwrap foil and put dough on work surface. Cut into 1/4-inch thick slices with sharp knife and place side-by-side on cookie sheet. Bake in oven for about 15 minutes, until cookies are golden.

Serve *speculaas* with a glass of milk or cup of warm cocoa. Dutch children sometimes press or cut the cookie dough into different designs and shapes.

Germany

German food can be generally characterized as substantial, centered around meat, and piled high. Foods of Germany are not always easy to describe because there are numerous regional specialties, and the class differences affect the foods eaten and even at what hour the people eat. For example rural people eat lunch at noon and dinner at six; upper class urban workers eat lunch at two o'clock and dinner much later. Some common threads are found, however. Five meals a days are the norm: two breakfasts, one early, the other around eleven in the morning; then the large meal of the day at lunch; coffee and cake or little sandwiches in the late afternoon; and supper in the evening. The first breakfast consists of coffee or hot chocolate with bread, butter, and jams. The second breakfast is around 10 or 11 a.m. Sandwiches of meat or cheese are eaten along with some fruit for the kids and coffee or beer for the adults. Lunch was traditionally taken at home, but now, with more women working, and people working far from home, this tradition is not as prevalent. Many employers help pay the cost of big lunches for their employees to keep them on the job and happy.

The main lunch meal was traditionally very heavy, and this is still true for rural folk engaged in hard manual labor. The city people don't need to eat as much, and when it was found in the 1970s in West Germany that one half of all deaths were circulatory and heart-related deaths, it shocked the nation into lighter eating habits. Now lunch consists of a meat, such as a roast (the national dish), potatoes, various garden vegetables, bread and butter; and dessert, such as rice or chocolate pudding. Coffee in the late afternoon comes with a nice slice of cake, or if it is a special occasion, dainty sandwiches. Supper is generally sliced bread with cold cuts, cheeses, and sausages. Everyone makes his or her own plate and eats the sandwich with a fork and knife!

The reunification of East and West Germany after more than four decades has had a major impact on the citizens. Economically, it has been hard on the former West Germans, the country known in economic circles as "the economic miracle" and the "little engine that could" because of the recovery it made after World War II and the strength of its currency. And what does this recent change have to do with the food eaten on each side? West Germans are not as well off as they were before the reunification. They can't afford as much as they used to. On the other hand, East Germans are better off, but they don't have food given to them as they did under communist rule. Now with a capitalist government, East Germans are free to go to any store. Since East Germany has the most fertile land, better farm methods will eventually be employed, which will make agriculture stronger than ever for Germany.

Rotkraut Mit Apfeln   Red Cabbage with Apples

Yield: serves 6 to 8

2 to 4 tablespoons vegetable shortening
2 pounds red cabbage, **shredded**
1/2 cup cider vinegar
1/2 cup dark brown sugar
1/4 cup hot water
1/2 cup seedless raisins
2 tablespoons currant jelly
1/2 teaspoon ground cloves
1 teaspoon caraway seeds

2 cups peeled, thinly sliced tart cooking apples
salt and pepper to taste

Equipment: Large-size saucepan with cover or **Dutch oven**, mixing spoon, small-size bowl

1. Heat 2 tablespoons oil in saucepan or Dutch oven over medium heat. Add cabbage, and, stirring frequently, cook for about 5 minutes or until wilted. Add more oil if necessary to prevent sticking.
2. Mix vinegar, sugar, and water in small bowl to dissolve sugar. Pour mixture on cabbage and mix well. Reduce to simmer, cover, and cook for about 15 minutes.
3. Add raisins, jelly, cloves, caraway, apples, and salt and pepper to taste. Mix well, cover, and continue simmering until apples are soft, about 15 minutes more.

Serve as a side dish with meat or poultry and lots of rye bread and butter.

Himmel und Erde
"Heaven and Earth"—Cooked Potatoes & Apple

The following recipe, blending fruit and vegetables, is typical German country cooking, giving a sweet and sour flavor to the dish. Perhaps it is named *himmel und erde* (heaven and earth) because apples grow on trees toward the heavens and potatoes grow in the earth.

Yield: serves 6 to 8

2 pounds new red potatoes, washed and quartered
6 cups water
1 tablespoon vinegar
2 pounds cooking apples, peeled and cut into chunks
6 slices bacon, finely **diced**
1/2 cup bread crumbs
salt and pepper to taste

Equipment: Medium-size saucepan with cover, medium-size skillet, mixing spoon

1. Put potatoes in saucepan and cover with water. Add vinegar and bring to a boil over high heat. Reduce heat to simmer, cover, and cook for 10 minutes. Add apple chunks, mix well, and continue cooking until potatoes are tender but not mushy, about 10 minutes more. Drain well.
2. While the potatoes and apples are cooking, fry bacon in skillet over medium-high heat until crisp. Reduce heat to medium, add bread crumbs, and mix well to coat crumbs. Fry for about 2 minutes more to heat through.
3. Add bacon mixture and salt and pepper to taste to potatoes and apples, toss gently, and transfer to serving bowl.

Serve *himmel und erde* hot, as a side dish with meat, poultry, or fish.

Denmark

Denmark is a little Scandinavian country with a big reputation for fine cheeses, pork products, and butter. Denmark is among the world's leaders in exporting these products, even though its labor force is engaged mostly in industrial, trade, and service industries and not agriculture. Other leading foods are cereals and root crops. Danish livestock include pigs, chickens, cattle, ducks, and turkeys. Potatoes are a staple in the Danish diet. The Danes like them boiled, peeled, and  then sprinkled with dill or covered with a white sauce. Endive or kale is also served with white sauce as a side dish. For special occasions, such as Christmas Eve, Danes like potatoes with caramel sugar. At one time a traditional Christmas Eve dinner began with rice pudding! Now they still have rice pudding, but it is served at the end of the meal along with cherries or strawberries. Soups, such as split pea, are favorite items on the menu. The Danes make enough to last the family several days. Pork is the preferred meat; herring the preferred fish. Eels are much loved and served with potatoes flavored with dill or a white sauce.

Smorrebrod — Open Sandwich

In Denmark, the *smorrebrod* literally means "bread and butter." They are really giant open-face sandwiches that are so large, one's a meal. All or any combination of the following ingredients can be added to give you just a small sampling of a Danish sandwich. Most combinations are given nicknames, such as the Northern Lights or the Big Wave. Roast beef with tartar sauce and crispy onions sprinkled on top is one favorite. You can make your own sandwich combination and name it.

Yield: serves 4

4 slices dark rye or pumpernickel bread
4 tablespoons butter or margarine
1/4 pound sliced liver sausage or salami
1/4 pound sliced roast beef, turkey breast, or ham (or combination)
2 tomatoes, sliced
4 hard-cooked eggs, peeled and sliced
12 slices fried bacon
8 tablespoons mayonnaise

Equipment: Clean hands

Butter each slice of bread with 1 tablespoon butter or margarine. Divide the other ingredients equally and layer them on the bread slices.

Serve *smorrebrod* with fork and knife; it's impossible to hold the open-face sandwiches in your hands.

Brunede Kartofler　　　　　　　Sugar-browned Potatoes

Yield: serves 4 to 6

1/2 cup butter or margarine
12 cooked, ping-pong-ball-size red potatoes, peeled, or canned whole potatoes, drained
1/4 cup sugar
salt and pepper to taste

Equipment: Large-size skillet, mixing spoon

Melt butter or margarine in skillet over medium heat. Add sugar, mix well, and cook until mixture turns golden. Add potatoes and toss to coat. Add salt and pepper to taste, and, stirring continually, cook until potatoes are glazed and golden on all sides, about 10 minutes.

Serve potatoes as a side dish with meat.

Ris a L'amande　　　　　　　　Rice Pudding

This traditional rice pudding is served on Christmas Eve. Mothers hide one whole almond in the pudding, and whoever finds it gets a special treat. A Danish friend said her dad used to hide it in his mouth until the end of the meal, if he got it, just to play a little joke on everyone. An everyday version is to serve it with brown sugar and cinnamon sprinkled on top.

Yield: 6 servings

2 cups milk
1/3 cup rice
1 teaspoon vanilla
2 tablespoons sugar, more or less as needed
1 cup heavy cream
1 cup strawberry or cherry preserve or marmalade
1/4 cup water
2 tablespoons **finely chopped, blanched** almonds, for garnish

Equipment: Medium-size saucepan with cover, mixing spoon, small-size saucepan

1. Put milk in medium saucepan and bring to a boil over medium heat. Mixing continually, add rice. Reduce to simmer, cover, and cook for 20 minutes.
2. Remove from heat and add sugar and vanilla. Mix well and cool to room temperature.
3. When cooled, add heavy cream and mix well. Transfer to individual serving bowls and set aside.
4. Put strawberry or cherry preserve in small saucepan, add water, and mix well. Heat over medium heat until heated through. Spoon warm sauce equally over individual servings of rice pudding. Sprinkle each serving with almonds for garnish.

Serve pudding at once while the sauce is still warm.

Norway

Norway, a Scandanavian country, is very mountainous and rugged, with only 3 percent of the land available for farming. Food crops include fruits, vegetables, and potatoes, but the majority of food is imported. A short growing season and long, cold winters make it necessary to store food for months, even years; smoked meats and cheeses, dried fruits, hard cookies and breads, cured fish, and root vegetables are just some of the foods Norwegians prepare to live on for months on end during the winters. Livestock are raised, but the fishing industry brings a large proportion of food to the table. Fish is served at most meals and plays an important role in the Norwegian diet. Big breakfasts start the day off, and even at this meal fish is served in different ways— smoked, salted, and fresh. Lots of meats, among them reindeer, sit side-by-side with cheese, boiled eggs, sour cream, berries, and waffles at the breakfast feasts. Lunch is simple, usually consisting of open-faced sandwiches. Dinner is served in the early evening and consists of soup and a main dish.

Lefse   Fried Potato Bread

Yield: about 15 pieces

4 cups warm mashed potatoes, fresh or instant (follow instructions on box)
1/4 cup vegetable oil
2 tablespoons milk
1 teaspoon salt
2 cups all-purpose flour

Equipment: Large-size mixing bowl with cover, mixing spoon, floured work surface, rolling pin, griddle or large-size heavy-bottom skillet, metal spatula or pancake turner, towel or wax paper

1. Put mashed potatoes, vegetable oil, milk, and salt in large bowl and mix until smooth and lump-free. Cover and refrigerate for about 2 hours, until chilled through.
2. Turn mixture onto floured work surface and **knead** in the 2 cups flour. Dough will have a soft texture. Divide dough into 15 equal parts and roll pieces into balls between palms of clean hands.
3. Flatten each ball on the work surface. Using a floured rolling pin, roll balls as thin as possible into an 8- or 10-inch circle. If it breaks apart, it's too thin. Add flour as needed to prevent sticking. Wrap circle of dough around rolling pin to transfer to the griddle or skillet.
4. Heat ungreased griddle or skillet over medium-high heat. Unroll the dough from rolling pin onto pan and cook until blisters form and brown spots appear on bottom, about 1 minute per side. Don't overcook; they should be soft, not crisp. Repeat, using all dough balls. Stack between towels or wax paper to prevent drying out.

Serve *lefse* spread with butter or sprinkled with brown sugar or cinnamon. Roll or **fold** to eat.

Toskakake   *Almond Caramel Topped Cake*

This easy-to-make almond- and caramel-topped cake is a favorite in all Scandinavian countries. Many, many years ago it was imported from Italy and made over in the great Scandinavian cooking tradition. This cake can be served as a representative dessert from Norway, Denmark, or Sweden.

Yield: serves 10 or 12

3 eggs, room temperature
1 1/2 cups sugar
1 1/2 cups all-purpose flour
1 1/2 teaspoons baking powder
1 cup melted butter (set aside 1/3 cup for topping)
3 tablespoons milk
1 teaspoon vanilla
1/2 cup *each* heavy cream and chopped almonds, walnuts, or pecans

Equipment: Large-size mixing bowl, **egg beater** or electric mixer, medium-size mixing bowl, **whisk** or mixing spoon, buttered 10-inch **springform pan**, small-size skillet, wire rack

Preheat oven to 350° F.

1. Mix eggs and 1 cup sugar with egg beater or electric mixer in large bowl until mixture is pale yellow and a ribbon forms when beaters are lifted (about 5 minutes).
2. Combine flour and baking powder in medium-size bowl, mix well, and **fold** into egg mixture using whisk or mixing spoon. Add 2/3 cup butter, milk, and vanilla and mix until smooth. Pour into springform pan. Bake in oven for about 35 minutes, until toothpick inserted in center comes out clean.
3. Prepare topping while cake is baking. Put remaining 1/3 cup butter in skillet over low heat, add remaining 1/2 cup sugar and cream, and mix well. Increase heat to medium high, bring to boil, and cook for 2 minutes. Remove from heat.
4. When cake is done remove from oven and immediately pour hot topping over it. Sprinkle with nuts, return to oven, and continue baking until top is bubbly and golden brown (about 10 minutes). Cool on wire rack.

Serve *toskakake* warm or at room temperature.

Sweden

Sweden has one of the highest standards of living in the world, despite its lack of usable land and harsh northern climate. Swedish cooks take pride in their foods and lovingly show off their national dishes. What better way to do this than with the *smorgasbord*, Sweden's most notable culinary contribution to the world. *Smorgasbord* is the hors d'oeuvres table, which is loaded with enough things to make an entire meal. The recipes listed in this section can all be used in the *smorgasbord*. Swedish baked goods are world famous and reign supreme in taste and variety. Spices are added sparingly and hot peppers are almost unheard of in Swedish kitchens. Dill grows in every herb garden and is used extensively in sauces and soups. The use of pickling spices and salt as food preservatives are important in traditional Swedish cooking because of the long, cold winters when preserved meats, fish, and vegetables are all many rural Swedish people have to eat. Agriculture in Sweden concentrates on dairy products such as milk and cheese. The Swedes grow grains, sugar beets, and potatoes. Cattle, chickens, pigs, goats, and sheep are all raised.

Among the many festivals celebrated in Sweden is one that takes place the first week in August; it is the beginning of crayfish season, and the eating of these little crustaceans is a national pleasure. There is no fancy way to cook or eat them; they're boiled in lots of salty water for about 10 minutes until they turn bright red. Crayfish are eaten like miniature lobsters; the meat in the tail section is eaten, and the heads are discarded.

Schmorr Gurken   Cucumbers with Bacon

Cucumbers make great pickles and add a pleasant crunchiness to salads. The following Swedish recipe requires cucumbers to be cooked. This is an old Swedish recipe, yet new to many who have never eaten cooked cucumbers.

Yield: serves 4 to 6

2 medium-size cucumbers, peeled and thinly sliced crosswise
1/2 teaspoon salt
4 slices lean bacon, **finely chopped**
1 tablespoon sugar
1 tablespoon vinegar
1 tablespoon flour

Equipment: Large-size plate, medium-size skillet with cover, mixing spoon, strainer, small-size bowl

1. Spread cucumber slices on the plate and sprinkle with salt. Let stand for about 30 minutes.
2. Fry bacon in skillet over medium heat, stirring frequently, until crisp.
3. Rinse cucumbers under cold water and drain well in strainer. Add cucumbers to bacon in the skillet.
4. Mix sugar, vinegar, and flour in small bowl, add to cucumbers, and mix well. Cover, reduce heat, and simmer for about 20 minutes.

Serve *schmorr gurken* hot as a side dish with meat or chicken.

Sausage Pâté

Among the great variety of dishes on a *smorgasbord* are *pâtés*. There are hundreds of different recipes but the following *sausage pâté* is easy to make.

Yield: serves 6 to 8

6 strips bacon, **coarsely chopped**
1/2 cup **finely chopped** onion

4 tablespoons chopped green onion tops
2 pounds bulk pork sausage
4 eggs
4 cups soft white bread crumbs
1/2 teaspoon *each* ground thyme, salt, and pepper
4 hard-cooked eggs, peeled
1 unbaked pie crust, fresh or frozen

Equipment: Small-size skillet, mixing spoon, large-size mixing bowl, nonstick or greased 9- x 5-inch loaf pan

Preheat oven to 350° F.

1. Fry bacon, onion, and green onion in skillet over medium-high heat until bacon is crisp. Remove skillet from heat.
2. Using clean hands, crumble sausage in the mixing bowl. With spoon, add bacon mixture, eggs, bread crumbs, thyme, and salt and pepper to taste and blend well.
3. Line pie crust dough on loaf pan bottom and halfway up the sides. An uneven edge up the sides is acceptable. Press half of the meat mixture onto pie crust, lining the bottom of the pan. Set whole hard-cooked eggs in a row, end to end, down the middle of meat, cover with remaining meat, and pat smooth. Bake in oven for about 45 minutes. Remove from oven and invert pan on platter. Cool to room temperature and refrigerate for about 2 hours. When cold, loaf should slide easily out of pan. If not, pry around edge with a small knife.

Serve *pâté* cold and slice so each piece has a slice of egg in the center. *Pâté* is excellent for sandwich filling.

Kjottboller   Swedish Meatballs

Swedish meatballs have gained popularity as an appetizer in many places of the world. It's probably because they're not only delicious but also small and easy to make and eat. Adding the touch of nutmeg makes them distinctly Swedish.

Yield: about 36 balls

1 pound ground lean beef
1/2 pound ground lean pork
1 cup bread crumbs
2 teaspoons sugar
1/4 cup milk
1 egg
1 onion, **finely chopped**
salt and pepper to taste
2 to 4 tablespoons vegetable oil
3 tablespoons butter or margarine
3 tablespoons all-purpose flour
2 1/2 cups half-and-half, slightly warm
1 teaspoon grated nutmeg

Equipment: Large-size mixing bowl, clean hands or mixing spoon, large-size skillet, metal spatula or slotted spoon, 9- x 13-inch baking pan, medium-size saucepan, **whisk** or mixing spoon

1. Put beef, pork, crumbs, sugar, milk, egg, onion, and salt and pepper to taste in large mixing bowl, and using clean hands or mixing spoon, blend well. Shape mixture into ping-pong-size balls by rolling between the palms of your wet hands. (Rinse hands in cold water to prevent sticking.) Place balls side-by-side on clean work surface.
2. Heat 2 tablespoons oil in skillet over medium heat. Add meatballs, a few at a time, so they can be rolled around to brown evenly. Cook for about 5 minutes; add more oil as needed. Using spatula or slotted spoon, remove and drain well. Transfer to baking pan and set aside.
3. Prepare sauce in saucepan. Melt butter or margarine over medium heat, add flour, and blend well using whisk or mixing spoon. Stirring continually, cook for about 2 minutes until smooth and thick. Do not allow mixture to brown. Continue stirring and slowly add half-and-half. Bring mixture to simmer, turn heat to low, and cook for about 5 minutes or until sauce thickens. Remove from heat and add salt to taste and grated nutmeg. Pour hot sauce over meatballs and, using a spoon, rotate meatballs to completely coat with sauce.

Serve *kjottboller* warm as an appetizer; they can be picked up with toothpicks.

Applecake with Vanilla Sauce

Yield: serves 8 to 10

1/2 cup (1/4 pound) butter or margarine
4 cups vanilla wafer crumbs (bought crushed or crushed with a rolling pin)
2 1/2 cups applesauce, homemade or canned

Equipment: Medium-size saucepan, mixing spoon, nonstick or greased 9-inch-round cake pan

Preheat oven to 350°F.
1. Melt butter or margarine in saucepan over medium heat. Add the crumbs and stir until coated (about 3 minutes).
2. Line cake pan bottom with a layer of crumbs and then alternate layers of applesauce and remaining crumbs, ending with crumbs on top. Bake in oven for about 25 minutes, until lightly brown. Cool before slicing.

To serve, cut into wedges and spoon vanilla sauce over each slice (see next recipe).

Vanilla Sauce

Yield: about 3 cups

6 **eggs, separated**
4 tablespoons sugar
2 cups heavy cream, slightly warm
4 teaspoons vanilla extract

Equipment: **Double boiler, egg beater** or electric mixer or **whisk**, mixing spoon, large-size mixing bowl, medium-size mixing bowl

1. Heat water in bottom pan of double boiler over high heat. In top pan, add egg yolks and sugar and mix well with egg beater or whisk for about 3 minutes. Slowly add

warm cream, stirring frequently until mixture thickens (about 10 minutes). Remove from heat.

2. Transfer to large-size mixing bowl. Using mixing spoon or whisk, blend in vanilla and cool to room temperature.
3. Using beater or electric mixer, beat egg whites in medium-size mixing bowl until stiff and dry. **Fold** whites into yolk mixture using whisk or spoon. Refrigerate until ready to serve.

Serve over slices of applecake for dessert.

Finland

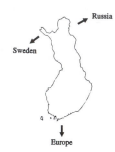

Russia

Sweden

Europe

In summer or winter, Finland is a fisher's paradise. No bigger than the state of Nevada, Finland has over 60,000 fish-filled lakes set among Europe's last great expanse of forest. The Finns love fish, and fishing is their favorite pastime, even through bitter cold Scandanavia winters. Food crops include sugar beets, potatoes, and cereals. Finland is 85 percent sufficient in foods but imports some grains. Livestock include poultry, cattle, pigs, reindeer, and sheep.

Sandwiches or porridge are served for breakfast in Finland; lunch consists of appetizers and a hot dish, such as racked trout or cheese bread pudding, and coffee; supper is served late, around 9:00 p.m., and once again sandwiches are served. The neighboring countries of Russia, Sweden, and Denmark have greatly influenced Finnish cooking. For example, the Swedish *smogasbords* are set up with the Finnish version of appetizers; the Finns eat lots of open-faced sandwiches like the Danes; and they eat the Russian soup *borscht* with sour cream and the Russian pancake, *blini.* Unique Finnish preferences include a taste for the salty, and for wild game birds, wild berries, and reindeer meat.

Ristinnaulittu Sikka   Racked Trout

The original recipe for *ristinnaulittu sikka* (racked trout) calls for the fish to be nailed to a hardwood plank and grilled by reflected heat from an open fire. The flavor will be wonderfully authentic if you have a wire grill basket for holding the fish over an open fire made with hardwood chips. We suggest preparing the fish under the oven broiler. It will still be delicious, lacking only the wood-burning flavor.

Yield: serves 2 to 4

1 trout fish, 2 to 4 pounds, fresh or frozen, thawed, head removed, skin-on, split open and boned. (Frozen, whole, skin-on rainbow trout, available at most supermarkets, are packaged bone-free. Most experienced fishmongers can bone fish from the inside.)
1/2 cup melted butter or margarine
1 teaspoon ground dry mustard
1/2 cup light brown sugar
1 teaspoon paprika
1 lemon cut in wedges for garnish
Equipment: Broiler pan, mixing spoon, metal spatula or pancake turner

Preheat oven broiler to high for about 10 minutes before broiling fish.

1. Rub the skin-side of the fish with melted butter. Open the fish and lay on broiler pan with buttered skin side down.
2. Add ground mustard, brown sugar, and paprika to remaining butter, mix well, and coat flesh side of fish generously with mixture. Place fish about 6 inches under broiler heat, and cook for about 25 minutes or until golden brown.

Serve the fish immediately, garnished with lemon wedges.

Cheddar Bread Pudding

Finland is a dairy country where great quantities of milk, cheeses, and butter are consumed along with an outstanding variety of breads. The inventive and frugal Finnish cooks do wonders with stale bread, making it into delicious puddings and desserts.

Yield: serves 4 to 6

2 cups 1/2-inch **cubes** stale white bread
1 cup grated cheddar cheese, either sharp or mild
1 1/2 cups milk
2 eggs, lightly beaten
3 tablespoons melted butter or margarine
2 teaspoons Dijon-style **prepared mustard**
1 teaspoon Worcestershire sauce
salt and pepper to taste

Equipment: Greased 2-quart baking dish, medium-size mixing bowl, mixing spoon or **whisk**

1. Alternate layers of bread cubes and cheese in the baking dish. Begin with half the bread cubes, then half the cheese, and then add remaining bread, and finish with remaining cheese on top.
2. Put milk, eggs, butter or margarine, mustard, Worcestershire sauce, and salt and pepper to taste in bowl and mix well. Pour mixture over the bread and cheese. Cover and chill for at least 1 hour before baking.
3. Preheat oven to 350° F.
4. Bake in oven for 1 hour, or until it is puffed and golden brown.

Serve the pudding as a side dish with meat, fish, or poultry or as the main dish for lunch.

Rikkaat Ritarit   Fried Bread Dessert

Yield: serves 4 to 6

8 tablespoons **finely chopped** almonds
8 tablespoons sugar
2 tablespoons all-purpose flour
1/2 teaspoon cinnamon
1 1/2 cups milk
2 eggs

12 slices white bread, crust trimmed off
4 tablespoons butter

Equipment: Small-size bowl, large-size mixing bowl, mixing spoon, large-size skillet, pancake turner

1. Put almonds and sugar in small bowl. Mix well and set aside.
2. Put flour, cinnamon, milk, and eggs in large bowl and mix until smooth. Dip each bread slice into mixture and coat on both sides. Sprinkle with almond-sugar mixture
3. Heat 4 tablespoons butter or margarine in large skillet over medium heat. Add bread slices and fry on both sides until crisp and golden (about 5 minutes per side). Use pancake turner to turn bread slices over. Add more butter as needed for frying all the slices.

Serve warm with plenty of jam or applesauce; allow 2 or 3 slices per person.

Poland

Poland is a low-lying country in central Europe that has lots of good grazing and farming land. Poles are meat eaters, and pork is their most favored meat. According to Polish tradition, a meatless meal is considered a snack or "going hungry." Meat is the most important food and everything else on the table is simply a side dish. The main foods of Poland are freshwater fish, ham, pork, sour cream, dark breads, mushrooms, cucumbers, sauerkraut, noodles and dumplings, buckwheat groats, game dishes, and rich cakes. Cucumbers are combined with sour cream for a salad treat. The favored side dishes are potatoes and cabbage; one or the other, or both, are served at almost every meal. Typical Polish meals are robust and filling, reflecting the cold climate and a heritage of food- and fun-loving people. Life in Poland has not been easy, and one of the great pleasures in the Poles' lives is eating, with generous servings for everyone.

Kluski Z Kapusta Po Polski   *Polish Noodles and Cabbage*

Yield: serves 4 to 6

1/4 cup butter or margarine
1 cup peeled and **coarsely chopped** onion
4 cups coarsely chopped green cabbage
1 teaspoon caraway seeds
8 ounces wide egg noodles (cook according to directions on package, drain well, and set aside)
1/2 teaspoon *each* salt and pepper, more or less to taste
1/2 cup sour cream

Equipment: Large-size skillet with cover, mixing spoon

1. Melt butter or margarine in skillet over medium-high heat. Add onions and fry until soft (about 3 minutes). Add cabbage while stirring frequently, reduce heat to medium, cover, and cook for about 10 minutes or until tender.
2. Add caraway seeds, noodles, and salt and pepper to taste and mix well. Remove from heat.
3. Add sour cream and mix thoroughly. Return to low heat and heat through (about 3 minutes).

To serve, transfer to a platter and eat while hot. This dish is very filling and can be the main meal most everywhere but in Poland, where it is only a side dish.

Pan-fried Mushrooms

Wild mushrooms grow especially well in northern Europe. Throughout the Polish countryside mushroom hunts had been a favorite family pastime until the Chernobyl nuclear accident in the spring of 1986. Since then, wild mushroom picking has been banned in many parts of Poland and neighboring countries. Mushrooms are still a popular food in Poland, as is reflected in this recipe and the following one.

Yield: serves 4 to 6

1 pound medium-size whole mushrooms, wipe lightly with paper towels, trim off and discard stems
2 eggs, beaten
1/2 cup water
1 cup dry bread crumbs
salt and pepper to taste
1/4 to 1/2 cup butter or margarine

Equipment: Small-size bowl, **whisk** or fork, small brown bag or plastic baggie, wax-paper-covered work surface, large-size skillet, slotted spoon

1. Put egg and water in small bowl and mix well using whisk or fork. Dip mushrooms, 2 or 3 at a time, into egg mixture.
2. Put crumbs in bag or baggie and add salt and pepper to taste. Holding top tightly closed, shake vigorously so crumbs will coat mushrooms. Carefully remove and set side-by-side on wax paper. Repeat dipping and coating all the mushrooms.
3. Melt 1/4 cup butter or margarine in skillet over medium heat and add mushrooms, a few at a time, leaving room to turn them. Fry until golden brown on all sides. Add remaining butter or margarine as needed. Remove mushrooms with slotted spoon to platter. Repeat until all mushrooms are fried.

Serve pan-fried mushrooms as an appetizer or side dish with meat.

Grzyby W Smietanie   Mushrooms in Sour Cream

Yield: serves 4 to 6

1/4 cup butter or margarine
1 onion, **finely chopped**
1 pound medium-size mushrooms, wipe lightly with paper towels, trim off and discard stems, cut into quarters

1 cup sour cream
salt and pepper to taste
paprika for garnish

Equipment: Medium-size skillet, mixing spoon

1. Melt butter or margarine in skillet over medium heat. Add onion and mushrooms, and, stirring frequently, fry until tender, about 5 minutes.
2. Remove from heat, add sour cream and salt and pepper to taste, and mix well. Return to low heat to heat through (about 5 minutes). Transfer to serving bowl and sprinkle with paprika for garnish.

Serve *grzyby w smietanie* as an appetizer, with toothpicks for picking up mushrooms, or as a side dish with meat.

Russia

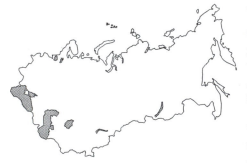

The dissolution of the Soviet Union has greatly changed this region of the world. Although most people thought of Russia and the Soviet Union as being one and the same, Russia was just one of 15 Soviet republics that have now become independent. It is still a very large country that is almost one-sixth of the earth's surface and stretches over two continents, from the frozen Siberian tundra to the marshes of St. Petersburg. (The map to the left shows the old Soviet Union, including the non-Russian republics.) Because of this vastness there are extreme variations in climate, and climatic conditions affect what will grow in each region of a country, which in turn affects what people cook and eat. To the north cold weather crops such as root crops, cabbage, and hearty wheats are grown. To the south a greater variety of crops is possible including vegetables, fruits, and grains. Russian cooking is a blending of many cultures, including European and Asian. Members of the Russian nobility, starting with Czar Peter the Great, as well as rich merchants, traveled throughout Europe, bringing back chefs from different countries. The conquest of Caucasia, a region between the Caspian and Black seas, covered with a profusion of vines, citrus groves, and tea plantations, also brought new foods to the old Russian empire.

Just as most Americans love milk and butter, the Russians have their *smetana* (sour cream), and they seem to use it in and on everything. Dill is the national herb of Russia, and it grows in almost every garden. Garlic is used with a "heavy hand" and is spread on bread, as we spread butter or peanut butter. Pickled beets, pickled cucumbers, and dried mushrooms are in every kitchen pantry. The most common side dishes are tomatoes and cucumbers. They are served at almost every meal (except breakfast!). In Russia, the staff of life is the beloved black bread. A bowl of *borscht*, the most popular Russian soup, with a chunk of black bread makes a hearty meal. *Borscht* was originally a Ukrainian dish, but now there are as many different recipes for *borscht* as there are Ukrainians.

For centuries Russian peasants have used cellars, underground storerooms placed below the freeze line, to keep vegetables edible. Beets, cabbage, and potatoes are the staple foods Russians depend upon to carry them through the terribly cold winters. They have created many different and unusual ways to cook these nourishing and filling vegetables.

Borscht — Vegetarian Beet Soup (Cold)

All Russian cooks have their own way of making *borscht*. The following recipe is a simple version of beet *borscht*. Usually vegetarian *borscht* is eaten cold and is very refreshing on a hot summer's day. Adding a cold boiled potato or hard-cooked egg to each serving of soup is not unusual and makes the *borscht* more filling. Chopped green onion tops sprinkled over the soup give it a little more flavor and interesting color.

Yield: serves 2

2 cups beets, cooked and **cubed**, or sliced beets, canned, including 3/4 cup juice (if necessary, add water to make 3/4 cup juice)
juice of 1 lemon
1 tablespoon sugar, more or less to taste
salt and pepper to taste
2 tablespoons sour cream

Equipment: Medium-size bowl, mixing spoon

Put beets with juice in bowl and add strained lemon juice and sugar. Mix well to blend and dissolve sugar. Chill until ready to serve.

Serve *borscht* cold in individual soup bowls with a **dollop** of sour cream in each serving. Have plenty of bread and butter to eat with it.

Cotletki — Meat Patties

Cotletki are fried meat patties. Sometimes they are wrapped in a pastry and baked. This recipe is popular in the cities.

Yield: serves 4 to 6

1 pound ground meat, any kind or combination
1 cup bread crumbs
1 egg
1 onion, **finely chopped**
5 tablespoons butter or margarine
salt and pepper to taste
1 cup sour cream

Equipment: Medium-size mixing bowl, medium-size skillet, mixing spoon, flat plate or pie pan, clean hands, spatula or pancake turner, oven-proof dish

1. Put meat, 1/2 cup crumbs, and egg in mixing bowl, mix well, and set aside.
2. Melt 2 tablespoons butter or margarine in skillet over medium heat, add onion, and fry until limp (about 5 minutes); stir frequently. Add onion to meat mixture, blend well, and add salt and pepper to taste.

3. Pour remaining bread crumbs in a flat plate or pie pan. Divide the meat into 4 equal balls. Using wet, clean, hands, shape each into slightly flat oval patties and coat each on all sides with bread crumbs.
4. Melt 3 tablespoons butter or margarine to skillet over medium heat. Add patties and fry about 5 minutes on each side until brown and fully cooked. Add more butter or margarine and reduce heat to low if necessary to keep from burning. Remove patties and set on oven-proof dish in a warm place.
5. Keep heat on low, add sour cream to drippings in the skillet and mix well to blend. Pour warm sour cream over patties.

Serve as a main dish with vegetables and plenty of dark bread. It is very natural to sop up sour cream gravy with chunks of bread.

Grechnevaia Kasha   Buckwheat Groats

There are several different kinds of groats (grains) that can be used to make *kasha*, Russian porridge. There are **millet**, oats, or pearl barley. In Russia buckwheat groats are the most popular grain for making *kasha*. *Kasha* is used in place of potatoes and is usually served with meat.

Yield: serves 4 to 6

2 tablespoons butter or margarine
1 onion, **finely chopped**
2 cups buckwheat groats, available from most supermarkets and health food stores
1 egg
1 teaspoon salt
2 cups boiling water

Equipment: Small-size skillet, mixing spoon, medium-size mixing bowl, greased baking dish

1. Melt 2 tablespoons butter or margarine in skillet over medium heat, add onion, and fry until soft (about 5 minutes). Set aside.
2. Preheat oven to 375° F.
3. Put groats, egg, and salt in mixing bowl and mix well. Transfer to baking dish. Slowly add as much boiling water to groats as they will absorb, stirring continually. They should not be soupy or too dry. Add onion and pan scrapings, mix well, and bake in oven for 30 minutes or until groats are tender.

Serve and eat *kasha* like mashed potatoes, with chicken or meat gravy.

Russki Salat   Russian Salad

Russian salads contain cooked vegetables and often include cooked meat, poultry, or fish. The salad dressing is simply oil and vinegar. This recipe is a wonderful way of using leftovers.

Yield: serves 4 to 6

1 cup **diced** cooked ham, beef, sausage, chicken, turkey or combination
2 cups peeled and diced beets, home cooked, or canned (drained)
2 cups diced, potatoes, home cooked or canned, skin-on or peeled
1 cup beans, homemade or canned (drained)—any kind can be used

1 onion, peeled and diced
1 fresh cucumber, thinly sliced
3 hard-cooked eggs, sliced
6 gherkins (small pickles), chopped
salt and pepper to taste
cruets of oil and vinegar for garnish

Equipment: Salad bowl, salad tools

Mix all ingredients in salad bowl, add salt and pepper to taste, and gently toss with salad tools.

Serve the salad in individual bowls. Serve with cruets of vinegar and oil. Let each person blend and add his or her own oil and vinegar to taste.

Omelet Smetanoi   *Omelet with Sour Cream*

Yield: serves 2

6 eggs
2 tablespoons chopped fresh parsley or 1 tablespoon dry flakes
4 tablespoons butter or margarine
2 tablespoons flour
3/4 cup hot milk
1 cup sour cream
salt and pepper to taste

Equipment: Small-size mixing bowl, fork or **whisk**, cup, 6-inch skillet with cover, heat-proof plate

1. Put 4 eggs in small bowl and mix in parsley. Melt 1 tablespoon butter or margarine in skillet over medium heat and add half the egg mixture. Swirl pan to coat, cover, and cook until set (about 3 minutes). Remove omelet to a warm plate. Add 1 tablespoon butter or margarine and make a second omelet exactly like the first. When done, stack it on top of the first omelet. Pour any pan drippings over it and keep warm.
2. Separate 2 remaining eggs and put yolks in a cup (refrigerate whites to use at another time).
3. Melt remaining butter or margarine in skillet over medium-low heat. Add flour and mix until smooth. Add hot milk, stirring continually until blended. Mix in sour cream and egg yolks and blend well. Stirring continually until smooth and thick, season with salt and pepper to taste. When ready to serve, pour hot sauce over the eggs.

Serve with pumpernickel or black bread for sopping the sauce. In Russia omelets are eaten at anytime of day or night.

Sibierskie Pelmeni   *Siberian Meat Dumplings*

Yield: serves 4 to 6

Pastry:
  1 cup flour
  4 tablespoons vegetable oil

6 tablespoons water
1/2 teaspoon salt
1/2 cup butter or margarine (for filling and sauce)
1 onion, **finely chopped**
1 cup finely chopped cooked beef, ham, sausage, or chicken
salt and pepper to taste
6 cups boiling water
Sauce:
1/2 cup lemon juice or vinegar
1 tablespoon chopped fresh parsley or 1 teaspoon dry flakes

Equipment: Medium-size mixing bowl, mixing spoon, floured work surface, clean kitchen towel, floured rolling pin, medium-size skillet, medium-size saucepan, slotted spoon, cookie cutter or firm water glass, fork

1. *Prepare pastry:* put 1/2 cup flour in mixing bowl, add oil, water, and salt, and mix until dough holds together. Transfer to work surface, and, using clean hands, **knead** remaining flour into dough until smooth and elastic. Transfer to bowl, cover, and chill for 1 hour.
2. Using rolling pin, roll dough out on the work surface, pie crust-thin, adding more flour to prevent sticking if necessary. Cut dough into 3-inch circles with cookie cutter or top rim of water glass. Stack circles and cover with slightly damp towel until ready to fill.
3. *Prepare filling:* melt 3 tablespoons butter or margarine in the skillet over medium heat. Add onion and fry for 3 minutes until soft. Add meat, mix well, and cook for 3 minutes more. Season with salt and pepper to taste and remove from heat.
4. Place a tablespoon of filling on each circle. Wet a finger with water and rub it along the circle edge. Draw the dough over the filling making a half circle. Press the edges firmly together using fork tines. Continue filling all circles of dough. Set aside on lightly floured work surface.
5. Keep water boiling in saucepan over high heat. Reduce heat to medium and add dumplings a few at a time. Don't crowd the pan. Cook for about 15 minutes, remove with slotted spoon, drain well, and put in bowl.
6. *Prepare sauce:* melt remaining butter in a small saucepan over medium heat, add lemon juice or vinegar and parsley flakes, and mix well. Pour butter mixture over dumplings when ready to serve.

Serve warm as the main dish or as an appetizer or snack.

Sharlotka   Apple Charlotte Dessert

The *sharlotka* is a classic Russian dessert. The original recipe calls for slices of buttered bread instead of bread crumbs. The Russians are masters of "leftovers," so it was always made with stale bread.

Yield: serves 4 to 6

1/2 cup butter or margarine
4 cups bread crumbs
1/4 to 1 cup sugar, more or less to taste
4 cups cooked apple slices, homemade or canned

Equipment: Large-size skillet, mixing spoon, medium-size bowl, nonstick or buttered 8-inch baking pan, wax paper

1. Melt butter or margarine in skillet over medium heat. Add bread crumbs and mix well to brown evenly. Add 1/4 cup sugar, reduce heat to low, and mix well to blend. Cook for 2 minutes and remove from heat. Set aside.
2. Put cooked apples in mixing bowl and add just enough remaining sugar to sweeten (canned apples are usually sweetened, and so no additional sugar is needed). Mix well.
3. Preheat oven to 350° F.
4. Cover the bottom of the baking pan with about 1/4-inch layer of crumbs. Alternate layers of apples and crumbs, ending with crumbs on top. Butter a piece of wax paper that will fit over the top of your pan. Put the buttered side of the paper on top of the crumbs. Bake in oven about 20 minutes, until golden brown. Remove wax paper.

Serve *sharlotka* hot or cold as dessert. It is delicious with ice cream.

Asia and the South Pacific

The foods of the region we call Asia and the South Pacific are as diverse as the people. The largest concentration of the earth's population lives in this part of the world. Some of the countries—such as China, Japan, India, Australia, and New Zealand—have a specific cooking style unique to the country. It might vary by regions within the country, but it is uniquely their own. The other countries in this region are a melting-pot for so many different cultures that they lack a specific style of their own. Except for Australia and New Zealand, they all have one food in common, rice. It is the staple in their diet. Rice growing is a painstaking hand operation, the hoe being almost the only tool used. In Indonesia rice is so highly regarded, a fine razor-type knife is used for cutting so it doesn't bruise the shafts. There are over 2,000 varieties of rice in the world to suit many types of soil, climate, and cultures.

You will get several cooking tips in this section. In most of the Asian countries, retaining the natural flavor of the main ingredient is very important. Steaming (a very healthy way to cook) and **stir fry** are the most common procedures. Spices are added with a sense of balance and harmony, never with a "heavy hand." The degree of hotness in some dishes is due not to the addition of herbs and spices but to capsicums (peppers).

Mongolia

The Mongolian people are meat eaters and the meat is usually lamb. They were a nomadic group, herding sheep, yaks, goats, camels, cattle, and horses on their windswept, flat grasslands, but now because political boundaries prevent free movement they are much more settled. Instead of keeping their flocks moving to eat fresh grass, they rely on growing grains to feed their livestock. Besides meat, dairy products such as cheese, milk, and yogurt are made from their animals. Everyone, including small children, drinks hot tea in this extremely cold, rugged country. It is prepared the traditional Tibetan way; butter and roasted barley are added to the brewing tea making it not only soothing but nourishing as well. Some vegetables, potatoes, and bread are eaten but only as side dishes to meat. In the past, only cold-tolerant vegetables could be raised. Thus, cabbage and onions were some of the few vegetables people ate.

Shaptak *Lamb in Spices*

Yield: serves 6

2 tablespoons vegetable oil
2 chopped onions
6 cloves garlic, **finely chopped,** or 2 teaspoons garlic granules
4 tablespoons finely chopped fresh ginger or 2 teaspoons ground ginger
1 tablespoon Oriental five-spice powder (available at most supermarkets and all Asian stores)
2 tablespoons soy sauce
1 tablespoon sesame oil, available at most supermarkets and all Asian stores
2 pounds lean boneless lamb, sliced in thin 2-inch strips (slightly freeze meat first to make slicing easier)
salt and pepper to taste

Equipment: **Wok** or large-size skillet, mixing spoon

1. Heat oil in wok or skillet over high heat. Add onions, garlic, ginger, five-spice powder, soy sauce, and sesame oil. Stirring continually, cook for 1 minute.
2. Add lamb and mix well. Add salt and pepper to taste and mix thoroughly.
3. Cook, stirring continually, until lamb is done (about 5 to 10 minutes). Reduce heat to medium if necessary to prevent sticking.

Serve lamb over a large platter of cooked rice and a side dish of **chutney**.

China

Chinese culture and cooking traditions are some of the oldest in the world. China also has the world's largest population. With well over one billion people to feed, nothing is thrown away in this country. Chinese food is economical, traditional, and delicious. It is one of the most popular foods worldwide. The chief food crops grown in China are rice, corn, and wheat. Over one-half of the population works in agriculture, mostly doing farming just to feed their families. Fishing is a large industry, producing the third largest catch in the world  yearly. In the cities both men and women share in the shopping and cooking. The national food of China is rice, and it is so much a part of their life that the Chinese word for rice, "fan," also means "meal."

The Chinese often eat more than three meals a day, all beginning with rice porridge for breakfast. When rice is soupy, as in porridge, it is called *congee*. When nothing chunky has been added to the rice it is called *jook*. The following recipe is for the basic *jook*. Five different *congee* recipes can be made with *jook*, and they can be seasoned with grated ginger, sugar, salt, pepper, and soy sauce according to your tastes. Garnish with chopped green onions. The recipes are as follows: for *ngau yook jook*, beef is added; for *sang choy jook*, lettuce is added; for *bok choy jook*, add bok choy (a Chinese vegetable meaning "white cabbage"—it's about the size of a stalk of celery with thick white stems and long, narrow green leaves; it is available at many supermarkets and Asian stores); add fish for *yueh jook*; and for *pie dan sau yook jook*, chopped preserved eggs and cooked pork are added.

Jook Congee   *Rice Porridge*

> 1 cup glutinous rice (available at many supermarkets and Asian stores)
> 4 cups water
> 4 cups chicken broth, homemade or canned
> salt and pepper to taste

Equipment: Strainer, medium-size saucepan with cover, mixing spoon

1. Put rice in strainer and rinse under cold running water.
2. Put water and chicken broth in saucepan, add rice, and bring to a boil over high heat. Reduce heat to simmer, cover, and cook for about 1 hour, stirring frequently to prevent sticking. Remove cover and cook for about 30 minutes more until *jook* is soupy thick. Add salt and pepper to taste.

Serve *jook* in soup bowls, to eat with soup spoons for breakfast or at the end of a meal.

Ch'a Yeh Tan   Tea Eggs

Eggs are economical, filling, and easy to digest, making them important in all Chinese cooking.

Yield: serves 4 to 6

6 eggs
8 cups water
1/2 cup black tea leaves
2 star anise (whole, available at many supermarkets and Asian stores)
1 teaspoon sugar
1 teaspoon soy sauce

Equipment: Small-size saucepan, spoon

1. Put eggs in small saucepan, cover with 6 cups water, and bring to a gentle boil over medium-high heat. Reduce heat to simmer and cook for 10 minutes. Cool under cold running water and drain. Using back of spoon, gently tap shells, making tiny cracks all over them, without breaking eggs open.
2. Fill saucepan with remaining 2 cups water and add tea leaves, anise, sugar, soy sauce and eggs and mix well. Bring to a boil, reduce to low heat, and cook for about 30 minutes. Remove from heat and let eggs sit in liquid. Carefully turn eggs several times so they will color well.
3. Remove eggs from liquid and peel off shells. Egg whites will be covered with a **marble**-like pattern. Refrigerate until ready to serve.

Serve tea eggs as a snack or as an edible garnish for rice.

Shao Pi K'u   Barbecued Ribs

Pork is the favorite meat of the Chinese, and the following recipe is easy to make. In China an extremely hot chili sauce would be added; we suggest adding ketchup instead. We also suggest baking the ribs for easy and more uniform cooking.

Yield: serves 4 to 6

1/4 cup soy sauce
1/2 cup brown sugar or honey
1/2 cup ketchup
1/4 cup Chinese black bean sauce, available at most supermarkets or Asian stores
3 cloves garlic, **finely chopped,** or 1 teaspoon garlic granules
salt and pepper to taste
4 pounds baby back spareribs (have butcher separate ribs and cut each in half, making short ribs)

Equipment: Large-size mixing bowl, clean hands, aluminum foil, broiler pan, mixing spoon, tongs

Preset oven to 350° F.

1. Put soy sauce, brown sugar, ketchup, brown bean sauce, garlic, and salt and pepper to taste in mixing bowl and mix well. Add ribs, and using clean hands, toss to coat with mixture. Cover ribs with foil and refrigerate, for about 1 hour; mix ribs in bowl 2 times to coat with mixture.
2. Place ribs side-by-side on broiler rack, and bake in oven for about 40 minutes, until browned and tender. **Baste** 1 or 2 times with **marinade** while ribs are baking.

Serve on a serving platter with extra marinade in a small bowl for dipping. In China, ribs are held with chopsticks; the Chinese do not touch food with their hands.

Broccoli and Carrots with Firm Tofu

Combining fresh vegetables with *tofu* (bean curd) is one of China's most popular dishes. *Tofu* is a white, soft, and easily digestible dried soybean product. It is high in protein, low in calories, and cholesterol free.

Yield: serves 6

4 tablespoons vegetable oil
1 tablespoon **finely chopped** ginger root or 1 teaspoon ground ginger
2 cloves garlic, finely chopped, or 1 teaspoon garlic granules
1 pound tofu (bean curd) (Momen if available), drained, cut into bite-size cubes (available at most supermarkets and all Asian stores)
2 cups broccoli flowerets
1 cup peeled, thinly sliced carrots
1 onion, sliced and separated into rings
1 cup chicken broth, homemade or canned
1 tablespoon cornstarch
1 tablespoon water

Equipment: **Wok** or large-size skillet with cover, slotted mixing spoon, paper towels, cup

1. Heat oil in wok or large skillet over high heat, add ginger root and garlic, and stirring continually for about 1 minute, cook until lightly brown. Reduce heat to medium, add tofu, and fry until golden brown (about 10 minutes); stir frequently. Remove tofu, drain on paper towels, and set aside.
2. Increase heat to medium high, add broccoli, carrots, and onion, and fry for 1 minute, stirring continually. Add chicken broth, cover, and and cook for about 3 minutes or until carrots are tender.
3. Mix cornstarch with water in cup, add to vegetable mixture, and mix well. Reduce heat to simmer. Add fried tofu to mixture, toss gently, and cook until mixture thickens and bean curd is heated through (about 2 minutes).

Serve **stir-fry** vegetables in a bowl with extra soy sauce. It is customary to serve other dishes at the same time and always include a bowl of rice.

Ch'ao Hsueh Tou   Stir-fried Snow Peas

The following can be served with the **stir-fry** vegetables above.

Yield: serves 4 to 6

1/2 pound pork with some fat, finely chopped
1 pound snow peas, washed, dried, and **trimmed**
1/2 cup chicken broth, homemade or canned
4 tablespoons water
1 tablespoon cornstarch
1 tablespoon soy sauce

Equipment: **Wok** or large-size skillet, mixing spoon, cup

1. Fry pork in wok or large skillet over medium high heat until crisp, and cooked through (about 2 minutes). Stirring continually, separate pieces of pork, add snow peas, reduce heat to medium, and cook for 1 minute. Stirring continually, add chicken broth and continue cooking until snow peas are tender but still crisp (about 2 minutes more).
2. Put water in a cup, add cornstarch and soy sauce, and mix well. Add mixture to pork and snow peas to thicken, mix well, and remove from heat.

Serve snow peas in a bowl as a side dish with other **stir-fry** dishes and rice.

Afghanistan

Afghanistan is a mountainous, land-locked country in central Asia. Agriculture is very important to Afghani society, although less than 10 percent of the rugged land is cultivated. Droughts and war have made raising food to eat very difficult. However, the majority of the people farm or herd animals. Clever underground water irrigation systems keep the Afghanis' water from evaporating before it gets to the fields. Wheat is a major crop, and corn, barley, and rice are also important. Afghanis enjoy *pilau*, rice dishes that include meat and vegetables as well. A spice called saffron is sometimes added. Lamb and chicken are the primary meats eaten in this Muslim society. Many fruits and vegetables are grown. Fruits are dried for storage so that they can be eaten much later. Mulberries grow wild and supplement the people's diets. A bread called *nan* is a staple; people like to tuck onions in their nan. Meals consist of soups, rice dishes, yogurt, kebabs, and tea. Tea, served in china bowls, is the national drink. Desserts can be puddings of rice or wheat. The food and eating habits of Afghanistan are similar to those of their neighboring countries, such as Pakistan, Iraq, and Iran.

Bonjan Borani   *Eggplant and Yogurt Casserole*

Yield: serves 6

4 to 6 tablespoons vegetable oil
1 onion, finely sliced
1 eggplant (about 1 3/4 pounds) cut into 1/2-inch, skin-on **cubes**
1 cup plain yogurt
3 cloves garlic, finely chopped or 1 teaspoon garlic granules
3 tablespoons chopped fresh mint or 2 teaspoons crushed dried mint
salt and pepper to taste
paprika for garnish

Equipment: Large-size skillet, slotted mixing spoon, oven-proof casserole or 9-inch baking pan, small-size bowl

1. Heat 4 tablespoons oil in skillet over medium-high heat, add onion and eggplant, and, stirring frequently, fry until golden (about 8 minutes). Add more oil if necessary.
2. Using slotted spoon, transfer mixture to casserole or baking pan and set aside.
3. Preheat oven to 350°F.
4. Put yogurt in bowl and add garlic, mint, and salt and pepper to taste. Mix well and pour over eggplant mixture. Sprinkle lightly with paprika.
5. Bake in oven for about 25 minutes or until bubbly and lightly brown on top.

Serve directly from the oven with side dish of rice and plenty of bread.

Pilau   *Rice Casserole*

Rice, vegetables, and loaves of flat bread are typical of an Afghan's meal. Rice is eaten at every meal, and adding to it a little chicken or mutton broth with the vegetables makes *pilau* more nourishing and flavorful.

Yield: serves 4 to 6

6 tablespoons butter, margarine, or **ghee**
2 onions, chopped
1 cup uncooked rice
3 cups chicken broth, homemade or canned
2 bay leaves
2 potatoes, peeled and **cubed**
2 carrots, cut lengthwise into 1-inch strips, peeled, and then quartered
1/2 cup seedless raisins
1/2 teaspoon curry powder
salt to taste
1 cup finely chopped spinach, fresh, well washed and drained or frozen and drained
1/4 cup slivered almonds for garnish

Equipment: Large-size saucepan with cover, mixing spoon, fork

1. Heat butter, margarine, or ghee in saucepan over medium heat. Add onions and cook, stirring frequently, until golden (about 5 minutes). Add rice, mix well, and cook for 5 minutes more. Add broth, bay leaves, potatoes, carrots, raisins, curry, and salt to taste, mix well, and bring to a boil over high heat. Reduce heat to simmer, cover, and cook for 20 minutes or until rice is tender. Remove from heat and remove bay leaves and discard.
2. Add spinach and mix with a fork. Cover and let sit for 10 minutes. Transfer to serving bowl and sprinkle with almonds.

Serve either as a side dish or on a platter with chicken or meat over it.

Pakistan

Pakistan was once part of the British Indian empire, but conflict between the Islamic Pakastanis and Hindu Indians led to the formation of separate nations after independence from Great Britain was declared in 1947. Nevertheless, food in Pakistan is similar to food in India except it is less spicy and it includes meat. Pakistanis are Muslim and follow Muslim dietary laws. Food is served on very large platters. Traditionally, people sat on the floor to eat, although today some, feeling European

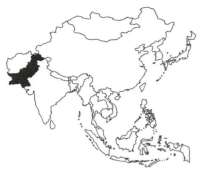

influences, have adapted to sitting at Western tables and using chairs and flatware.

Along the coast, fishing is an important industry, but agriculture plays a much greater role in the economy. Pakastanis grow wheat, rice, and sugar cane. Wheat is the staple crop. The northern and western parts of the country are dry, and thus, the majority of agricultural activity in those areas involves raising livestock. Pakistanis keep sheep, cattle, water buffalo, and donkeys.

Pakistanis are big eaters, having two big meals a day, at lunch and dinner. Each big meal consists of a main dish of lamb, chicken, or beef; rice; a curried vegetable; and side dishes of salads or curds and whey. Side dishes served during a Pakistani meal are called *sambals* (sahm-bahls). *Sambals* are carefully selected to compliment each other—hot and cool flavors, smooth or crisp textures, and balanced color contrasts. *Sambals* are often more important than the main dish. They can be simply pickles and **chutneys,** cooked dried peas, beans, or any selection of fruit and vegetables. Scarcely a meal is served without a *sambal* or main dish containing some kind of beans or dried peas. These dishes serve as a bland contrast to hot curries. Desserts are sweet and are like those found in India. In this group of recipes a complete meal is included except for the dessert. The carrot pudding of India can be used to end this meal.

Chapli Kabab   Meat Patties

Chapli kababs aren't kababs at all—they're meat patties. Adding curry powder gives them the unique flavor characteristic of Pakistani cooking.

Yield: serves 2 to 4

1 pound finely ground beef or lamb
1 egg
2 teaspoons curry powder
juice of 1/2 lemon
1 green chili pepper or jalapeno **seeded**, finely chopped, fresh or canned, **cored** and seeded
3 to 5 tablespoons **ghee** or vegetable oil
1 onion, thinly sliced for garnish
1 tablespoon chopped fresh **coriander** for garnish

Equipment: Medium-size mixing bowl, mixing spoon or electric mixer, medium-size skillet, metal spatula or pancake turner

1. Put meat, egg, curry powder, lemon juice, and chili pepper in bowl, and using spoon or electric mixer, mix into smooth paste. Divide mixture into 4 oval-shaped patties, each a 1/2 inch thick.
2. Heat 3 tablespoons ghee or oil in skillet over medium-high heat. Add patties, reduce heat to medium, and fry about 8 minutes on each side or until brown. (Add more oil if necessary.) Put on serving platter, garnish with onion slices, and sprinkle with coriander.

Serve with any number of side dishes: Chopped pickles, **chutney**, peanuts, coconut, chopped hard-cooked egg, chopped tomatoes, chopped bananas, and recipes that follow. To fully enjoy the contrast in flavors, with each mouthful of meat, add a dab from a different side dish.

Chana Dahl   Chickpeas

Yield: serves 4

2 to 4 tablespoons **ghee**, butter, or margarine
1 onion, **finely chopped**
1 teaspoon *each* curry powder and ground cumin
1/2 teaspoon *each* ground ginger and ground red pepper
1 cup cooked chickpeas, homemade or canned (drain liquid and set aside 1/2 cup of liquid or 1/2 cup water)
1 cooked potato, peeled and **cubed**
1 teaspoon sugar
salt and pepper to taste

Equipment: Medium-size skillet, mixing spoon

1. Heat 2 tablespoons **ghee**, butter, or margarine in skillet over medium heat. Add onion and fry until golden brown, about 5 minutes. Add curry powder, cumin, ginger, and red pepper and mix well.
2. Reduce heat to low and add chickpeas, drained liquid or water, potato, sugar, and salt and pepper to taste. Mix well and add more ghee, butter, or margarine if necessary to prevent sticking.
3. Increase heat to medium and cook for about 5 minutes to heat through.

Serve *chana dahl* as a side dish with curried meat, poultry or fish.

Kachoomber

Kachoomber is raw salad flavored with fresh herbs. Any variety of vegetables and fruit can be combined to make *kachoomber*. Adding vinegar, sugar, and other fresh herbs, such as mint, and any combination of spices is perfectly acceptable. *Kachoomber* is a cooling *sambal*, an excellent contrast to fiery hot curries.

Yield: about 1 1/2 cups

1 green bell pepper, **seeded** and **finely chopped**
1 *each* small cucumber, tomato, white onion, finely chopped
1 green chili pepper, fresh or canned, **cored**, seeded, and finely chopped
4 tablespoons white vinegar, more or less to taste
sugar and salt to taste
1 tablespoon finely chopped fresh **coriander** leaves or 1 teaspoon dried ground coriander

Equipment: Small bowl with cover

Put green pepper, cucumber, tomato, onion, chili pepper, vinegar, sugar, salt to taste, and coriander in bowl and mix well. Cover and refrigerate. Mix before serving.

Serve in a small bowl as salad or condiment to accompany other dishes.

India

Next to China, India is the most populous nation in the world. Indians enjoy a worldwide reputation for fine food. India is known as the "land of curry"; its people have been combining and blending spices for thousands of years. At first spices were only used as medicine. Now spices are used mostly for flavoring. It is interesting that curry powder is not sold in India as it is in Western countries. Each cook mixes her or his own spices to make curry powder. These blended spices are then mixed with foods, either meat or fish or vegetables, to make curries!

A curry meal is not complete without mountains of rice and lots of condiments, each served in its own little dish. The condiments, or *sambals* as they are called, must always include a **chutney** and a variety of taste sensations to awaken the taste buds. Shredded coconut or raisins for sweet, something lemony for sour, salted nuts or **capers** for salty, slices of fresh melon or yogurt for cooling, pickles for pungent, and sliced apple for tart.

There are many different kinds of foods in India, and many different kinds of people with special food habits. For example, the Muslims don't eat pork, and the Hindu people do not believe in eating meat; they are vegetarians. The Jains are a small special group of Hindus that believe all living things have souls. They sweep the ground in front of them to avoid stepping on bugs. They avoid eating tubers, such as sweet potatoes, because tubers grow underground, and they fear that while pulling up the plant an insect may be accidently hurt.

Agriculture is very important to India, with over 70 percent of the population involved in growing rice, cereals, legumes (peas, **groundnuts**, and **lentils**), and other crops. Indians began using modern farming methods in the 1970s and increased food production to the point where they can now feed their people.

Ghee   *Indian Butter*

Ghee is clarified butter; the water and nonfat solids are separated and removed by gently heating and straining. There are several advantages to cooking with *ghee*: it doesn't sputter or burn since the water and solids are removed; it has an excellent flavor; and it will keep almost indefinitely, even when left unrefrigerated.

Usli ghee is the clarified butter made from the rich milk of water buffalo and yak. For centuries it has been used not only for cooking but also for religious ceremonies. During the "Festival of Lights," thousands of clay lamps are fueled with *ghee*, and every Indian, rich and poor alike, looks forward to the joyous festival that begins the winter season. Every home glows from the flickering light of these simple lamps.

Ghee is available at supermarkets that carry foreign foods and at Indian food markets. You can make it at home following this recipe.

Yield: about 1 cup

1 pound butter

Equipment: Medium-size saucepan, spoon, bulb baster or fine-hole strainer, small-size bowl

1. Melt butter in saucepan over low heat without browning. Cook undisturbed for about 45 minutes or until it separates, with the solids on the bottom and clear oil on top.
2. The clear oil (*ghee*) can be carefully spooned off, removed with a bulb baster, or slowly poured through a strainer into the bowl. Save the residue to add to and enrich soups or sauces. Cool *ghee* to room temperature, cover, and refrigerate.

Serve *ghee* over vegetables or fish, use it in making many sauces, or use it in place of oil for stir-frying.

Chapati   Flat Bread

Very little meat is eaten in India, so bread is important and is truly the staff of life. Bread and grains are used in sacred rituals and ceremonies marking major life events, from birth to death. *Chapati* is unleavened bread, made today as it was in ancient times. The flour has become more refined, but the end result is pretty much the same.

Yield: makes 6

3/4 cup unbleached all-purpose flour (set aside 1/4 cup)
1 cup whole-wheat flour
3/4 cup warm water
2 to 4 tablespoons butter, margarine, or **ghee**

Equipment: Large-size mixing bowl, floured work surface, large-size griddle or heavy-bottomed skillet, metal spatula or pancake turner

1. Combine all-purpose and whole-wheat flours in bowl, make a hole in the center, and add water. Mix flour into water and with clean hands **knead** into a very smooth dough for about 5 minutes.
2. Divide dough into 6 equal egg-size balls. Press each piece between the palms of your hands or on a work surface. Each ball should flatten out to a circle of about 6-inch diameter. If balls seem sticky, dust lightly with flour.
3. Heat butter, margarine, or *ghee* on griddle or skillet over high heat. Cook dough circles, one at a time for about 15 seconds per side. Brown spots will appear on the underside. Press *chapati* down around the edges with spatula or pancake turner. The center should bubble up.

To serve, brush one side with butter, margarine, or *ghee* and eat while warm.

Kari   Chicken Curry

Food holds a high place in the aesthetic and intellectual level of Indian life. Creating curries is an art; it takes skill and patience to prepare the right balance of flavors. Indian cooks blend their own, but ready-mixed curries, available at supermarkets, are time and labor savers. Today curries are enjoyed all over the world for the unique flavor they add to everything edible.

Yield: serves 4 to 6

2 to 4 tablespoons vegetable oil, more or less as needed
2 to 3 pounds chicken, cut into serving-size pieces
2 onions **finely chopped**
3 cloves finely chopped garlic or 1 teaspoon garlic granules
4 teaspoons ground curry powder
1 teaspoon salt
1 cup water
1 cup finely chopped fresh tomatoes
1/2 cup plain yogurt

Equipment: Large-size skillet with cover or **Dutch oven**, tongs or metal spatula, mixing spoon, small-size bowl

1. Heat 2 tablespoons oil in skillet or Dutch oven over high heat, add chicken, and fry for about 8 minutes per side, until browned. (Add more oil if necessary.) Using tongs or spatula, remove chicken from pan and keep warm. Reduce heat to low, add onions and garlic, cover, and cook for about 3 minutes, until onions are soft. Mix well.
2. Mix curry powder, salt, and water in small bowl. Add to onion mixture in skillet and mix well. Add tomatoes and yogurt and mix thoroughly. Continue to heat on simmer.
3. Return chicken to skillet, turning pieces to coat evenly with sauce. Cover and simmer for about 30 minutes, until tender.

Serve chicken on a platter and pour sauce from the skillet over it. Serve a large bowl full of hot cooked rice and assorted condiments in small individual bowls. Always serve **chutney** and select at least 3 or 4 of the following: chopped peanuts, chopped green onions, mandarine orange slices, raisins, coconut flakes, yogurt, and chunks of mango, melon, pineapple, and apples.

Am Ki Chatni   *Fresh Mango and Coconut Chutney*

Curries without **chutneys** are incomplete; they lack sparkle and the finishing touch.

Yield: about 2 cups

1 mango (about 1 pound), peeled, **seeded**, and cut in chunks
1/2 cup **shredded** coconut, fresh (see recipe page 208), frozen, or canned
1/4 cup **finely chopped** fresh **coriander** leaves
1 tablespoon finely chopped fresh ginger or 1 teaspoon ground ginger
1/2 teaspoon *each* salt and dried red pepper flakes

Equipment: Small-size bowl, mixing spoon

Put mangos, coconut, coriander, ginger, salt, and red pepper in the bowl, toss gently until completely mixed, and chill.

Serve in a separate bowl as condiment with curries. With every mouthful of the curry meat or chicken, add a dab of chutney or one of the other condiments is added.

Nimbu Chatni   Date and Lemon Chutney

Yield: 1 1/2 cups

8 ounces **pitted** dates, **finely chopped** (cut with scissors for best results)
1/2 cup **shredded** coconut
1/4 cup fresh lemon juice
2 tablespoons fresh grated ginger or 1 teaspoon ground ginger
1 tablespoon finely chopped fresh **coriander** leaf (no stems) or 1 teaspoon dried coriander
1/2 teaspoon *each* ground fennel seeds, salt, and black pepper

Equipment: Small bowl, mixing spoon

Combine dates, coconut, lemon juice, ginger, coriander, fennel, salt, and pepper; toss gently until completely mixed; and chill.

Serve in a small bowl and use as a condiment with curries.

Gajar Halva   Sweet Carrot Pudding

Yield: serves 6 to 8

6 carrots (about 1 pound), scraped and finely **shredded**
2 cups half-and-half
1/2 cup dark brown sugar
1/2 cup golden seedless raisins (soaked in warm water for 20 minutes and drained well)
1/4 cup butter, margarine, or **ghee**
1/2 teaspoon ground **cardamom**
salt to taste
1 cup finely chopped almonds or pistachios, **blanched**
1/2 cup chopped nuts of your choice for garnish

Equipment: Medium-size saucepan with cover, mixing spoon

1. Put carrots and half-and-half in saucepan and bring to a boil over medium-high heat. Reduce heat to simmer, cover, and cook until liquid is almost absorbed, about 1 hour.
2. Add brown sugar, raisins, butter or margarine, or ghee, cardamom, and salt and mix well. Reduce heat to low and stir continually until sugar is dissolved (about 2 minutes).

To serve as they do in India, spoon the carrot pudding into a mound in the center of a dish, garnish with chopped nuts, and serve warm.

Sri Lanka

Way down at the tip of India you will find this island nation, separate from India, yet close in culture and culinary tastes. The ocean presents Sri Lankans with a daily bountiful harvest. They have developed special foods based on what is most readily available to them—fish, coconuts, and tropical fruits, which they lay out on platters in beautiful designs. Rice is the staple grain and provides the backdrop for their nutritious and delicious meals.

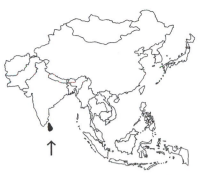

Sri Lanka is famous for its "white curries" always made with coconut and coconut milk, and for its spices and hot peppers. Side dishes of cooling fresh tropical fruit are a pleasing contrast to hot curry. Orange slices, bananas, mango, chopped plums, sliced kiwi, and **cubed** melon are just a few of the fruits that grow in Sri Lanka. Farmers provide enough food here to feed the entire population. Irrigation systems were developed, and so most of the island can be used to grow rice, coconuts, spices, fruits, vegetables, and tea. Sri Lanka is third in the world for tea production. Tea was brought by the British colonist in the 1800s and is a valuable cash crop.

Meen Molee   *Fish Coconut Curry*

Molee is a coconut milk curry made with precooked vegetables, fish, or poultry. The following recipe can be made with poultry (4 chicken breasts) or vegetables cut into chunks (4 cups), or shrimp instead of fish **fillets**. Just reduce the cooking time.

Yield: serves 4 to 6

1 teaspoon *each* **turmeric** and salt
6 fish fillets, skin on, about 6 to 8 ounces each—washed and patted dry
4 to 6 tablespoons butter, margarine, or **ghee**
2 onions, **finely chopped**
4 green chili peppers, **seeded** and cut in thin strips
1 tablespoon grated fresh ginger or 1 teaspoon ground ginger
1 teaspoon curry powder
1 cup coconut milk, fresh (see recipe page 208), frozen, or canned
1/4 cup lemon juice
1/2 cup shredded coconut for garnish

Equipment: Large-size skillet, pancake turner or metal spatula, mixing spoon, 13- x 9- inch baking pan

Preheat oven to 350°F.
1. Mix turmeric and salt in small bowl and rub on fish fillets.
2. Heat 2 tablespoons butter, margarine, or *ghee* in skillet over medium heat. Add fillets and fry on both sides until golden brown (about 5 minutes per side). Transfer to baking pan and place fillets side-by-side, skin-side down. Do not stack fish.
3. Add more fat to the same skillet if necessary. Add onions, chilies, ginger, and curry powder. Mix well, and fry over medium heat for about 5 minutes or until onions are soft. Remove from heat, stir in coconut milk and lemon juice, mix well, and pour over fish.
4. Put fillets in oven to heat through, about 10 minutes. Remove and sprinkle with shredded coconut for garnish.

Serve hot with side dishes of lentils, rice, and condiments of your choice.

Dried beans and peas are protein-rich meat substitutes called *dals (duls)* in India and throughout most of Southeast Asia where little meat is eaten. *Dal* is the Hindi name for members of the legume (beans) and pulse (edible seeds) family. There are at least 60 varieties of *dals* to choose from—either fresh or dried. *Dals* are cheap and easy to cook into tasty nourishing meals. Red kidney beans; yellow, red and brown **lentils**; split peas; black-eyed peas; and pigeon-peas are the most popular. The recipe is the same regardless of which *dals* are used; they can be mashed or left whole. The mild flavor is a good buffer for hot and spicy Sri Lanka curries. *Dals* can be spooned over rice or served separately as side dishes with curries. Lentil *dal* is the most popular in Sri Lanka. Soup can be made from leftover *dal* by just adding water and heating; that is, if you ever have any leftovers of this tasty dish.

Yield: serves 4 to 6

1 cup dried **lentils** (red, brown, or yellow) or split peas
3 cups water
2 tablespoons vegetable oil
1 teaspoon *each* salt, ground cumin, and ground **turmeric**
3 cloves garlic, finely chopped, or 1 teaspoon garlic granules
1 onion, **finely chopped**
4 to 6 lemon wedges

Equipment: Large-size saucepan with cover, mixing spoon, small-size skillet

1. Put lentils or split peas and water in saucepan and bring to a boil over high heat. Reduce heat to simmer, cover, and cook until tender (about 45 minutes); stir frequently.
2. Heat oil in skillet over medium-high heat. Add salt, cumin, turmeric, garlic, and onion, mix well, cook until tender (about 5 minutes).
3. Stir the onion mixture into the lentils and simmer, uncovered, for about 20 minutes, stirring frequently to prevent sticking.

Serve warm as a side dish with curries.

Bangladesh

Bangladesh was formed in 1971 after breaking away from Pakistan, more than 1,000 miles to its west. Previously known as East Pakistan, the Bengalis of Bangladesh are different from Pakistanis in dress, language, and food. Rice is the main food crop grown, accounting for approximately 80 percent of the fields cultivated. Fishing is an important industry along the rivers and extensive coastline. Seafood is sold locally and exported. Low-lying marshes are home to millions of frogs, whose tasty legs show up on fancy restaurant menus around the world. Seafood such as flounder is spiced with hot chilies or turmeric, and then cooked in mustard oil called *bhajhi*. Soy oil is replacing mustard oil because it is more economical and healthy. Highly seasoned curried vegetables accompany the fish, followed by a soup made from *dal*. For dessert, mild, sweetened, soft white cheese sprinkled with rose water gently ends the meal. Tea or water are the principal drinks. Hot milk is sometimes served after dinner. Because of poor harvests, bad weather, and regular flooding Bangladesh needs assistance in feeding its people. It is one of the poorest countries in the world.

Bata Ne Tameta   Potatoes with Gravy

The following recipe of potatoes and gravy is not like the meat-juice version of gravy many of us are accustomed to. The gravy is simply seasoned potato water. It's inexpensive, nourishing, and easy to make.

Yield: serves 4 to 6

2 to 4 tablespoons vegetable oil
4 potatoes, peeled and **cubed**
4 cups water
1 tablespoon vinegar
1 tomato, cubed
1/2 teaspoon *each* dry ground mustard, ground **coriander**, crushed red pepper flakes, ground ginger, ground **turmeric**
1 teaspoon sugar
salt and pepper to taste

Equipment: Large-size skillet with cover, mixing spoon

1. Heat oil in skillet over medium heat, add potatoes, and, stirring continually to coat with oil, fry for 3 minutes. Add water and vinegar, cover, and cook for about 15 minutes.
2. Add tomato, mustard, **coriander**, red pepper, ginger, turmeric, sugar, and salt and pepper to taste, mix well, and cook until potatoes are tender (about 5 minutes).

Serve *bata ne tameta* as a side dish with rice and curried fish or meat.

Myanmar (Burma)

Once known as Burma, Myanmar was at one time the richest country in Southeast Asia. It was ruled by the British as part of India until 1937, when it became an independent country. It was originally settled by Tibetans, in about the ninth century, who are now considered native Burmans. They follow Buddhist teachings, and most are vegetarians; however, many do eat fish. The cuisine is a blending of Indian curries with Chinese **stir-fry** using native tropical fruits and vegetables.

Rice is a staple of the Myanmar diet and is eaten as porridge or in simple plain, snowy white form. Small farms with rice paddies dot the countryside, and all the work, from seeding to harvesting, is done by hand. Farming is very hard work, and children are taught at a young age to respect food and waste nothing. They believe vegetables are "nature's gift to people." Every vegetable has its growing season, and when it's green bean time, everyone eats green beans at every meal.

Many Chinese customs are followed in Myanmar, except in the use of chopsticks. Burmans eat with their hands and are offended if chopsticks are suggested. They like using Indian ingredients, such as **ghee**, and Chinese cooking equipment, such as the wok, which is a very efficient cooking utensil. The rounded bottom distributes heat evenly, and less oil is needed for cooking than in a conventional skillet.

Stir-fried Green Beans

Yield: serves 4 to 6

2 to 4 tablespoons vegetable oil
2 pounds whole green beans, fresh (**trimmed**) or frozen (thawed)
1 onion, **finely chopped**
1/4 cup water
1 tablespoon sesame oil
salt and pepper to taste
1/2 cup sesame seeds

Equipment: **Wok** or large-size skillet, mixing spoon

1. Heat 2 tablespoons vegetable oil in wok or skillet over high heat and add beans and onion, stirring continually to coat with oil. (Add more vegetable oil if necessary.) Add water to keep beans moist and prevent burning.
2. **Stir-fry** until beans are emerald green in color and still crunchy, but not raw, about 5 minutes. Add sesame oil, salt and pepper to taste, and sesame seeds and toss to blend.

Serve hot with a large bowl of rice. A fish sauce such as *nuoc nam* (see page 177) is often sprinkled on the vegetables for added flavor.

Tupa Menda   Buttered Fruit Rice

Yield: serves 4 to 6

1/4 cup butter or **ghee**
1 cup uncooked rice, rinsed and drained
1 3/4 cups water
1/4 teaspoon salt
1/2 cup seedless raisins
1/2 cup **finely chopped** dried apricots

Equipment: **Wok** with cover or medium-size skillet with cover, mixing spoon

1. Melt butter or ghee in wok or skillet over medium heat. Add rice and stir until golden, about 3 minutes. Add water and salt, mix well, and bring to a boil. Reduce heat to simmer, cover, and cook 5 minutes.
2. Add raisins and apricots, mix well, cover, and continue simmering until rice is dry and soft (about 12 minutes).

3. Turn off heat and let rice stand covered 15 minutes before serving. Serve rice as a side dish with **stir-fry** vegetables.

Thailand

Thailand, a country in Southeast Asia, is on the other side of the world from New York City. Not only are these two opposite each other geographically, their lifestyles and cultures are also diametrically opposed. Thai people have a reputation for being very easy going and relaxed. Most people are involved in agriculture, living in small villages and farming the good Thailand soil. Rice is the staple food. They enjoy hot and spicy curried dishes of fish, meat, or chicken. Rice and a cooling cucumber salad are usually served with every meal to help cool off the diner's mouth. Favorite spices include **cardamom**, coriander, ginger, turmeric, lemon grass, garlic, chili peppers, and tamarind. Desserts are very sweet rice or banana dishes cooked with coconut.

Martabak   *Ground Beef Omelete*

A popular Bangkok street food is *martabak*, made with fried bread. We're suggesting easier to work with eggroll skins, available at most supermarkets. This recipe would do well anywhere; its so easy to fix and delicious to eat it will be a hit at food festivals or pot lucks; it reheats well.

Yield: serves 4 to 6

1 cup ground beef
6 eggs, beaten
1/2 cup **finely chopped** green onions
salt and pepper to taste
1 to 2 tablespoons vegetable oil
6 to 10 eggroll skins, fresh or frozen (thawed)

Equipment: Medium-size skillet, mixing spoon, medium-size bowl, pancake turner or metal spatula

1. Brown beef in skillet over medium-high heat until no longer pink, about 4 minutes. Remove from heat to cool.
2. Put eggs and green onions in mixing bowl, add meat and salt and pepper to taste, and mix well.
3. Place 1 eggroll skin on work surface and spoon about 2 tablespoons of egg mixture in the center. Bring top and bottom edges up, overlapping them envelope-fashion. Set aside on work surface and repeat filling other eggroll skins until mixture is used up. (Wrap and refrigerate or refreeze any remaining eggroll skins to use at another time.)

4. Wash and dry skillet and add 1 tablespoon oil. Heat oil over medium-low heat and place 2 or 3 eggroll packages, overlapping side down, in the skillet. Lightly press down on eggroll packages with back of pancake turner or spatula and cook for about 2 minutes or until lightly brown. Turn over and cook other side for about 3 minutes, until lightly brown. Repeat until all packages are fried. Add more oil if necessary. Set aside in warm place until ready to serve.
5. On work surface, cut each eggroll package into 4 pieces, cutting across folded edge.

Serve *martabak* warm or cold, as a light lunch or snack. You may pick them up either with your hands or with chopsticks. A small serving of cucumber salad is usually eaten with them.

Meat Satay

Mention Thailand cooking and everyone seems to know about the famous and delicious thinly sliced, **marinated**, skewered, and grilled meat-on-sticks served with dipping sauces.

Cooking tip: Cut the meat while slightly frozen; it will be easier to cut into thin strips.

Yield: serves 6 to 8

1/2 pound *each* skinless, boneless chicken breast, and either boneless beef or pork loin, cut as thinly as possible into strips
1 teaspoon curry powder
salt and pepper to taste
1/2 cup unsweetened coconut milk, homemade (see recipe page 208), canned, or frozen (thawed)
1/2 cup apple cider vinegar
2 tablespoons sugar
2 tablespoons dried, crushed red pepper, more or less to taste
1 onion, **finely chopped**
1 tablespoon fresh **coriander**, finely chopped, or 1/2 teaspoon dried

Equipment: Large-size shallow dish, medium-size bowl, 24 6- to 12-inch long water-soaked bamboo skewers (more or less as needed, or use metal skewers), baking sheet

1. Put strips of chicken and meat in large shallow dish.
2. Put curry powder, salt and pepper to taste, coconut milk, vinegar, sugar, red pepper, onion, and coriander in medium mixing bowl, add strips, and mix well to coat. Refrigerate for 1 hour, mixing frequently to coat strips.
3. Set oven rack about 6-inches under broiler and preheat to high.
4. If using wooden skewers, you **must** soak skewers in water for about 30 minutes. Thread chicken and meat strips onto separate skewers. Place skewers side-by-side on baking sheet and broil for about 3 minutes, until lightly browned. Turn strips over and broil other side until cooked through and browned (about 3 minutes).

To serve *satays*, place skewers on large platter and give each person a small dish of peanut dipping sauce. Everyone picks up a skewer and dips the end to be eaten in the dipping sauce.

Peanut Dipping Sauce

Cooks in Thailand and other Asian countries prepare many different dipping sauces to use with *satays*, but the peanut sauce is the most popular. Thais usually grind peanuts to a paste for the following recipe, and coconut milk is sweetened. We're suggesting a simpler procedure that will provide similar results.

Yield: about 1 1/8 cup

1/2 cup smooth peanut butter
1/2 cup coconut cream, canned (available at most supermarkets)
3 tablespoons soy sauce

Equipment: Mixing spoon or electric blender, small-size bowl

Use mixing spoon or blender, combine peanut butter, coconut cream, and soy sauce until thoroughly mixed. Refrigerate until ready to serve.

Serve each person about 2 tablespoons of dipping sauce with *satay*.

Laos

Climatically, Cambodia, Vietnam, and Laos are very much alike; they're all entirely tropical. Laos, however, differs from its neighboring countries by having no coastline. It is a mountainous, forest-covered land that makes entry difficult; so difficult, in fact, that a great part of the country is still unexplored. The only low flatland is on the eastern shore of the Mekong River, where the majority of people live. It is here that the staple crop of rice is grown using wet-rice farming techniques. Laotians are not able to grow enough food to feed the entire population, and so imports and gifts have to be acquired.

Laos, along with Vietnam and Cambodia, was once part of French Indochina, yet the cooking in Laos reflects little of the French style. It is a blending of neighboring Southern Chinese cooking and Thai spices and foods. The foods of Laos are basically simple, quite spicy, and always colorful. Unlike many other Asian countries, Laotians eat with their hands instead of using chopsticks and spoons. They prefer sticky rice as an eating tool; the rice is taken little by little with the fingers, **kneaded** slightly, and used as a "pusher" or for sopping up juices.

Like other Asian countries, rice is eaten at almost every meal. The day begins with a hearty bowl of porridge referred to as the "national breakfast soup." In Laos, it is made of spiced coconut milk and rice-like noodles, and it is called *khao poon*. In the cities khao poon stands are set up early each morning where Laotians can hurriedly buy and eat bowls of porridge on their way to work or school. The name *khao poon* means "rice vermicelli," and a variety of dishes are made with it as the basic ingredient. Italian vermicelli noodles, available at all supermarkets, are made with wheat flour and should not be used in place of rice noodles. Oriental vermicelli noodles are made with rice flour. It is not necessary to cook dried rice noodles because they are already cooked. To make them edible, they need only to be **reconstituted**. To do that, soak the noodles in water for about 15 minutes to soften them and remove some of the starch. If the rice noodles are thick, they might need to soak a little longer. Once the noodles are soft they can be added to hot broth or **stir-fry**.

Khao Poon with Chicken

Yield: serves 4 to 6

1 chicken, quartered
3 cups water, more or less as needed
2 teaspoons peeled, grated fresh ginger or 1 teaspoon ground ginger
2 tablespoons chopped, fresh **coriander** (also called **cilantro**) or 1 teaspoon ground coriander
6 green onions, **trimmed** and **finely chopped** (set aside half for serving)
3 tablespoons fish sauce (*nuoc mam*), homemade (see recipe page 177), or bottled (available at Asian stores)
6 ounces rice vermicelli (prepare according to directions on package, drain, and rinse with cold water—available at some supermarkets and all Asian food stores)
1 cup finely chopped Chinese cabbage (also called Napa)
1 small papaya, peeled, **seeded**, thinly sliced
1/2 cup chopped canned bamboo shoots (available at most supermarkets)
1 teaspoon ground hot red pepper, more or less to taste, for serving
2 tablespoons sugar, for serving bowl
salt to taste, for serving

Equipment: Large-size saucepan with cover, mixing spoon, large serving bowl, strainer

1. Put chicken in saucepan and add water to cover, add ginger, coriander, half the green onions, and 1 tablespoon fish sauce. Bring to a boil over high heat, reduce to simmer, cover, and cook for about 1 hour until tender. Remove chicken from broth and set aside to cool. Continue simmering the broth, uncovered, for about 1/2 hour more or until broth is reduced to about 2 cups.
2. Using clean hands, remove skin from cooled chicken and discard. Pull meat off the bones and cut into bite-size strips. Set aside.
3. Arrange cabbage, papaya slices, and bamboo shoots in center of serving bowl and cover with noodles and then shredded chicken. Pour about 1 cup of strained broth over the mixture and sprinkle with remaining green onions.

Serve with small side dishes of remaining fish sauce, ground red pepper, sugar, salt to taste, and remaining chicken broth.

Kay Patkhin Ginger

Asians love chicken and have many flavorful, yet simple, ways of preparing it. The following recipe is a good example. The dish can be prepared with cooked and **diced** leftover chicken and is still wonderfully delicious.

Yield: serves 4 to 6

6 cups finely **diced** chicken meat (removed from bones)
salt and pepper to taste

2 to 4 tablespoons vegetable oil
1 garlic clove, **finely chopped,** or 1/2 teaspoon garlic granules
1 onion, sliced
1 piece fresh ginger, about 1 inch long, finely chopped or 1 teaspoon ground ginger
6 green onions, finely chopped

Equipment: Medium-size mixing bowl, **wok** or large-size skillet, mixing spoon or metal spatula

1. Put chicken in bowl and season with salt and pepper to taste.
2. Heat 2 tablespoons oil in wok or skillet over high heat. Add garlic, onion, and ginger, mix well, and reduce to low. Cook for about 3 minutes until onions are soft. Add chicken and mix well. Increase heat to medium-high, and, stirring continually, cook until chicken pieces are golden brown, adding more oil if necessary. Reduce heat to medium and cook for about 8 minutes until chicken is fully cooked. Remove from heat and mix in green onions.

Serve *kay patkhin* hot with side bowls of either noodles or rice.

Cambodia

Cambodia is a tiny country tucked between Thailand, Laos, and Vietnam. The Cambodians are mostly village people, whose lives have been plagued with wars and starvation. Most of the people live in the center of the country where annual flooding makes the land rich and fertile for growing rice. The Mekong River and the Tonle Sap Lake are centrally located, making fish a primary source of food for the people. Fish farming is practiced in the Tonle Sap. Fish is eaten fresh or can be  dried or salted for storage and eaten later. Salted fish is soaked in water to leach out the salt. Besides fish, other crops include sweet potatoes, onions, chili peppers, oranges, bananas, pineapple, coconuts, tomatoes, and corn.

Chopsticks are used, as are little tables that people squat around. Tea is the main drink. Meals consist of steamed or fried rice mixed with fish. Seasonings include chilies, mint, or garlic. Famous sauces are made of fish and are called *tuk trei*; these sauces and a fish paste called *prahoc* are used in cooking and flavoring meals. On special occasions shrimp may be served. Roasted sunflower seeds are tasty snacks. The people of the coast have the treasures from the Gulf of Thailand to catch and eat. Squid are plentiful in the waters off the Cambodian coast, and it's common to see thousands of squid drying in the sun on bamboo poles suspended over the boat decks, hanging like crystal prisms from a chandelier.

Stir-fried Squid

Squid, often called by the Italian name *calamari*, are cheap and very easy to cook. To clean squid can be tricky and so it is best to buy them already cleaned. Cleaned and frozen squid are available at many supermarkets, and most fresh fish markets carry a goodly supply since squid thrive in American coastal waters.

Yield: serves 2

2 tablespoons sesame oil
1 tablespoon fresh grated ginger
1 clove **finely chopped** garlic or 1/2 teaspoon garlic granules
1 red pepper, **cored, seeded**, cut into thin strips
8-ounces squid, fresh or frozen, thawed, cleaned and cut into 1/4-inch wide rings
1 cup whole string beans, fresh (**blanched**) or frozen (thawed)
1 tablespoon sugar, more or less to taste
1 tablespoon soy sauce, more or less to taste
salt and pepper to taste

Equipment: **Wok** or medium-size skillet, mixing spoon

1. Heat oil in wok or skillet over medium-high heat. Add ginger and garlic, mix, and cook a few seconds to flavor the oil. Add red peppers and mix to coat, about 1 minute.
2. Add squid, and, stirring continually, cook until they become **opaque white** and firm, about 3 minutes.
3. Add string beans, sprinkle with sugar, soy sauce, and salt and pepper to taste, and mix well. Cook just long enough to heat through. Do not overcook or squid become tough (about 4 minutes).

Serve stir-fried squid over rice or noodles.

Vietnam

Vietnam is a long, narrow country bordering the South China Sea. Vietnamese people are of Chinese descent. They migrated from the north, bringing with them the cooking of their homeland and applying it to the native tropical foods of their new surroundings. The Vietnamese dishes and flavors are unique and distinctive, unlike any others. For the Vietnamese, fish and shellfish are important, along with duck; vegetables, however, are eaten with rice at almost every meal. If rice isn't eaten as a grain it's eaten in the form of noodles made from rice flour. The favorite soup, called *pho*, uses a brittle noodle called "rice sticks." Commonly used spices include ginger, lemon grass, chilies, garlic, and star anise. Besides rice, sweet potatoes, corn, **sorghum**, citrus fruits, bananas, melons, and garden vegetables are grown. The best locations for farming are along the rich soils of the Red River delta and the Mekong River delta.

Fishing is a very important industry. Nothing is wasted—sauces are made from crustacean shells and fish heads and bones to give flavor to soups and stews. It seems as though every Vietnamese recipe includes a few spoonfuls of fish sauce called *nuoc mam*. *Nuoc mam* is made from salt and fish that has fermented for nine to twelve months. We believe the following recipe using anchovy paste is a good substitute if you cannot find *nuoc mam* in the store. Bottled *nuoc mam* is available at some supermarkets and most Asian markets.

Nuoc Mam   *Fish Dipping Sauce*

Yield: about 1 cup

1/2 cup soy sauce
1 teaspoon anchovy paste, more or less to taste
3 cloves **finely chopped** garlic or 1 teaspoon garlic granules
1/2 teaspoon dried red pepper flakes, more or less to taste
1 tablespoon lemon juice
1 tablespoon sugar
1/8 cup water

Equipment: Small-size jar with cover

Put soy sauce, anchovy paste, garlic, red pepper, lemon juice, sugar, and water in jar, cover, and shake until well blended.

To serve *nuoc mam*, put the jar on the table for people to use as they like. Refrigerate and use as needed in Asian recipes.

Nem Nuong   *Grilled Meatballs*

Very often, hot spicy meat is wrapped in lettuce leaves and eaten like a sandwich. The meat and ingredients are pulverized to a smooth paste. Unless you have a food processor, this is time consuming and difficult to do. We suggest chopping the ingredients as finely as possible; you will still taste the flavors of Vietnam with an added pleasant crunchiness.

Yield: serves 4 to 6

1 pound extra finely ground pork
1 onion, **finely chopped**
2 cloves, finely chopped garlic or 1/2 teaspoon garlic granules
1 teaspoon sugar
1 tablespoon all-purpose flour
salt and pepper to taste
6 or 8 large lettuce leaves, washed and dried

Equipment: Medium-size mixing bowl, mixing spoons aluminum foil, broiler pan with rack, oven mitts, tongs

Place broiler tray on top shelf in oven, about 6 inches under broiler heat, and preheat broiler to medium hot.
1. Put pork, onion, garlic, sugar, flour, and salt and pepper to taste in mixing bowl and mix until well blended.
2. Using wet hands, form meat into ping-pong-size balls.
3. Place meatballs side-by-side on broiler rack. Broil in oven until firm and fully cooked. Brown evenly on all sides, turn 2 or 3 times wearing oven mitts and using metal tongs (about 5 to 8 minutes total broiling time.)

Serve meatballs on platter surrounded with lettuce leaves. Serve with a side dish of vermicelli rice and dipping sauce. To eat the meatballs, slide them onto a lettuce leaf, add a spoonful of rice, and sprinkle with *nuoc mam*. Wrap the leaf around the mixture, making sure nothing can fall out, and then pick it up in your hands to eat.

Korea (North and South)

Sweet potatoes, soy beans, rice, corn, wheat, barley, and fruit trees all grow well in Korean soil along with most garden vegetables, such as carrots, onions, and lettuce. They are all staples of the Korean diet. There is one vegetable, however, that stands out from all others and is the most treasured food of all, cabbage. For thousands of years pickled cabbage called *kimchi* has been Korea's national dish and is eaten at every meal. It is packed in school lunch boxes, taken on picnics, put in and on everything from breakfast to late night snacks. If *kimchi* isn't on the table, the meal isn't complete. Koreans often organize work parties and help each other prepare huge batches of this pungent smelling dish. Throughout Korea, from every city-dweller's balcony to farmhouse roofs, vats of Chinese cabbage are fermenting, turning into the beloved *kimchi*.

Koreans like meat, especially beef. A single 12-ounce T-bone steak can easily feed a Korean family of six because no Korean would ever think of eating large amounts of meat as Americans do. Meat is cut into bite-size pieces or thin strips making a little go a long way. It is always served and mixed with other filling foods. Meat is either stir fried or quick grilled over hot charcoal. Koreans eat with chopsticks and spoons.

Bul Ko Kee   *Barbecued Beef*

Barbecued beef, *kimchi*, and a scoop of rice, wrapped together in a lettuce leaf, and eaten like a sandwich, is a popular dish in Korea.

Yield: serves 4 to 6

1/4 cup soy sauce
2 to 4 tablespoons vegetable oil
1/4 teaspoon pepper
3 green onions, **finely chopped**
2 cloves garlic, finely chopped or 1/2 teaspoon garlic granules
2 tablespoons vegetable oil
2 pounds lean boneless beef, cut across grain, 1/4-inch-thick by 2-inch slices (for easier cutting, freeze beef for 1 hour)
2 teaspoons sesame seeds

Equipment: Large-size mixing bowl, mixing spoon, **wok** or large-size skillet

1. Put soy sauce, 2 tablespoons vegetable oil, pepper, green onions, and garlic in bowl and mix well. Add meat and coat with mixture; cover and refrigerate for 30 minutes. Mix several times to make sure meat is well coated with mixture.
2. Heat remaining oil in wok or skillet over high heat. Drain beef over the bowl and add to hot oil, stirring continually until cooked through (about 3 minutes). Transfer to serving platter and sprinkle with sesame seeds.

Serve with a side dish of *kimchi* and either boiled noodles or boiled rice.

Kimchi   Pickled Cabbage

There are many variations for *kimchi*, such as adding other vegetables with the cabbage. It can also be made hotter and more spicy, because the longer kimchi ferments the stronger and spicier it gets.

Yield: about 4 cups

2 cups chopped Chinese cabbage (also called Napa cabbage), washed and drained
1/2 cup coarse (kosher) salt
4 green onions (including tops), **finely chopped**
1 cup finely shredded carrots
1 tablespoon peeled, grated fresh ginger or 1/2 teaspoon ground ginger
3 cloves garlic, finely chopped or 1 teaspoon garlic granules
1 teaspoon sugar
4 tablespoons dried red pepper flakes

Equipment: Large-size mixing bowl, **colander** or strainer, 2-quart crock or glass jar with cover

1. Toss cabbage with salt in large mixing bowl to coat evenly. Set aside for 30 minutes; toss frequently.
2. Transfer cabbage to colander or strainer, rinse under cold water, and drain well. Return to large bowl and add green onions, carrots, ginger, garlic, sugar, red pepper flakes, and mix well to blend.
3. Pack mixture in crock or jar, cover, and keep at room temperature for about 2 days, then refrigerate.

Serve as a relish with other dishes or add to meat, soup, or stews.

Japan

Japan is made up of four separate islands located off the coast of eastern Asia. Japanese people are known worldwide for their artistic presentation of food. Everything is precisely cut into bite-sized pieces, which are easy and fast to cook and easy to eat with chopsticks. **Stir-frying** foods helps them to retain their natural flavors. At every meal you will find rice: Japanese rice is short and of sticky consistency. A home-cooked Japanese meal is simple

and frugal, usually consisting of rice, soybeans in some form such as miso soup, and pickles, fish and seaweed. For some special occasions, however, up to 26 side dishes will be served.

Fishing is a large food industry in Japan, and fish are important in the Japanese diet as are an extensive variety of vegetables. Beef is enjoyed, but fish is the predominate source of protein in Japan. Noodles, for those of you who get in trouble for slurping food, are the food to slurp. No one will look at you twice if you slurp hot noodles in Japan, for it is felt that you need to cool the hot noodles a bit by pulling some cool air in before they enter your mouth.

Sweet desserts are rare in Japan, and fresh fruit is preferred as a fitting end to the meal. Mango, peeled, sliced, and served with a bit of lemon juice, is a favorite among the Japanese. Orange trees and golden persimmon seem to grow in every yard, and the choice of other fruits is overwhelming.

Chicken Egg Soup

Yield: serves 4 to 6

6 cups chicken broth, homemade or canned
1/4 cup **finely chopped** celery
1/4 cup finely chopped carrots
1/4 cup finely chopped onion
1 egg, beaten
salt and pepper to taste
1 green onion top, finely sliced diagonally, for garnish

Equipment: Medium-size saucepan, strainer, medium-size bowl, mixing spoon

1. Put chicken broth, celery, carrots, and onion in saucepan. Bring soup to a boil, reduce heat to simmer, and cook for 1/2 hour.
2. **Strain** soup into bowl. (Refrigerate or freeze vegetables to use at another time.) Pour liquid back into saucepan, bring to a boil, and reduce to simmer. Stirring continually, slowly pour egg into soup, heat through, add salt and pepper to taste, and serve.

To serve soup, ladle into bowls and float green onion garnish on top of each.

Sunomono   Cucumber & Shrimp Salad

Sunomono is a tangy salad often made with fish stock. The arrangement of food on the plate, color balance, and contrasts are as important as the taste is to the Japanese cooks.

Yield: serves 4 to 6

1/2 pound cooked shrimp, peeled and **deveined,** (26-30 count)
1 cucumber, peeled and thinly sliced
1/2 cup rice vinegar, available at most supermarkets or Asian stores
1/4 cup sugar
4 tablespoons soy sauce, more or less to taste
4 to 6 leaf lettuce leaves, washed, dried, (refrigerate to crisp)

Equipment: Medium-size mixing bowl, mixing spoon, jar with cover

1. Put shrimp and cucumbers in mixing bowl.
2. *Prepare dressing:* Combine vinegar, sugar, and soy sauce in small jar, cover, and shake well. Pour dressing over shrimp and cucumbers, toss gently, and refrigerate until ready to serve. Toss again before serving.

To serve, put a lettuce leaf on each individual salad plate. Divide cucumber slices equally among plates and arrange on lettuce. Arrange an equal number of shrimp on each serving.

Teriyaki   Marinated Beef

Yield: serves 4 to 6

1/2 cup teriyaki sauce, available at most supermarkets
1 tablespoon peeled and **finely chopped** fresh ginger or 1 teaspoon ground ginger
2 pounds lean beef, sirloin, or round steak, cut into 3- to 4-inch strips, 1/4 inch thick

Equipment: Large-size mixing bowl or large-size plastic baggie, mixing spoon, tongs or long-handled fork

1. Put teriyaki sauce and ginger in bowl or baggie and mix well. Add beef strips and coat with mixture for at least 30 minutes, stirring frequently.
2. Set broiler tray about 6 inches under heat and preheat broiler to medium.
3. Lay meat strips side-by-side on broiler pan. Broil on one side for about 3 minutes, then, carefully using tongs or long-handled fork to turn meat, broil on other side for about 3 minutes, or to desired doneness.

Serve *teriyaki* on a platter with side bowls of boiled rice. Guests help themselves using chopsticks.

Gohan   Boiled Rice

There are many different kinds of rice in the world. Japanese rice is short grained and cooks to a very sticky consistency, making it ideal to eat with chopsticks.

Yield: serves 4

1 cup Japanese uncooked short grain rice, available at most supermarkets and Asian food stores
1 1/4 cups water

Equipment: **Colander** or strainer, medium-size saucepan with cover

1. Wash rice under running water until water runs clear. Allow rice to soak in saucepan for about 30 minutes and then drain in colander or strainer.
2. Return drained rice to saucepan, add water, and bring to a boil over high heat. Reduce heat to simmer, cover, and cook for about 15 minutes until water has been absorbed by rice. Reduce heat to warm and keep covered, allowing rice to steam for about 15 minutes.

Serve rice in individual bowls to be eaten with chopsticks. The rice bowl is held in the left hand, close to the mouth. The chopsticks are used to push the rice into the mouth as the bowl is slowly rotated in the hand.

The following recipe is a very popular Japanese meal-in-a-bowl called *domburi*. The one we have selected, *oyako domburi*, is made with chicken and eggs. *Oyako* means "mother and child," referring to the chicken and egg. *Domburi* means "big bowl." Deep bowls of rice are topped with an assortment of vegetables and mixed with egg, meat, or poutry. *Domburi* are inexpensive and easy to prepare.

Yield: serves 2

4 mushrooms, sliced
3 green onions, finely sliced diagonally (set aside half of onion slices for garnish)
1 skinless, boneless chicken breast, cut into bite-size pieces
1/4 cup chicken broth
2 tablespoons soy sauce
1 teaspoon ginger, fresh, **finely chopped** or 1/2 teaspoon ground
1 teaspoon sesame oil
2 tablespoons vegetable oil
4 eggs, beaten
2 cups warm cooked rice (short-grain preferred)
1/2 teaspoon sesame seeds, for garnish

Equipment: Medium-size bowl, small-size bowl, medium-size skillet or **wok** with cover, mixing spoon

1. Put mushrooms, green onions, and chicken in medium-size bowl and mix well.
2. Put chicken broth, soy sauce, ginger, and sesame oil in small bowl, mix well, and pour over chicken mixture. Mix well to coat.
3. Heat oil in skillet or wok over medium-high heat. Add chicken mixture, and, stirring continually, cook until chicken is cooked through (about 3 minutes). Add eggs, mix well, cover, and cook for about 3 minutes, until eggs are set. Remove from heat, keep covered, and let mixture steam for about 3 minutes, depending on how firm you want your eggs.
4. Put warm rice in individual bowls. Divide and spoon egg mixture equally on top of rice. Sprinkle with sesame seeds and the rest of the green onions for garnish.

Serve as the main meal with extra soy sauce on the side.

Philippines

The Philippines are a group of mountainous islands off the coast of mainland Asia. Most Filipinos are of Malaysian descent and are very "westernized." Spaniards settled in the Philippines, uniting the country with Christianity and a common language, Spanish. Families are closely knit, with strong family ties. Everyone, including grandparents, children, aunts, uncles, and even sometimes godparents live and work together for a better way of life. Each meal, including breakfast, is a group project, with many people sharing the kitchen work and food. The Philippines have long been the crossroad for migrating people from all corners of the world, and the food reflects the blending of many cultures. Pineapples, coconuts, sugar cane, rice, and corn are among the crops grown in the Philippines. Fish and shellfish are plentiful, but the people also raise chickens and pigs, which contribute greatly to the Filipinos' diet. The national dish, *adobo*, is made with chicken and pork.

Adobo   Chicken and Pork Stew

Yield: serves 6

2 to 3 pounds chicken, cut into serving-size pieces
1 pound pork, cut into 1-inch cubes
3 cloves garlic, **finely chopped,** or 1 teaspoon garlic granules
1/2 cup cider vinegar
1 tablespoon sugar
4 whole allspice
salt and pepper to taste
2 cups water

Equipment: Large-size saucepan with cover or **Dutch oven**, mixing spoon

1. Put chicken, pork, garlic, vinegar, sugar, allspice, and salt and pepper to taste in saucepan or Dutch oven, add water, and bring to a boil over high heat. Reduce heat to simmer, cover, and cook for about 1 1/2 hours, stirring frequently to prevent sticking.
2. Remove cover and continue cooking until liquid thickens like gravy (about 15 minutes). The mixture should be rather dry, not soupy.

Serve *adobo* hot, transfer to a serving platter, with a side dish of rice.

Misua   Angel Hair Noodles in Soup

Noodle shops are a fast-food craze in the Philippines. For a few pesos a heaping plate of noodles is quickly served up with choice of toppings . The Philippine noodles used in the following recipe are extremely thin. We suggest substituting angel hair noodles, available in most supermarkets.

Yield: serves 4 to 6

2 tablespoons vegetable oil
3 cloves garlic, **finely chopped,** or 1 teaspoon garlic granules
4 green onions, finely chopped
1 yellow onion, finely chopped
6 cups chicken broth, homemade or canned
2 cups finely chopped spinach, fresh or frozen (thawed)
salt and pepper to taste
3 ounces Angel hair noodles or Filipino fine wheat vermicelli noodles

Equipment: Large-size saucepan with cover, mixing spoon, ladle

1. Heat oil in saucepan over medium-high heat, add garlic, green onions, and yellow onion, and fry until soft, about 3 minutes. Add chicken broth, mix well, and bring to

a boil. Add spinach, reduce heat to simmer, and cook for about 2 minutes. Add salt and pepper to taste. Mix well.

2. Remove from heat and add noodles over the top of soup. Do not mix. Push noodles down with back of spoon as they soften and absorb liquid, cover, and simmer for about 5 minutes, or until soft. Remove from heat and let stand, covered, until soft, not soggy (about 5 minutes).

Serve *misua* immediately in individual soup bowls so noodles don't get soggy. Spoon a heaping serving of noodles in bowl and fill with spinach soup.

Maja Blanca   Coconut Cake

In the Phillipines, coconuts are used in and on everything. The following recipe is a firm, custard-like cake requiring no baking—the oven is used only to toast grated coconut. The cake is very unusual but easy to make.

Yield: serves about 6-8

2 cups tightly packed, finely **shredded** coconut, fresh (see recipe page 208), frozen, or canned (sweetened)
3 tablespoons granulated sugar, more or less to taste
4 tablespoons butter or margarine
1/2 cup cornstarch
1/2 cup tightly packed light brown sugar
1/4 cup water
2 cups coconut milk, fresh (see recipe page 208), frozen, or canned (unsweetened)
3 egg yolks (refrigerate egg white to use at another time)
whipped topping for garnish

Equipment: Medium-size mixing bowl, 9-inch pie pan, **whisk** or mixing spoon, medium-size saucepan

1. Preheat oven to 325°F.
2. If using freshly grated unsweetened coconut, add about 3 tablespoons of granulated sugar, more or less to taste. No sugar is needed if canned sweetened coconut is used.
3. Put coconut and melted butter or margarine in medium mixing bowl, and, using clean fingers, blend well. Using fingers, press coconut onto pie pan bottom and up sides, making a pie crust. Put in oven and bake for about 5 minutes, until lightly golden. Remove from oven and cool to room temperature.
4. Put cornstarch and sugar in medium saucepan, add water, and mix well to dissolve cornstarch. Add coconut milk and egg yolks, and, stirring continually, heat over medium-high heat until mixture boils. Reduce heat to low and stir vigorously, until smooth and thick (about 5 minutes). Remove from heat and pour mixture into coconut pie crust. Cool to room temperature and refrigerate for about 3 hours to set.

To serve, cut into wedges and add a dollop of whipped topping.

Philippine Fruit Salad

The following fruit salad is a mixture of many different fruits growing in the tropical Philippines. It makes a colorful and delicious salad or dessert as well as a decorative **buffet** presentation. Slice and add bananas just before serving for best flavor and color.

Yield: serves 4 to 6

2 pineapples
1 pint strawberries, rinsed, hulled, and halved (leave 4 whole for garnish)
1 cantaloupe, cut in half, **seeded**, and cut into balls
1 honeydew melon, cut in half, seeded, and cut into balls
2 kiwifruit, peeled, sliced in rounds, about 1/4 inch thick
1 cup **shredded** coconut, fresh (see recipe on page 208), frozen, or canned
2 bananas, peeled and sliced in rounds, about 1/4 inch thick
1 cup heavy cream, whipped, or frozen whipped topping (thawed)

Equipment: Melon baller, large-size **serrated knife**, grapefruit knife or sharp paring knife, large-size bowl with cover, mixing spoon

1. Put pineapples on work surface, and, using serrated knife, cut each in half, lengthwise, including top leaves. Carefully scoop out flesh from each half, leaving about 1/2-inch shell all around, making pineapple bowls. Set aside.
2. Cut scooped-out pineapple flesh into bite-size pieces and put into mixing bowl. Add strawberries, melon balls, kiwi, and coconut and toss gently, using clean hands. Cover and refrigerate until ready to serve.
3. Set pineapple shells on large round serving platter with their tops hanging over the outer edge. Remove fruit from refrigerator, add bananas and whipped cream or whipped topping, and toss gently to blend. Transfer mixture to pineapple shells and pile high. Garnish with whole strawberries.

Serve with a large serving spoon, as salad or dessert for a luncheon or **buffet**. Have guests help themselves to the salad.

Malaysia / Singapore

Malaysia consists of a long, narrow peninsula and part of the island of Borneo. It sits just north of the equator where it is extremely hot and humid. With a range of 65 to 200 inches of yearly rainfall, the ground is pretty muddy most of the time, and the people must build their homes on high posts to keep dry. Most Malaysians have small plots of land where they grow their staples—rice, sweet potatoes, and sago (which is a starch extracted from the stem of the sago palm and which is used as a thickener in food). Everyone, including inlanders, enjoys fish. It is often salted and dried. Fruit trees such as coconut, banana, guava, and papaya thrive in the tropical climate. Another popular fruit, not soon to be exported widely from the region, is the *durian*, which is known by Westerners more for its highly offensive odor than for its taste, since few have had the grit to sample it.

Three ethnic groups live side-by-side in Malaysia—Chinese, Indians, and native Malaysians. Each group has its distinct habits and traditions. Malaysians are Muslim, and therefore do not eat pork. The Hindu Indians are vegetarians, but Sikh Indians living in Malaysia are not. The Chinese have imported Chinese cookery and enjoy pork very much. Each group borrows from each other at times, but still retains the original cooking traditions. A Malay specialty food is *satay*, a grilled kebab of **marinated** chicken, beef, or mutton, similar to the Thai food of the same name (see page 172 for the recipe).

Singapore is small, independent nation just south of the Malay Peninsula. It comprises Singapore Island and 60 islets. Singapore City, the capital, is one of the world's busiest ports. A Singapore cooking style has developed known as *Peranaken*. It is a multiethnic blend of old Chinese immigrant cooking with Indonesian, Malaysian, and Indian cooking styles. Coconut milk is used in many of the dishes. "Hawker food," for which Singapore was famous, was sold by street vendors who trundled their carts through the streets of Singapore. They now operate in modern food centers, licensed by the government.

Lemon Rice

Yield: serves 6

1 cup brown uncooked long-grain rice, washed, available at most supermarkets, Asian food stores, or health food stores
2 cups hot water
4 tablespoons butter, margarine, or **ghee**
1/4 cup lemon juice
salt to taste

Equipment: Medium-size saucepan with cover or **Dutch oven**, mixing spoon

1. Heat rice in dry saucepan or Dutch oven over medium heat, stirring continually until rice "pops" or is lightly browned, about 6 minutes.
2. Add hot water; butter, margarine, or *ghee;* and lemon juice. Mix well and bring to a boil over high heat. Reduce heat to simmer, cover, and cook until liquid is absorbed and rice is tender (about 25 minutes).
3. Remove from heat but keep covered for about 5 minutes to steam. Season with salt to taste and mix well.

Serve *lemon rice* as a side dish with fish or chicken.

Pengat Pisang   Banana Porridge

Yield: serves 6 to 8

4 cups coconut milk, homemade (see recipe page 208), canned, or frozen (thawed)
3 teaspoons grated fresh ginger or 1 1/2 teaspoons ground ginger
1 cup sugar, more or less to taste
6 ripe bananas, mashed
1 tablespoon **tapioca** pearls

Equipment: Medium-size saucepan, mixing spoon, medium-size serving bowl

Put coconut milk and ginger in saucepan, bring to a boil over medium-high heat, and then reduce to simmer. Add sugar, bananas, and tapioca, stirring continually until mixture thickens, about 6 minutes. Remove from heat, pour into service bowl, cool to room temperature, and refrigerate.

Serve porridge hot or cold, for dessert or breakfast.

Biryani is an Indian dish that the Sikh Indians must have imported to Singapore; it is very popular in Singapore.

Yield: serves 4 to 6

1 pound boneless lamb shoulder cut into 1-inch **cubes**
1/2 cup plain yogurt, homemade or commercial
2 tablespoons vegetable oil
1 cup **finely chopped** onion
3 cloves garlic, finely chopped or 1 teaspoon garlic granules
2 cups chicken broth, homemade or canned
2 teaspoons ground cinnamon
1 tablespoon ground cumin
2 teaspoons finely chopped fresh ginger or 1 teaspoon ground ginger
salt and pepper to taste

Equipment: Medium-size bowl, mixing spoon, medium-size skillet with cover

1. Put lamb in bowl, add yogurt, and mix well. Set aside to **marinate** for about 30 minutes.
2. Heat oil in skillet over high heat and add onion and garlic. Stirring continually, fry for about 3 minutes until golden. Add meat and yogurt mixture, chicken broth, cinnamon, cumin, ginger, and salt and pepper to taste to skillet and mix well. Bring to a boil, reduce heat to simmer, cover, and cook for about 40 minutes until meat is tender.

Serve over *biryani rice* (recipe follows).

Biryani Rice

Yield: serves 4 to 6

1 cup uncooked basmati rice, available at most supermarkets and Middle East stores
3 cups water
1 teaspoon ground cinnamon
1/2 teaspoon ground cloves
1/4 teaspoon ground **turmeric**
salt to taste
4 **hard-cooked eggs**, peeled and quartered, for garnish

Equipment: Strainer, medium-size saucepan with cover, wooden mixing spoon

1. Put rice in strainer and rinse under running water. Drain well.
2. Put water in saucepan, add rice, and bring to a boil over high heat. Reduce heat to simmer, add cinnamon, cloves, turmeric, and salt to taste and mix well. Cover and cook for about 10 minutes, until water is absorbed. Stir frequently to prevent sticking. Reduce heat to low and keep covered to steam rice for about 20 minutes until tender. **Fluff** rice with a fork before serving.

To serve, transfer rice to a large bowl, arrange *biryani* (recipe above) on top, and garnish with hard-cooked egg wedges. *Biryani rice* is also served with *satay*.

Indonesia

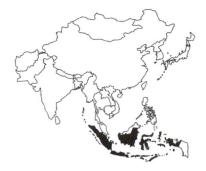

For centuries Indonesia, now a nation of 3,000 islands which include Java, Sumatra, Sulawesi, parts of Borneo and New Guinea, and Baki, was known to Westerners as the source of spices. The Moluccas, also a part of this diverse nation, were called the "spice islands." Today Indonesia not only exports cloves and pepper, but is also a fertile supplier of rice, sweet potatoes, coffee, tea, peanuts, soybeans, and sugar cane. The Dutch controlled the Indonesian Archipelago from the seventeenth century to 1949, when under internal and international pressure they granted Indonesia independence. To this day, Dutch remains the common language of many islanders. Rather than bring Dutch food to Indonesians, the Dutch brought Indonesian food to the world, creating a style of dining known as *rijsttafel*, meaning "rice table" in Dutch, in which as many as 30 dishes are placed on a large table and guests serve themselves. Most dishes are vegetarian; very little meat is eaten, and when it is, a little goes a long way. Huge bowls of cooked dry white rice are served with every meal, and some of the dishes are simply bowls of fresh sliced pineapple, fresh and fried bananas, peanuts, pistachios, fresh coconuts, mango, cucumbers, and fish. Vendors sell many foods on the streets. Cakes and breads, noodles and meatballs, and rice with fish are just a few of the offerings of these hard-working vendors.

Timor Achar   *Pepper Salad with Sesame Seeds*

Yield: serves 6

1/4 cup apple cider vinegar
1 teaspoon sugar
1/2 teaspoon salt
2 tablespoons sesame seeds
1/4 pound snow peas, **trimmed** and cut lengthwise into thin strips
1 red onion, thinly sliced
1 green bell pepper, **cored, seeded**, finely sliced
1 red bell pepper, cored, seeded, finely sliced
1 tomato, cut in 6 wedges

Equipment: Small-size jar with cover, small-size skillet, salad bowl, salad tools

1. Put vinegar, sugar, and salt in jar, cover, and shake to blend; refrigerate.
2. Heat sesame seeds in small skillet over medium heat, tossing until browned (about 3 minutes). Set aside.
3. Put snow peas, onion, and green and red bell peppers into salad bowl, pour over the dressing, and toss to blend using salad tools. Sprinkle with sesame seeds.

Serve the salad chilled with rice and other dishes.

Gado-gado   Cooked Vegetable Salad

This traditional cooked vegetable salad with savory peanut dressing makes a refreshing lunch on a hot summer day.

Yield: serves 6

1 tablespoon vegetable oil
1 cup bean curd (tofu), **cubed**
1 cup **shredded** cabbage, fresh, **blanched**
1/2 cup sliced carrots, fresh (blanched) or frozen (thawed)
1/2 cup diagonally sliced green beans, fresh (blanched) or frozen (thawed)
2 tomatoes, sliced
1 cucumber, peeled, sliced
3 cooked potatoes, peeled and sliced
salt and pepper to taste
2 **hard-cooked eggs**, peeled and sliced
Peanut sauce (*katjang saos*) (see recipe below)

Equipment: Small-size skillet, slotted spoon, paper towels, salad bowl, salad tools

1. Heat oil in skillet over medium-high heat, add bean curd, and fry for about 8 minutes until lightly browned. Remove with slotted spoon and then drain on paper towels.
2. Arrange cabbage, carrots, green beans, tomatoes, cucumber, and potatoes in salad bowl. Add salt and pepper to taste and eggs for garnish. Drizzle with *katjang saos* (peanut sauce) and serve.

Serve salad with extra peanut sauce.

Katjang Saos   Peanut Sauce

Yield: about 1 cup

1/2 cup peanut butter, chunky or plain
3 tablespoons fresh lemon juice
3 tablespoons sugar
2 tablespoons soy sauce
1 teaspoon fresh peeled and grated ginger or 1/4 teaspoon ground ginger
2 cloves **finely chopped** garlic or 1 teaspoon garlic granules
1/2 teaspoon ground red pepper
1/4 cup water

Equipment: Electric blender

Using blender, combine peanut butter, lemon juice, sugar, soy sauce, ginger, garlic, red pepper, and water into a smooth paste.

Serve sauce in little individual bowls. Have guests dip the *sate ajam* (see recipe on page 190) in their dishes of sauce. The chicken is eaten off the stick, like eating a corn dog. The sauce is also used as a salad dressing on the *gado-gado* (cooked vegetable salad).

Nasi Goreng   *Fried Rice*

Nasi goreng is one of the best known Indonesian rice dishes. (Either fried or plain boiled rice is served at every meal.)

Yield: serves 4 to 6

4 tablespoons vegetable oil
3 eggs, lightly beaten
4 onions, chopped
2 garlic cloves, **finely chopped**
1 cup cooked, thinly sliced chicken or turkey
5 cups cooked rice
2 tablespoons soy sauce
1 teaspoon brown sugar
salt and pepper to taste
1/2 cup chopped peanuts for garnish

Equipment: Large-size skillet, mixing spoon, plate

1. Heat 1 tablespoon oil in skillet over medium-high heat, add eggs, and spread out like thin pancake. When firm, remove from heat, transfer to plate, and cut into thin strips. Set aside for garnish.
2. Add remaining oil to same skillet and heat over medium heat. Add onions and garlic, mix well, and cook until soft, but not brown (about 3 minutes). Add chicken or turkey, rice, soy sauce, sugar, and salt and pepper to taste. Cook until heated through. Sprinkle with egg strips and peanuts.

Serve rice hot as a main dish or as a side dish with *sate ajam*, for which recipe follows.

Saté Ajam   *Skewered Chicken*

Yield: serve 4 to 6

2 tablespoons soy sauce
1 tablespoon sugar
1 tablespoon peanut oil
1 clove garlic, **finely chopped**
1 tablespoon fresh ginger, peeled and finely chopped, or 1 teaspoon ground ginger
4 chicken breasts, skinless and boneless, cut in 1-inch cubes.

Equipment: Medium mixing bowl, mixing spoon, 8 or 10 12-inch wooden skewers (or metal skewers), either lightly greased oven broiler pan or lightly greased baking sheet with raised edge, tongs, oven mitts

Set broiler rack about 6 inches under broiler and preheat broiler.
1. Put soy sauce, sugar, oil, garlic, and ginger in medium bowl, and mix well. Add chicken, mix well, and **marinate** for 1 hour in refrigerator. While in refrigerator, mix to coat with **marinade** several times.
2. Set top shelf in oven directly under broiler heat (about 4 inches). Preheat oven broiler to medium.
3. If using wooden skewers, you **must** soak skewers in water for about 30 minutes. Thread about 6 chicken cubes on each skewer and place side-by-side on broiler pan

or baking pan. Place under broiler to broil for about 3 minutes on each side. Turn chicken once as it browns, using tongs and oven mitts. Do not overcook.

Serve *sate ajam* with *katjang saos* (peanut sauce) for dipping (recipe above) and rice.

Lontong   *Indonesian Rice Rolls*

Lontong is the traditional bread dish served at a **buffet**.

Yield: serves 6

3 cups water
1 cup uncooked long-grain rice, rinsed in cold water
2 1/2 quarts water

Equipment: Medium-size saucepan with cover, 2 (10 x 16") aluminum foil sheets, large-size saucepan with cover, potholder or oven mitt

1. Put rice and water in saucepan and bring to a boil over high heat. Reduce to simmer, cover, and cook for 15 mintues. Remove from heat, keep covered, and set aside for 10 minutes. Uncover and cool at room temperature for 15 minutes.
2. Place 2 sheets of foil side-by-side on work surface and divide cooked rice equally between them. Moisten hands, and, one at a time, form each mound of rice into a sausage-shape, about 2 inches thick and 6 inches long down the center of the foil. To wrap the rice, bring the 2 long edges of foil up over the rice, and holding them together, fold over several times and press each fold to tightly seal in the rice. Twist the ends and bend them over, making the package waterproof.
3. Fill the large saucepan with 2 1/2 quarts water, bring to a boil over high heat, and add foil-wrapped rice. Bring back to a boil, reduce to simmer, cover, and cook for 1 hour. Wearing oven mitts and using tongs, remove packages of rice from water and place on work surface to cool to room temperature. Refrigerate wrapped until ready to serve.

To serve, carefully unwrap and discard foil. Place *lontong* on service dish and cut into 1-inch slices (moistened knife helps with cutting). Serve at room temperature.

Papua New Guinea

Papua New Guinea occupies the eastern half of New Guinea, the second largest island on earth, and 600 smaller islands. Vegetation flourishes in the tropical climate of this Southeast Asian island. The chief foods are starchy *sago* from the **pith** of the sago palm, yams, coconuts, and shellfish and fish for the people who live along the coast and rivers. Sweet potatoes and *pandanus nuts* are the staple foods for mountain dwellers. Everyone raises pigs; in fact, the people of New Guinea relish  pork more than any other food. They have village feasts where pigs are cooked for about eight hours over hot stones set in a large hole in the ground called an earth oven. Along with the pig, yams, sweet potatoes, and greens are also cooked.

Long, shallow, canoe-like boats are used for fishing. Fish, shellfish, and ocean vegetation are prepared simply; there are no fancy sauces or garnishes.

Boiled Shrimp

Boiled shrimp are always cooked in the shell to preserve flavor. To be eaten, shrimp must first be cooked, then peeled. To peel, hold the shrimp by the tail with one hand and place the thumbnail of the other hand under the legs, separating the shell and then pull off the shell; it peels easily over and off. Shrimp are often eaten without removing the dark vein that runs along the back, especially if they are small, but they are cleaner when **deveined**, because in large shrimp the vein contains grit. To devein shrimp, make a very shallow cut down the back to the tail with a small knife to reveal the black intestinal vein. Using the point of a knife or skewer, scrape out the black line and rinse the shrimp under cold running water. Allow at least 1/2 pound per person of raw shrimp when serving shell-on boiled shrimp.

Yield: 4 to 6

3 pounds raw, headless shrimp, fresh or frozen (thawed)
2 quarts water
3 tablespoons salt

Equipment: **Colander** or strainer, large-size saucepan, mixing spoon

1. Rinse shrimp in colander or strainer under cold water and drain well.
2. Heat water in saucepan over high heat, add salt, bring to a boil, and add shrimp. The water will cool when shrimp are added, so bring back to a boil, then reduce to simmer, and cook for about 3 to 6 minutes, depending upon shrimp size. Large shrimp take a little longer to cook. Very tiny shrimp are cooked almost as soon as they hit the boiling water. Shrimp are done when the meat becomes **opaque** white.
3. Remove at once from the boiling water and rinse in colander or strainer under cold water or ice to stop the cooking action.

Serve shell-on shrimp either warm or chilled. Provide an extra plate or paper to hold the shells and extra napkins or damp towels and a piece of lemon for hand-wiping.

Grilled Fish

On the island of New Guinea, grilling is the most common way to cook. To keep food moist and juicy, it is first wrapped securely in leaves before placing over the hot coals. For the following recipe we suggest using aluminum foil instead of leaves. Islanders always prepare whole, head-on, bone-in fish; we are using fish fillets instead. It is also easier to bake the fish in the oven but the more adventuresome can use the grill. (We advise wearing rubber gloves or baggies on your hands when handling the jalapeno pepper.)

Yield: serves 6

4 onions, **finely chopped**
1 pickled jalapeno pepper, **cored**, **seeded**, finely chopped

3 cloves garlic, finely chopped, or 1 teaspoon garlic granules

1 teaspoon ground **turmeric**

2 tablespoons finely chopped fresh ginger or 2 teaspoons ground ginger

2 teaspoons finely chopped lemon grass (also called sorrel) or juice of 1 lemon

1 cup grated unsweetened coconut, homemade (see recipe page 208), or frozen (thawed), or canned

salt to taste

6 (6 to 8 ounce each) red snapper, trout, or other firm fish **fillets**

Equipment: Rubber gloves or baggies to cover hands, small-size mixing bowl, mixing spoon, 6 (8 x 10 inch) aluminum foil sheets, work surface, 1 or 2 baking sheets

Preheat oven to 350° F.

1. Put onions, jalapeno, garlic, turmeric, ginger, lemon grass or juice, and grated coconut in small bowl and mix well. Set aside.
2. Place 6 sheets of foil side-by-side on work surface and place one fillet down the center of each. Spread the same amount of mixture equally over the 6 fillets.
3. To wrap the fillets in foil, bring the 2 long edges of foil up over the fillets, and holding them together, fold over several times and press each fold to tightly seal the package. Bend the ends over to make it airtight.
4. Place packages of fish side-by-side, seam-side up, on baking sheet (use 2 if necessary), and bake in the oven for about 25 minutes. The fish is fully cooked when the flesh is **opaque white** and **flakes** easily when poked with a fork.

To serve, each person at the dinner table is served a fish package with the seam-side up. As they open it, the wonderful aroma can be enjoyed along with the delicious treat inside.

Australia

Australia is inhabited by two basic groups of people: Aborigines, who are the natives, and people whose ancestors migrated from the United Kingdom (UK). The first British settlements were, in fact, penal colonies. Traditionally the Aborigines were hunters and gatherers. All kinds of native plants and animals were consumed. Kangaroos, snakes, lizards, and wombats were eaten. Boomerangs were used for knocking down birds in flight. That probably took some practice! Edible vegetation was gathered, and  fruits growing wild, such as green plums and berries, made for great sweet treats. Today the Aborigine people combine old traditional hunting and gathering techniques with foods and cooking styles adopted from the descendents of the settlers from the UK.

The pioneer settlers from the UK wanted no part of the Aborigines and retained their British cooking and eating habits, fitting them into their new sparse environment. Traditions such as tea time are still kept today. Simple and practical sums up the cooking style that originated with the Aussie pioneer women. The same straightforward approach is still practiced today in Australian kitchens. Australians are known as "meat and potato" eaters. Sunday dinner is traditionally a roast of lamb or beef called a "joint," with boiled vegetables and some kind of potatoes. Potatoes are known as spuds, taties, or murphies.

Even though Australia is surrounded by waters brimming with wonderful fish and seafood, beef and lamb are most important in the Australian diet. Australia has vast plains for animal grazing, and its beef and lamb are of the finest quality, shipped and enjoyed by people all around the world. Because beef and lamb have been cheap and plentiful, raising pigs never became popular. Pork was hard to obtain, making it expensive, to be eaten only on special occasions like Christmas or Easter.

Kangaroo Soup

Kangaroo was the meat of the early Australian settlers. Today it is against the law to kill them, so skinned kangaroo tails are not easy to come by to throw into the soup kettle! For a similar taste adventure, substitute beef, pretending it's kangaroo. Today Australians do this and still call it kangaroo soup.

Yield: serves 4 to 6

1 pound lean beef, cut into bite-size chunks
3 tablespoons barley
3 cups beef broth, homemade or canned
2 bay leaves
3 cups water
2 *each* onions, **coarsely chopped** and carrots, peeled and thinly sliced
3 celery ribs, finely sliced
salt and pepper to taste
4 teaspoons chopped green onions

Equipment: Large-size saucepan with cover or **Dutch oven**, mixing spoon

1. Put meat, barley, beef broth, bay leaves, and water in saucepan and bring to a boil over high heat. Reduce to simmer, cover, and cook for 1 hour.
2. Add onions, carrots and celery, cover and cook for 30 minutes more. Add salt and pepper to taste. Remove bay leaves and discard.

To serve, sprinkle each serving with green onions. Aussies eat *kangaroo soup* with hot buttered toast.

Pineapple and Cabbage Salad

Exceptional exotic fruits grow in Australia's tropical climate. Fresh fruit salads and desserts are popular throughout the country.

Yield: 4 to 6

2 cups finely **shredded** white cabbage
1 large ripe pineapple, **peeled, cored**, and **cubed**
1 grapefruit, peeled and separated into segments
1 orange, peeled and separated into segments
1/2 cucumber, peel-on, sliced into thin rounds

1 red bell pepper, seeded and sliced into thin strips
1 cup **finely chopped** cooked ham

Equipment: Salad bowl, salad tools

1. Put cabbage, pineapple, grapefruit, orange, cucumber, bell pepper, and ham in salad bowl and toss gently using salad tools. Refrigerate until ready to serve.
2. Pour dressing (recipe follows) over salad and toss gently to blend.

Dressing

Yield: about 1 cup

1 tablespoon grated orange rind
4 tablespoons olive oil or vegetable oil
2 tablespoons apple cider vinegar
2 tablespoons mayonnaise
2 tablespoons heavy cream
salt and pepper to taste

Equipment: Small-size bowl, **whisk** or mixing spoon

Put orange rind, oil, vinegar, mayonnaise, and cream in small bowl and add salt and pepper to taste. Mix well with whisk or mixing spoon.

Serve salad on individual plates lined with lettuce leaves.

Toad-in-the-Hole   Meat Baked in Batter

Toad-in-the-hole is originally an English recipe brought to Australia by the early settlers. *Toad-in-the-hole* is a great way to use up leftover cooked meat. In England it's traditionally made with sausages, and the batter is poured into the sausage grease. This meat in batter dish is popular for breakfast, lunch, or tea time. The Aussies' tea time is the evening meal we know as supper or dinner.

Yield: serves 6

1 1/2 cups all-purpose flour
1/2 teaspoon baking powder
2 cups milk
2 eggs, beaten lightly
3 cups bite-size pieces cooked chicken, sausage, or roast beef
3 tablespoons **finely chopped** fresh or dried parsley
salt and pepper to taste

Equipment: Flour sifter, medium-size mixing bowl, **whisk** or egg beater, mixing spoon, greased 7- x 11-inch baking dish

Preheat oven to 375°F.
1. **Sift** flour and baking powder into mixing bowl. Add milk and eggs and mix until smooth using whisk or egg beater.
2. Cover bottom of baking dish with chicken, sausage, or beef, sprinkle with parsley flakes, and add salt and pepper to taste. Pour batter over the meat and spread smooth. Bake in oven until puffed and golden brown (about 45 minutes).

Serve either hot or cold, cut in squares. Australians pour lots of catsup on it.

If Australians have a national dish it would have to be *pasties*. Pasties are the country's favorite fast food. They are a combination of meat and vegetables encased in pie dough. The variety of sizes, shapes, and fillings are endless and any combination of meat and vegetables seems to be acceptable.

Yield: serves 2 or 3

1/2 pound lean ground beef
1 *each* carrot, onion, and potato, peeled and **finely chopped**
salt and pepper to taste
1 prepared 9-inch pie crust, homemade or frozen, thawed
1 egg, beaten

Equipment: Medium-size skillet, mixing spoon, nonstick or lightly greased baking sheet, fork, pastry brush, aluminum foil

Preheat oven to 350°F.
1. Put meat in skillet and, mixing continually, brown over medium heat, about 3 minutes. Add carrot, onion, potato, and salt and pepper to taste, mix well, and cook for about 3 minutes more.
2. Place prepared pie crust in center of baking sheet. Spoon meat mixture on it, keeping to one side and about 1 inch inside the edges. Moisten the edges by running a slightly wet finger around the crust. Fold unfilled side over the filling, making a half circle. Using the bottom side of fork tines, press it gently into the crust edges to seal the filling in. Using fork tines, poke about 5 vents into the top crust.
3. Using a pastry brush, brush the top with beaten egg. Put in oven and bake for about 30 minutes until crust is golden.

Serve *pasties* hot with plenty of catsup as they do in Australia.

Dandenong Squares   Cookies from the City of Dandenong

These great cookies are fun to make and just right for the holiday season.

Yield: about 15 pieces

1/4 cup butter or margarine
1/4 cup sugar
1 cup pitted, chopped dates (cut with scissors for best results)
3 cups rice krispies
2 cups chocolate chips, melted

Equipment: Medium-size saucepan, wooden mixing spoon, medium-size mixing bowl, 9-inch shallow baking pan, metal spatula or spoon

1. Put butter or margarine, sugar, and dates in saucepan and heat over low heat, stirring continually until mixture begins to thicken. Remove from heat when it thickens.
2. Put rice krispies in mixing bowl and blend in date mixture. Mix well, using wooden spoon. Transfer mixture to baking pan and flatten to cover pan bottom.

3. Pour melted chocolate over mixture, using metal spatula or back of spoon to spread it evenly. Refrigerate to set (about 1 hour).

To serve, cut into about 2-inch squares and eat as a sweet snack.

New Zealand

New Zealand native inhabitants are the Maori people, who number over 300,000. They are Polynesians who migrated to New Zealand in the fourteenth century and intermarried with the people already there, the Tangata Whenua. Captain Cook was one of the first Europeans to set foot in New Zealand, and he brought with him pigs and potatoes. Thus began a long process of importing animals and foods to an island that had no animals. Thus, every type of sheep, cat, possum, chicken, pig, dog, kangaroo, mouse, horse, and freshwater fish that lives in New Zealand was brought there originally by humans. Today with millions of sheep, exotic fruit, and a wonderful fishing industry, New Zealand is an island rich with amazing culinary treasures.

New Zealand was settled principally by the British who turned their hand to farming and ranching. Over the centuries, under British rule, Polynesian foods and customs were of little interest to the English settlers. There are a couple exceptions, such as the *hangi* (a feast, like a *luau*) which took place in tribal villages. During the *hangi*, food is wrapped in burlap sacks and buried in the ground to cook over hot stones. Served along with the hot food was a table full of cold seafood, vegetables, fruit, and bread.

Kumara and Apple Casserole

Sweet Potato and Apple Casserole

Cultivated by the Polynesians is the *kumara* a mealy, not-white vegetable with sweet potato-like flavor. Because *kumara* is not readily available, we suggest using sweet potatoes.

Yield: serves 6

4 boiled sweet potatoes, cooled, then peeled and **cubed**
4 cooking apples, peeled, **cored** and thinly sliced
1/2 cup brown sugar
1/2 teaspoon salt
4 tablespoons butter or margarine

Equipment: Large-size mixing bowl, mixing spoon, nonstick or greased 8-inch-square baking pan

Preheat oven to 350° F.
1. Put potatoes and apples in mixing bowl and sprinkle with brown sugar and salt. Gently mix to blend. Transfer mixture to baking pan and dot top with butter or margarine.

2. Bake in oven for 1 hour or until apples are tender and top is brown.

Serve *kumara and apple casserole* as a side dish with meat or as a dessert.

Rock Cakes

One of the oldest written New Zealand recipes is for *rock cakes*. How they got their name seems to be a mystery, but one recipe dating back to 1861 said the dough should be made to look as rough as possible. Rock cakes are quick, simple, and inexpensive to prepare and cook. In New Zealand *rock cakes* were popular tea-time treats with original English settlers.

Yield: serves 6 or 8

1 cup all-purpose flour
1/2 teaspoon salt
1/2 cup *each* butter or margarine, sugar, and seedless raisins
2 tablespoons orange marmalade
1 egg, lightly beaten

Equipment: Flour **sifter,** large-size mixing bowl, mixing spoon, fork, greased or nonstick cookie sheet

Preheat oven to 425° F.

1. **Sift** flour and salt into mixing bowl and blend in butter or margarine using clean hands until it is like fine bread crumbs.
2. Add sugar, raisins, and marmalade and mix well with the spoon. Add egg and blend into flour mixture until stiff and rocky. The mixture must be stiff, or it will lose shape when baking. Pull off golf ball-size chunks of dough and drop on cookie sheet about 1-inch apart. Do not smooth out dough pieces.
3. Bake in oven for 15 minutes until lightly browned. Remove from oven and turn rock cakes bottom side up to cool.

Serve *rock cakes* as a snack with milk or tea.

Kiwi Sorbet   Dessert Sherbert

Yield: serves 4 to 6

1/2 cup sugar
1/2 cup water
7 kiwi, peeled and mashed (set aside one to slice for garnish)
3 tablespoons lemon juice or juice of 1 lemon
1 egg white, beaten to stiff peaks

Equipment: Small-size saucepan, mixing spoon, medium-size metal bowl, aluminum foil

1. Put sugar and water in small saucepan and cook over medium heat for about 2 minutes, stirring continually to dissolve the sugar. Bring to a boil and remove at once from heat. Cool to room temperature.
2. Put mashed kiwi and lemon juice in metal bowl, add sugar mixture, and mix well. Cover with foil, place in freezer, and chill until slightly thickened (about 1 to 1 1/2 hours).

3. Remove from freezer, and, mixing continually, add whipped egg white. Cover with foil and return to freezer until firm (about 2 to 3 hours). When ready to serve, place in refrigerator for 5 to 10 minutes, if mixture is too firm.

To serve, spoon sherbert into individual dessert bowls and garnish each with a slice of kiwi.

Pavlova   Meringue Fruit Dessert

The *pavlova*, a dessert named in honor of a once world famous Russian ballerina, is very popular in both New Zealand and Australia. Simple to make with just egg whites and the fruit of your choice, the *pavlova* is similar to many meringue desserts found in American and western European cooking. The *pavlova*, unlike other baked meringues, has a moist sticky center, much like marshmallow cream.

Yield: serves 8

4 egg whites, at room temperature
1/2 teaspoon salt
1 cup sugar
2 teaspoons *each* cornstarch and apple cider vinegar
1 1/2 cups heavy cream, whipped or 3 cups prepared frozen whipped topping, thawed
4 fresh kiwi, peeled and sliced across (about 2 to 3 cups)

Equipment: 8-inch pie pan or plate, greased and lightly floured cookie sheet, medium-size mixing bowl, **egg beater** or electric mixer, small bowl, spoon or spatula

Preheat oven to 300° F.
1. Place an 8-inch pie pan or plate upside down on the greased and floured cookie sheet and trace around it with your clean fingertip to mark a circle in the flour.
2. Put egg whites and salt in medium bowl and use egg beater or electric mixer to whip into soft peaks. Add sugar, a little at a time, beating after each addition until smooth and glossy.
3. Mix cornstarch and vinegar until smooth in small bowl and using spoon or spatula **fold** into whipped egg whites until well blended. Then pour whites into center of circle marked on cookie sheet. Spread meringue evenly to edges of circle, building up edges more than center.
4. Place on middle shelf in oven, reduce oven heat to 250° F and bake until outside of meringue is firm and pale tan in color, about 1 hour. Remove from oven and cool for 15 minutes and then carefully remove from cookie sheet. Let stand at room temperature until ready to serve. Do not cover or chill.

To serve, spread top and sides with whipped cream or whipped topping to cover meringue. Decorate top with slices of kiwi.

Fiji

In the South Pacific, between Australia and Hawaii, sits a group of tiny islands known as Fiji. Fiji is home to Melanesian and Polynesian natives and a very large group of East Indians, brought to the islands by the English in the nineteenth century to work the sugar cane plantations. There are many cultural differences between the Indian

descendants, following the Muslim and Hindu rituals of their homeland, and native Fijians, who prefer to live in undeveloped communal villages, much as their ancestors have done for hundreds of years. Rice, coconuts, and sugar cane are the main island crops. Bananas, watermelons, pineapples, taro, yams, and corn are also grown. Livestock include cattle, pigs, and poultry. Every household has its yard full of chickens and pigs. Pork is the favorite meat. The islands are surrounded by wonderful fishing grounds with an overwhelming variety of seafood such as giant prawns, sea urchins, rock snails, clams, and turtles of all sizes.

Fijians are inventive and creative people. Food is prepared and cooked simply, using whatever is at hand; an example is wrapping food in native plant leaves and then cooking it with steam. They prefer their fish whole—heads on, bones in. For the following recipe we suggest, instead, using boneless fish **fillets** and placing them on shredded cabbage in a **steamer basket** or wrapping them in **blanched** cabbage or leaf lettuce leaves. Coconuts are everywhere on the islands and coconut oil is used in cooking. We suggest healthier vegetable oil.

I'A   *Steamed Fish with Sweet Potatoes*

Yield: serves 4

4 (about 8 ounces each) skin-on fish **fillets**, such as snapper or mullet
2 to 4 tablespoons vegetable oil
juice of 1 lemon
salt and pepper to taste
4 sweet potatoes, peeled and cut into 1/2 inch chunks
1/2 cup butter or margarine, more or less as needed

Equipment: Aluminum foil, paper towels, roasting pan with wire rack and cover, medium-size skillet with cover or **Dutch oven**

Preheat oven to 350° F.
1. Cut foil into 4 (8-inch) squares and place side-by-side on work surface.
2. Rinse fish fillets and gently pat dry, using paper towels. Rub both sides with oil and place a fillet, skin-side down, in the center of each foil square. Sprinkle with lemon juice and salt and pepper to taste. Wrap each fillet securely in foil, tightly sealing the edges.
3. Set foil packages, seam-side up on wire rack in the roasting pan and pour about 1 or 2 inches of boiling water into the pan. (The water can touch, but not cover, the foil packages.) Cover and place in oven for about 20 minutes or until the fish flesh **flakes** easily when tested with a fork.
4. *Preparing sweet potatoes:* Melt butter or margarine in skillet or Dutch oven over medium-high heat, add potatoes, and brown on all sides, mixing gently, about 5 to 8 minutes. Reduce heat to low, cover, and cook until tender, about 10 minutes; add more butter or margarine, if necessary, to prevent sticking.

To serve, give each person a fish package and serve sweet potatoes separately.

The Caribbean

The Caribbean Islands are a large group of islands running from the southern coast of North America to the northern coast of South America. They encompass the islands of Aruba, the Bahamas, Cuba, Curacao, the Greater Antilles, Hispaniola (Dominican Republic and Haiti), Jamaica, Puerto Rico, Trinidad, and many smaller islands.

Caribbean cooking is a blending of many cultures that have influenced the region, making it unique. It is a mixture of the traditions of the Spanish, Portuguese, Dutch, French, and English who came to colonize the islands, and the methods of the involuntary migrants: the West Africans brought as slaves and the Chinese and East Indians brought as cheap laborers for the plantations. Pinpointing cooking differences between the islands is difficult. The same fruits, vegetables, animals, and seafood thrive on all of the islands, and native cooks frequently move from island to island, preparing the same dishes. The most common Caribbean ingredients are coconuts, squash, tomatoes, corn, the green leaf from the **taro** root, and root vegetables: yams, **cassava**, and sweet potatoes. The main spices are allspice, thyme, and chilies (especially the very hot Scotch Bonnet), curry powder, and **coriander**. Allspice is grown in such abundance in Jamaica that it is called Jamaica pepper, and it is found in many recipes of the region.

Trinidad and Tobago

Carib and Arawak Indians, among the first Native Americans to inhabit the islands, still live on Trinidad and Tobago. The islands have a long history of migration of varied peoples including Spanish, French, English, and Asians from India and China. Customs from each of these countries are part of the unique makeup of Trinidad and Tobago. The British were the last to rule the islands before granting independence in 1962.

Tobago does not have the natural resources that Trinidad, the larger island, has, and so it relies more on tourist trade than Trinidad. Food has to be imported to each of these islands even though conditions for agriculture are good on Trinidad. The principal crops are rice, bananas, citrus, cocoa, coffee, and sugar cane. Livestock include pigs, goats, sheep, buffalo, and cattle.

Fungi   *Cornmeal Cake*

Fungi, also called *cou-cou (coo coo)* and *funchi*, is the Caribbean "comfort food" made with cornmeal mush and okra. Most natives have their own way of fixing it, adding whatever is available from the garden or market. This recipe can be used for all the Caribbean countries. When *fungi* gets cold it is sliced and eaten like bread.

Yield: serves 6

6 tablespoons butter or margarine
1/2 cup chopped onions
1/2 cup stemmed and **coarsely chopped** okra, fresh or frozen (thawed)
2 1/2 cups water
1 1/2 cups yellow stone-ground cornmeal
salt and pepper to taste

Equipment: Small-size skillet, wooden mixing spoon, medium-size saucepan with cover, greased or nonstick cookie sheet, spatula

1. Melt 3 tablespoons butter or margarine in skillet over medium heat. Add onions and okra and cook for 5 minutes or until vegetables are soft, stirring frequently. Remove from heat and set aside.
2. Put water in saucepan and bring to a boil over high heat. While stirring continually with wooden spoon, slowly pour in cornmeal. Reduce heat to lowest setting, cover, and cook for 10 minutes. Add onions, okra, and skillet scrapings and mix well. Add salt and pepper to taste. Increase heat so that mixture simmers and cook for about 4 minutes more, until mixture pulls away from sides of the pan.
3. Pour mixture in a pile in the center of the baking sheet. Using spatula, spread mixture out into a smooth circle about 1-inch thick. Dot top with remaining butter or margarine.

Serve *fungi* either warm or cold. The Islanders set the *fungi* in the center of the table, and everyone eats from it.

Arima   *Almond Chicken*

The following dish is typical of the strong Chinese influence on Caribbean cooking.

Yield: serves 4 to 6

1/2 cup chopped onion
1/2 cup peeled and chopped cucumber
1/2 cup chopped carrots
1 cup sliced water chestnuts (canned, drained)
1 cup sliced bamboo shoots, (canned, drained)
2 cups boiling water
2 cups raw, bite-size pieces chicken
2 to 4 tablespoons vegetable oil, more or less as needed
salt and pepper to taste
1/2 cup coarsely chopped almonds, pecan, walnuts, or peanuts

Equipment: Large-size bowl with cover; mixing spoon; large-size skillet, **Dutch oven,** or wok; **colander** or strainer

1. Put onion, cucumber, carrots, water chestnuts, and bamboo shoots in bowl and add boiling water. Cover and let sit 10 minutes.
2. Heat 2 tablespoons oil in skillet, Dutch oven, or wok over high heat, add chicken, and stir to coat with oil. Reduce heat to simmer, cover, and cook for about 20 minutes until chicken is cooked through.
3. Drain vegetables in colander or strainer and discard water. Increase heat under chicken to medium-high and add vegetables. Add remaining 2 tablespoons oil, if necessary, to prevent sticking. Mixing continually, cook for 4 minutes, and add salt and pepper to taste. Just before serving sprinkle with nuts.

Serve *arima* hot over rice or combination of rice and beans.

Bammy   *Pan Fried Bread*

Bammy, a flat pancake-like bread, is a popular Caribbean snack. African slaves deserve the credit for creating bammies, not as a snack but as survival food. The slaves were given little to eat, so they turned simple greens or roots into nourishing and tasty meals.

Yield: serves 4 to 6

4 cups peeled, finely grated fresh **cassava** (yucca root) or yams
1 1/2 teaspoons salt
2 to 4 tablespoons vegetable oil

Equipment: Medium-size mixing bowl, mixing spoon, 6-inch skillet, pancake turner or spatula, 9-inch plate

1. Using the mixing spoon, mix cassava or yams and salt in medium bowl.
2. Heat 1 tablespoon oil in skillet over medium heat, swirling oil to cover bottom and about 1 inch up the side.
3. Add 1 cup of cassava or yam mixture to skillet and press it down with back of spoon to fill the pan. When steam starts to rise and edges pull away slightly from

the sides of skillet, press mixture flat again with back of spoon. Cook for about 5 minutes, remove from heat, and turn over on a plate. Using pancake turner or spatula, put *bammy* back into skillet with uncooked side down. Cook for 5 minutes or until lightly brown. Repeat process until all mixture is used.

Serve *bammies* hot or cold.

Grenada

Grenada is known as the "spice island" because it grows and exports nutmeg, pepper, cinnamon, cloves, and mace. Even a few miles off the coast people can smell spices as they approach the island. Other food crops include cocoa and bananas. Naturally, food has to be imported to this island because the specialized crops can't support the local food needs. Culture on Grenada has been influenced by the French and the British, who both ruled here in the past. Caribbean Is-

landers make well-seasoned soups and stews, and the people of Grenada are no exception. Local fish, shellfish, pork, and chicken are added to the pot, creating a cook's masterpiece. The degree of thickness makes the difference between soup and stew.

Callaloo   *Vegetable Stew with Greens*

The Caribbean stews called *callaloo* are similar to the one-pot meals found throughout Africa. Some African one-pots are also called *callaloo*, and they are made with whatever is available at cooking time. The same is true of Caribbean *callaloo*, except a locally grown vegetable green is always added, either spinach or kale.

Yield: serves 4 to 6

2 pounds spinach or kale, fresh (washed and drained, leaves cut into 4 pieces) or frozen (thawed)
6 cups water
1 cup **coarsely chopped** celery
1 cup **trimmed** and sliced okra, fresh or frozen (thawed)
1 cup corn kernels, fresh, scraped off the cob or frozen (thawed)
1 onion, coarsely chopped
1 cup green bell pepper, stemmed, **seeded,** and coarsely chopped
1 tablespoon sugar
3 cloves garlic, **finely chopped,** or 1 teaspoon garlic granules
1 jalapeno pepper or Scotch Bonnet pepper, seeded and finely chopped
salt and pepper to taste

Equipment: Large-size saucepan with cover or **Dutch oven**, mixing spoon

Put spinach or kale, water, celery, okra, corn, onion, bell pepper, sugar, garlic, and jalapeno in saucepan or Dutch oven and bring to a boil over high heat. Reduce heat to simmer, mix well, cover, and cook until tender, about one hour. Add salt and pepper to taste and mix well.

Serve *callaloo* in individual bowls over rice, beans, or both.

Spice Squares

Yield: makes 48 pieces

2 1/2 cups all-purpose flour
1 1/2 teaspoons baking soda
1 1/2 teaspoons ground allspice
1 teaspoon ground ginger
1/4 teaspoon salt
1 cup molasses
1 cup milk
1/2 cup butter or margarine, softened at room temperature
1/2 cup dark brown sugar
1 egg

Equipment: Flour **sifter**, medium-size bowl, small-size mixing bowl, large-size mixing bowl, wooden mixing spoon or electric mixer, nonstick or greased 13-x 9-inch baking pan

Preheat oven to 325° F.

1. **Sift** flour, baking soda, allspice, ginger, and salt together in the medium bowl and set aside.
2. Mix molasses and milk together in small bowl.
3. In large bowl, cream butter, using mixing spoon or electric mixer. Gradually add sugar, and continue mixing until fluffy, about 3 minutes. Add egg and mix well. Stirring continually, slowly add flour mixture and alternate with molasses mixture. Mix for about 3 minutes until blended.
4. Pour mixture into baking pan. Bake in oven for about 45 minutes or until toothpick inserted in center comes out clean. Cool in pan before cutting into 1 1/2-inch squares.

Serve *spice squares* as a snack with a cool glass of milk.

Nutmeg Ice Cream

Of all the spices grown on Grenada, nutmeg is Grenada's most outstanding. It's a small round nut with an aroma and flavor that is at its best when freshly grated.

Yield: serves 6 to 8

2 cups milk
1 cup half-and-half
4 eggs
3/4 cup sugar
3/4 cup sweetened condensed milk (14 1/2-ounce can)
2 whole nutmegs, freshly grated, or 1 teaspoon ground nutmeg
1 1/2 cups heavy cream

Equpment: Large-size saucepan, mixing spoon, medium-size mixing bowl, **whisk** or electric mixer, ice cream freezer

1. Heat milk and half-and-half in saucepan over medium-high heat. Bring to bubbling around the edges but DO NOT BOIL. Reduce heat to low.
2. In medium bowl blend eggs and sugar using whisk or mixer. Add small amount of hot milk to egg mixture, mix well, and add this to remaining hot milk mixture in saucepan. Stirring continually, cook over low heat until it thickens to custard consistency. Increase heat to medium, if necessary to achieve desired thickness, but again, DO NOT BOIL. When thick, remove from heat.
3. Add condensed milk and grated nutmeg, mix well, and cool to room temperature. Add heavy cream, mix well, and refrigerate for 2 hours.
4. Transfer to ice-cream freezer and continue according to manufacturer's directions.

Serve *nutmeg ice cream* as a snack or dessert on sweet potato or pumpkin pie.

Dominican Republic

The Dominican Republic is located on the eastern half of Hispaniola Island, which it shares with Haiti. Rule of the island has passed among French, Spanish, Haitians, and the United States, but it is now an independent country. Chief food crops include rice, sugar cane, coffee, and corn. The best land goes to the big sugar plantations, and farmers contend with small hillside lots that are likely to erode when the trees are removed for farming. Conditions in the rural communities are poor, and many people migrate to the cities in the hope of finding work and a better life. Unfortunately, work is hard to find, and city living standards tend to be low. People are predominantly Spanish-speaking Catholics and are of mixed European and African descent.

Orange Pumpkin Soup

The tropical tastes of the Caribbean are classic in this cold soup made with locally grown oranges, pumpkins, and coconuts. Islanders prefer their fruits and vegetables cooked until very well-done, never raw and crunchy.

Yield: serves 6 to 8

1 tablespoon butter or margarine
3 tablespoons **finely chopped** onions
2 cups orange juice, fresh or frozen
4 cups cooked mashed pumpkin, fresh, frozen, or canned
1/2 teaspoon salt
1 teaspoon ground ginger
1/2 teaspoon ground nutmeg

1 cup half-and-half or canned evaporated milk
salt and white pepper to taste
1 orange, peeled, **pith** removed, and thinly sliced for garnish

Equipment: Large-size saucepan or **Dutch oven**, mixing spoon

1. Melt butter or margarine in saucepan over medium-high heat, add onions, and cook until tender (about 5 minutes). Add orange juice and pumpkin, mix well, and simmer for 30 minutes.
2. Stir in ginger, nutmeg, half-and-half or evaporated milk, and salt and pepper to taste. Continue cooking to heat through (about 5 minutes). Cool to room temperature and then refrigerate until ready to serve.

Serve in individual soup bowls; garnish each with 1 or 2 orange slices.

Coconut Buying and Opening

Coconuts play an important role in Caribbean cooking, and in the cooking of many other regions in the world. The following advice for buying coconuts and making shredded coconut and coconut milk can be used when these ingredients are called for elsewhere in this book. To select a fresh coconut, shake it to feel the sloshing of liquid inside. A cracked or an old coconut will be empty and dry.

1. *Opening the coconut:* Pierce the brown eye-like spots at one end with sharp point. Drain and discard liquid.
2. Preheat oven to 400° F.
3. Place the coconut in oven for 15 minutes, remove, wrap in clean kitchen towel, and carefully crack open with a hammer. The coconut meat should be broken away carefully from the shell. If a portion of it hasn't, return coconut to oven for a few minutes.

Making Shredded Coconut

You can either grate the white meat from the brown shell using the fine side of a hand grater, or you can peel the meat from the brown shell with a vegetable peeler, and then shred it in a food processor or with a sharp knife. One coconut yields about 4 cups grated coconut.

Coconut Milk

Homemade coconut milk is at its best when freshly made. Even under refrigeration it quickly loses its flavor.

Yield: 1 1/2 to 2 cups

2 cups grated coconut meat (see recipe above—or, canned or frozen unsweetened, shredded coconut is available at most supermarkets)
2 cups boiling water

Equipment: Small-size bowl, blender or food processor, 8-inch square of cheesecloth (surgical gauze can be used) or 8-inch square of clean nylon stocking

1. Put grated coconut in small bowl, add boiling water and let set for 30 minutes. *If using a blender or food processor*, add boiling water and blend for 1 minute. Let cool for 5 minutes.
2. **Strain** liquid through cheesecloth or nylon. Squeeze and twist cloth to extract all milk from the coconut meat.
3. Repeat the process if additional coconut milk is needed.

Sweet Potato Balls

For centuries tubers—yams, **cassavas**, and sweet potatoes—have been a prime nutritious food source in a large part of the world. Shiploads of slaves survived on yams during their long imprisoned journey from Africa. This recipe uses sweet potatoes.

Yield: about 24 balls

2 pounds cooked sweet potatoes, peeled and cubed, fresh or canned (32-ounce) water pack (drained)
1/2 cup coconut milk (see recipe above) or heavy cream
1/4 to 1 cup sugar, as needed, depending upon individual preference
2 egg yolks (refrigerate egg whites to use at another time)
2 tablespoons ground cinnamon for garnish

Equipment: Large-size mixing bowl, potato masher or electric blender, large-size saucepan, wooden mixing spoon, pie pan or flat plate

1. Put potatoes in mixing bowl and blend smooth with potato masher or in electric blender. Transfer potatoes to saucepan, add coconut milk or cream, sugar, and egg yolk, and mix well. Cook over medium heat, stirring continually until mixture pulls away from sides of pan. Remove from heat and let mixture sit until cool enough to handle. Shape into ping-pong-size balls.
2. Put cinnamon into a pie pan or flat plate and coat potato balls one at a time. Place side-by-side on platter and refrigerate.

Serve *sweet potato balls* cold as a candy treat.

Haiti

Haiti occupies the western half of the Hispaniola Island, which also is home to the Dominican Republic. Haitian farmers till the soil on their own plots, which are remnants of the old plantations that have been divided among the many. There they grow their own food, usually garden vegetables such as black-eyed peas, squash, pumpkins, and **cassava**. Haiti is a poor nation and many Haitians barely get by the growing season with enough food. The have been know to subsist on only one food item, such as mangos, until the next crop is ready to harvest. Cassava, made into a flour material

and baked into a bread, and coffee are breakfast for most rural people. Cassava is mostly starch, though, and it isn't very nutritious by itself. Dinner is the main meal of the day and usually consists of rice and beans or a stew.

A surprising fact is that, even though Haiti is surrounded by waters full of fish, the Haitian fleet is not seaworthy enough to gain the full benefit of the ocean. Inland waters have fish, but getting them to the people is a problem because of a lack of refrigeration.

The following recipes are typical of Haitian cooking.

Sweet Red Pepper Soup

Yield: serves 4 to 6

1 1/2 cups chicken broth, canned or homemade
4 red bell peppers, **seeded** and **finely chopped**
1 1/2 cups heavy cream or canned evaporated milk
2 tablespoons tomato paste
salt and pepper to taste
1/2 cup coconut milk, canned, frozen, or fresh (recipe on page 208)
sprinkle of paprika for garnish

Equipment: Medium-size saucepan, mixing spoon or **whisk**

1. Pour chicken broth into saucepan, bring to a boil over high heat, and mix in peppers. Reduce heat to simmer, cover, and cook for 20 minutes. Add cream or evaporated milk, tomato paste and salt and pepper to taste and mix well. Increase heat and bring to a boil for 1 minute. Remove from heat, cool to room temperature, and refrigerate.
2. Before serving, add coconut milk, mix well, and sprinkle with paprika.

Serve *sweet red pepper soup* cold, in individual bowls.

Pois et Ris   Kidney Beans and Rice

This recipe, a combination of kidney beans and rice, is the national dish of Haiti. The amounts of beans and rice Haitians use makes no difference, and the end result always seems to taste good. The French Haitians call kidney beans and rice *pois et ris*. This can be misleading since *pois* in French means peas, not beans.

Yield: serves 6

1 cup **finely chopped** bacon, ham, or sausage, or combination
3 cloves garlic, finely chopped
1/2 teaspoon ground thyme
2 cups kidney beans, homemade or canned (with juice)
1 cup hot water
2 cups cooked rice (cooked according to directions on package)
salt and pepper to taste

Equipment: Large-size skillet with cover or **Dutch oven**, mixing spoon

1. Heat bacon, ham, or sausage, or combination in skillet or Dutch oven, over medium-high heat, add garlic and thyme, and mix continually, until meat browns (about 4 minutes).
2. Add beans with juice, water, cooked rice, and salt and pepper to taste and mix well. Reduce heat to low and cook for about 10 minutes, stirring frequently. Cover, remove from heat, and allow flavors to blend for about 10 minutes.

Serve *pois et ris* in individual bowls.

Sweet Potato Pudding Cake

Yield: serves 4 to 6

1 cup cooked, mashed sweet potatoes, fresh or canned
2 ripe bananas, mashed
1 cup milk
2 tablespoons sugar
1/2 teaspoon salt
3 egg yolks, beaten (refrigerate whites to use at another time)
3 tablespoons **finely chopped** raisins

Equipment: Medium-size mixing bowl, mixing spoon or electric mixer, greased or non-stick 9-inch cake pan, cake rack

Preheat oven to 300° F.
1. Put sweet potatoes and bananas in mixing bowl, and blend, using spoon or electric mixer. Add milk, sugar, salt, yolks, and raisins and mix well.
2. Pour batter into cake pan and bake in oven for 45 minutes or until cake is set, firm to the touch, and top is golden brown. Remove from oven and place on cake rack to cool at room temperature.

Serve as dessert, cut into wedges.

Accra (also called Calas)   Black-eyed Pea Patties

Black-eyed peas were brought to the Caribbean from Africa in the seventeenth century. Either fresh or dried, black-eyed peas were survival food for slaves. Today Islanders love their black-eyed peas, and the tradition of eating them on New Year's Eve means luck for the coming year.

Yield: serves 4 to 6

4 cups cooked black-eyed peas, homemade or canned (drained)
1 egg
1 teaspoon ground red pepper, more or less to taste
salt to taste
2 to 4 tablespoons vegetable oil

Equipment: Strainer, medium-size mixing bowl, potato masher or food processor, mixing spoon, large-size skillet, pancake turner or metal spatula, paper towels

1. Put cooked peas in strainer, drain well, and press out all moisture.

2. Transfer peas to mixing bowl and mash with potato masher or put in food processor and mash until smooth and free of lumps. Mix in egg, red pepper, and salt. Continue mixing until light and fluffy.
3. Heat 2 tablespoons oil in skillet over medium-high heat. Heat until a drop of water sizzles on contact. Drop spoonfuls of pea mixture into the pan. Flatten into 2-inch patties, pressing with back of spoon. Add more oil if necessary and continue making patties until mixture is all used. Fry each patty for about 5 minutes on each side, until golden brown. Remove from skillet and drain on paper towels.

Serve *accra* at any time of day; they are a great lunch or picnic snack.

Jamaica

When traveling around the kitchens of the world, it is surprising to learn there are so many different fruits and vegetables that have never made it to U.S. gardens or supermarkets. For instance, in Jamaica there is a fruit so common and plentiful it is nicknamed "free food." The fruit is ackee, and it is the basic ingredient in one of Jamaica's national dishes. Although it grows well on other Caribbean Islands, the fruit is not considered edible; perhaps because if it is not fully ripe when picked, the fruit is poisonous.

The unusual ackee has an equally unusual history. It was brought to Jamaica from West Africa in 1778 by a slave ship, and it was Captain William Bligh of "Mutiny on the Bounty" fame who brought the unknown plant to England, where the botanical name (*Blighia sapida*) was given in his honor. Ackee is used as a vegetable, often mixing with savory ingredients such as pork, salt fish, onions, green peppers, eggs, and tomatoes.

Breadfruit, another favorite of Jamaicans, is usually baked and served at almost all meals. A few other interesting tropical fruits are jack fruit, soursop, tangelos, pawpaw (another name for papaya, which is used as meat tenderizer), and ugli, a cross between grapefruit, orange, and tangerine. (It is called ugli because of its ugly, lumpy appearance.)

Escovitch   *Fried Fish in Marinade*

A very old method of preserving fish, meat, and fowl is to keep it in a vinegar **marinade** such as *escovitch*. The name and method derive from Spain. (In Spain and France, a similar dish is called *escabèche*.) Every island has its own variation.

Yield: 6 to 8

2 to 4 tablespoons olive oil
2 pounds fish **fillets** or steaks, fresh or frozen (thawed)
1 cup white vinegar

1 onion, sliced paper thin
2 carrots, scraped and sliced in rounds
2 bay leaves
3 cloves garlic, finely sliced, or 1 teaspoon garlic granules
1 teaspoon *each* whole allspice, salt, dried crushed red pepper flakes

Equipment: Large-size skillet; pancake turner or metal spatula; paper towels; glass or enamel bowl with cover, plastic wrap, or aluminum foil; small-size saucepan

1. Heat 2 tablespoons oil in skillet over medium-high heat. Add fish pieces and fry on both sides for about 5 minutes per side until golden brown, adding more oil if necessary. Drain fish well on paper towels and place pieces, slightly overlapping, in bowl.
2. *Prepare* **marinade**: put vinegar in saucepan and bring to a boil over high heat. Add onion, carrots, bay leaves, garlic, allspice, salt, and red pepper, mix well, remove from heat, and cool to room temperature.
3. Pour marinade to completely cover fish pieces. Cover the bowl with lid, plastic wrap, or foil, and refrigerate for at least 24 hours. Discard bay leaves.

Serve cold as an appetizer or for lunch.

Jerked Pork & Chicken

Allspice is not a blend of several different spices as many people think when buying ground allspice; it is one berry with combined flavors of cloves, cinnamon, and nutmeg. Jerked meat is a Caribbean Island speciality and is no relation to beef jerky, made famous by the American pioneers settling the west. According to legend, runaway Jamaican slaves survived on the meat of wild pigs roaming the island and used the wild herbs and spices to enhance the flavor. Allspice grew wild and was in great abundance. It is now a cultivated crop on the island. Allspice is an important ingredient in the following recipe. Jerked meat is made with pork or chicken in Jamaica; beef is seldom used because it's too scarce and expensive.

Yield: serves 6 to 8

4 tablespoons ground allspice
2 onions, **finely chopped**
2 green chili peppers or jalapeno peppers, **seeded** and finely chopped
3 cloves fresh garlic, finely chopped, or 1 teaspoon garlic granules
1 teaspoon *each* ground cinnamon and ground or freshly grated nutmeg
6 bay leaves, crumbled
1 teaspoon *each* salt and pepper
3 tablespoons vinegar
1 cup vegetable oil
2 pounds lean pork loin or pork shoulder, cut into strips, about 4 inches long and about 1 inch thick
1 chicken cut into serving-size pieces

Equipment: Small-size mixing bowl, mixing spoon, rubber gloves or plastic wrap for hands, large-size bowl with cover or plastic bag, outdoor grill and tongs or roasting pan with cover

1. *Prepare **marinade**:* Put allspice, onions, chilies, garlic, cinnamon, nutmeg, bay leaves, salt, pepper, vinegar, and oil in bowl and blend to a paste-like mixture.
2. Wearing rubber gloves or plastic wrap on your hands, rub pork and chicken with mixture. Put pieces in a bowl with a cover or in a plastic bag, seal, and refrigerate for at least 2 hours.

Grill Cooking: ready the coals to medium heat.

Place the pieces on grill as far from direct heat as possible. Cover grill and cook until done, about 2 hours. Using tongs, turn at least once during the cooking.

OR Oven Cooking: preheat oven to 350° F.

Put pork and chicken in roasting pan, cover, and cook for about 1 hour. The meat should be very well done.

To serve as they do in the Caribbean, cut pork into bite-size pieces. Transfer pork and chicken to a platter and serve with raw onion slices.

Stamp and Go

Jamaicans love to snack, and one of their favorite foods is *stamp and go*, sold by street vendors at almost every bus stop on the island. Bus riders jump off their bus, grab a *stamp and go*, and hop back on to continue their trip. Traditionally made with soaked salt codfish in Jamaica, we will substitute more readily available codfish **fillets**; all other ingredients are the same. If codfish is in short supply, other firm-flesh fish can be substituted.

Yield: serves 4 to 6

4 codfish **fillets**, skin removed, fresh or frozen (thawed)
6 cups water
1 onion, **finely chopped**
1 clove garlic, finely chopped or 1/4 teaspoon garlic granules
1/2 teaspoon ground thyme
2 eggs
salt and pepper to taste
1/2 cup all-purpose flour
1 teaspoon vinegar
2 to 4 tablespoons vegetable oil

Equipment: Medium-size saucepan, **colander** or strainer, large-size mixing bowl, mixing spoon, small-size bowl, large-size skillet, pancake turner or metal spatula, paper towels

1. Put fillets in saucepan, cover with water, and bring to a boil over high heat. Reduce heat and simmer until fish **flakes** easily with fork (about 10 minutes). Drain in colander or strainer and discard water. Transfer fish to large bowl and break up into small pieces. Add onion, garlic, thyme, eggs, salt and pepper to taste, and mix well to blend smooth.
2. Mix flour and vinegar in small bowl, add to mixture, mix well.
3. Heat 2 tablespoons oil in skillet over medium-high heat. When hot but not smoking, drop tablespoons of mixture into skillet. Flatten to about 2-inches across, with back of spoon. Fry on both sides until golden brown (about 5 minutes per side). Remove patties from skillet and drain on paper towels. Continue frying until all mixture is used (adding more oil if necessary).

Serve *stamp and go* hot or cold, as a finger food with lime or lemon wedges.

Rice and Peas

What Americans know as kidney beans or red beans are called "red peas" in Jamaica. The beloved combination of rice and red peas is one of their national dishes. It can be thick like a stew or soupy. Jamaicans call anything that is soupy "tea." By adding fish, chicken, or meat broth to the following recipe it becomes Jamaican tea.

Yield: serves 4 to 6

4 cups cooked kidney beans, dried (cooked according to directions on package) or canned
4 cups coconut milk, canned, frozen, or fresh (recipe on page 208)
1/2 cup chopped green onions
1/2 teaspoon ground thyme
1 cup uncooked rice
1 or 2 cups water (optional)

Equipment: Large-size saucepan with cover or **Dutch oven**, mixing spoon

Put cooked beans in saucepan or Dutch oven. Add coconut milk, onions, thyme, and rice, and mix well. Bring to a boil over high heat, reduce heat to simmer, cover, and cook for about 25 minutes, until rice is fluffy. If necessary add a little water to prevent sticking.

Serve as main dish or as side dish with any combination of island dishes.

Cuba

Fishing, sugar plantations, coffee plantations, and cattle raising are the main food industries of Cuba. Potatoes and rice are grown as well as vegetables and fruits. The people of Cuba today are poor, but they are not undernourished.

A major culinary difference between countries is how herbs and spices are used. Tropical limes and an aromatic bitter-orange concentrate are distinctively Cuban seasonings. They add a mild and blander flavor to traditional Spanish-style cooking used throughout Latin America. Black beans are the national food of Cuba, and in almost every Cuban household a pot of black beans is simmering on the stove, either soupy or thick, ready to feed a hungry family. *Sofrito*, a mixture of sauteed garlic, onions, green pepper, and tomatoes, dominates Cuban cooking. Tamarind is used as a flavoring for beverages, candies, meat sauces, and salsa. It comes from a tropical tree and is popular in Latin American countries, Italy, and India as a flavoring in cooking and refreshing drinks.

La Sopa Frijoles Negros   Black Bean Soup

Yield: serves 6 to 8

2 cups dried black beans (washed, and any foreign matter removed)
10 cups water
2 green peppers, **finely chopped**
1 onion, finely chopped
4 cloves garlic, finely chopped, or 1 tablespoon garlic granules
2 bay leaves
1/2 pound bacon, fried crisp and finely chopped
salt and pepper to taste
3 cups cooked rice (cooked according to directions on package)

Equipment: Large-size saucepan with cover or **Dutch oven**, mixing spoon

1. Add beans to water in large saucepan or Dutch oven and bring to a boil over high heat.
2. Reduce heat to medium, add green peppers, onion, garlic, bay leaves, bacon, and salt and pepper to taste, and mix well. Cover and cook for about 2 hours or until beans are tender.
3. Remove from heat and discard bay leaves.

To serve, put cooked rice in each soup bowl and ladle the soup over it.

Frijoles Negros   Black Beans

Yield: serves 4

2 to 4 tablespoons olive oil
1 green pepper, chopped
1 onion, chopped
4 cloves garlic, **finely chopped**, or 1 tablespoon garlic granules
2 cups cooked black beans, homemade (cooked according to directions on package), or canned
1 teaspoon *each* ground cumin and dried oregano flakes
salt and pepper to taste
2 cups cooked rice (cooked according to directions on package) for serving

Equipment: Large-size skillet with cover, mixing spoon

1. Heat 2 tablespoons oil in the skillet over medium-high heat, add green pepper, onion, garlic, and, stirring frequently, fry for about 3 minutes, until soft. Add more oil if necessary to prevent sticking.
2. Add beans, cumin, oregano flakes, salt and pepper to taste, and mix well. Reduce heat to simmer, cover, and cook for 5 minutes.

Serve black beans over cooked rice. Spoon 1/2 cup beans over 1/2 cup rice for each serving.

Yield: 4 to 6

2 to 3 pounds chicken, cut in serving-size pieces
1/2 cup lime juice
3 cloves garlic, **finely chopped**, or 1 teaspoon garlic granules
4 to 6 tablespoons vegetable oil
1 *each* green pepper, **cored, seeded**, chopped, and onion, chopped
1/2 cup raisins
2 bay leaves
1 cup tomato sauce, canned
4 cups chicken broth, homemade or canned
2 cups rice
salt and pepper to taste
1/2 cup sliced **pimento**, canned (drained)
2 cups green peas, fresh or frozen
4 eggs, hard-cooked and quartered, for garnish
2 limes cut into wedges for garnish

Equipment: Large-size skillet or **Dutch oven**, mixing spoon

1. Rub chicken with juice and garlic, cover, and refrigerate for 30 minutes.
2. Heat 2 tablespoons oil in skillet or Dutch oven over medium-high heat. Add chicken and brown on both sides, about 8 minutes per side. Add more oil as needed. Remove browned chicken and set aside.
3. Add green pepper, onion, raisins, bay leaves, tomato sauce, broth, and rice to skillet. Mix well and bring to a boil over high heat. Reduce heat to simmer, return chicken pieces to mixture, cover, and cook until chicken and rice are done, about 25 minutes. Add salt and pepper to taste. Remove from heat and remove and discard bay leaves. Sprinkle with pimento and peas and garnish with egg and lime wedges.

Serve from the skillet. *Arroz con pollo* can vary in consistency; some cooks prefer it soupy and others prefer a drier mix; either way is delicious.

Masa Real   *Marmalade Tart*

Yield: 24 pieces

1 1/2 cups sugar
1 1/4 cups vegetable oil
1 egg
2 tablespoons vanilla extract
5 cups cake flour
2 1/2 tablespoons baking powder
1/2 teaspoon salt
1/2 cup milk
3 tablespoons cornstarch
3 cups guava or pineapple marmalade
all-purpose flour for work surface
1 egg, beaten
1 tablespoon milk

Equipment: Large-size mixing bowl, mixing spoon or electric mixer, medium-size bowl, wooden mixing spoon, small-size saucepan, floured work surface, rolling pin, 9- x 12-inch baking sheet, **whisk** or fork, small-size bowl, pastry brush

1. *Prepare dough:* in large mixing bowl or electric mixer, cream together sugar and oil until smooth and fluffy, about 3 minutes. Add egg and vanilla and mix well.
2. In medium bowl, mix flour, baking powder, and salt together. Add flour mixture and milk alternately to sugar mixture, being careful not to overmix; just blend together. Cover and refrigerate for 2 hours.
3. *Prepare filling:* using wooden spoon, mix cornstarch with 1/2 cup marmalade to a smooth paste in saucepan. Add remaining marmalade and blend well. Cook over medium heat until thick, stirring frequently. Set aside to cool.
4. Place dough on work surface and divide in half. Using as little flour as possible, roll each piece to fit the bottom of the baking sheet; they should be about 1/2-inch thick.
5. Spread out 1 sheet of dough into the pan and gently pull the edges up so they can overlap the top crust. Spread filling evenly over the dough in the pan. Cover with second sheet of dough and press top and bottom edges together to seal.
6. Preheat the oven to 375° F.
7. *Prepare glaze:* in a small bowl beat egg with milk. Using the pastry brush, brush the top piece of dough with glaze. Using fork tines, poke vent holes into the dough.
8. Bake for 20 minutes or until the top crust begins to brown. Reduce heat to 350° F. and bake for 30 minutes more or until the top is firm and dry.

To serve, cool to room temperature and cut into squares 2 x 2 1/2-inches.

Ajiaco   Pork and Vegetable Stew

Yield: serves 6

1 1/2 pounds lean pork, cut into 2-inch cubes
1 pound pork bones
3 quarts water
3 yams or sweet potatoes, peeled and cut into chunks
2 ears of corn, fresh or frozen (cut crosswise into 4 pieces)
2 summer squash, **trimmed**, skin-on and finely chopped
4 **plantains**, peeled and cut in chunks (if available)
2 tablespoons vegetable oil
1 *each* onion, chopped and green bell pepper, **cored**, **seeded**, chopped
2 tomatoes, chopped
3 cloves garlic or 1 tablespoon garlic granules
juice of 2 limes
salt and pepper to taste
3 cups cooked rice (prepared according to directions on package)

Equipment: Large-size saucepan with cover or **Dutch oven**, tongs, spoon, medium-size skillet

1. Put pork, bones, and water in the saucepan or Dutch oven and bring to a boil over high heat. With spoon, skim off any film that comes to the top. Reduce heat to simmer, cover, and cook for 1 hour or until meat is almost tender. Add yams, corn, squash, and **plantains**, simmer for 30 minutes, and remove bones.

2. Heat oil in skillet over medium heat, add onion, green pepper, tomatoes, and garlic, and, stirring continually, fry about 5 minutes until soft. Add to stew, with lime juice and salt and pepper to taste and mix well.

Serve *ajiaco* over cooked rice.

Bahamas

The Bahamas are a group of 700 sparsely settled islands that stretch for 590 miles just off the southeast tip of Florida. It is populated mostly by people of African descent. The British established a colony in the Bahamas in 1629 and granted full independence in 1973. British foods such as pickled onions, dark English fruitcake and plum pudding at Christmas, and pound cakes served at weddings are common in the Bahamas. The pickled onions have red pepper added to them and the fruitcake has rum added for that zing Bahamians appreciate. The very British tradition of tea time has not carried over for the general population. Most of the islands will not support very much agriculture, and so the people rely on earning money from tourism to purchase food. On the southeastern islands, small-scale farming and fishing are practiced. People raise fruits and vegetables, goats, pigs, turkeys, and sheep.

Curried Bananas

Yield: serves 4 to 6

1 cup butter or margarine
2 tablespoons dark brown sugar
1 tablespoon curry powder
6 bananas, peeled and sliced in 1/4-inch rounds

Equipment: Medium-size skillet, mixing spoon

1. Melt butter or margarine in skillet over medium heat. Add brown sugar and curry powder, and blend well. Add bananas and gently turn to coat.
2. Reduce heat to low and cook for 6 minutes or until bananas are lightly browned.

Serve *curried bananas* as a side dish with chicken or meat. It also makes a fine dessert.

Banana Pudding

Like British puddings, this Bahamian desert resembles cake more than it does an American pudding.

Yield: serves 4 to 6

6 ripe bananas, mashed
1/2 cup all-purpose flour
1 cup sugar
1 tablespoon melted butter
1 teaspoon ground nutmeg
confectioners' sugar for garnish

Equipment: Large-size mixing bowl, mixing spoon, greased 8-inch baking pan

Preheat oven to 325°F.
1. Put bananas in mixing bowl, add flour, sugar, butter, and nutmeg, and mix well.
2. Pour batter in baking pan and bake in oven about 40 minutes until top is golden brown. Cool to room temperature, cut in squares, and sprinkle with confectioners' sugar.

Serve warm or cold as dessert.

Conkies   Sweet Coconut Snack

Conkies are made for Guy Fawkes Day on November 5, an English celebration marking the anniversary of the Gunpowder Plot to blow up King James I and the British Parliament in 1605. The plot failed and all plotters, Guy Fawkes among them, were executed. The celebration is full of good food and fun. This same recipe can be used for the other Caribbean Islands. Islanders wrap **plantain**, almond, or banana leaves around the filling mixture when making *conkies*. We suggest instead aluminum foil.

Yield: makes 12

1 1/2 cups grated coconut meat, canned or fresh (see recipe page 208)
1 cup peeled and grated pumpkin, fresh or frozen (thawed)
1 cup sweet potatoes, peeled and grated
1 1/2 cups brown sugar
1 teaspoon *each* ground allspice and ground nutmeg
1 teaspoon almond extract
1/2 cup seedless raisins
1/4 cup all-purpose flour
1 cup white or yellow cornmeal
1 teaspoon salt more or less to taste
1 cup *each* melted butter or margarine and milk
4 to 10 cups water

Equipment: Large-size mixing bowl, wooden mixing spoon or electric mixer, 12 6-inch squares of aluminum foil, large-size saucepan with cover, fitted with steamer rack or basket

1. Combine coconut, pumpkin, sweet potatoes, brown sugar, allspice, nutmeg, almond extract, raisins, flour, cornmeal, and salt in mixing bowl, using spoon or electric mixer and mix well. Slowly add butter or margarine and milk, mixing into smooth paste.
2. Put 2 tablespoons of mixture in middle of each foil square, fold in edges making a tightly sealed package.

3. Put about 2 or 3 inches of water in saucepan and fit with steamer rack or basket (the water should not touch basket). Stack packages in steamer, bring water to a boil over high heat and cover tightly. Reduce heat to simmer and steam for 1 hour or until mixture in packages is thoroughly cooked. Check frequently to make sure water has not boiled out. If necessary, add more hot water, but be careful of steam when you are adding it.

Serve *conkies* hot; open the package and eat the mixture inside.

Latin America

Latin America includes South and Central America and Mexico. The geography, as much as the history, has influenced the development of each country and its culture. At one time the Andes, the 4,000-mile mountain range that runs parallel with the Pacific coast, kept not only the countries isolated from one another but also kept apart different cultures within each country. The foods of Latin American countries are a blending of Native American with Portuguese and Spanish techniques and flavors. In most large cities the life-style of the people is very continental. The cooking has a strong European influence, and foods are imported from all over the world. The rural and village people cook and eat very much as their ancestors have for centuries. In South America the llama has played an important role in the lives of farmers and is a beast of burden as well as a source of wool for clothes, meat for food, and milk. Today Latin America is a melting-pot of the ancient with the new, of indigenous foods prepared in hundreds of different ways, all exciting and delicious. In this section we have modified some of the hot peppers added to many Latin dishes. If you prefer, they may be omitted all together.

Chile

Chile is a very Europeanized South American nation that skirts the western coast of South America. Most of the inhabitants are *mestizo*, that is, the descendants of Europeans and Native American people who long ago married and raised families. There are not many Native Americans left in Chile as a distinct group.

Although Spaniards were the dominant settlers, other Europeans settled there as well. The settlers found Native Americans growing corn, potatoes, squash, beans, cucumbers, papayas, avocados, and prickly pear. The settlers continued to grow these crops and began to import their own favorite foods. Grapes were imported and now are an important crop in Chile. Wine is made from them and is a popular drink. Chilean wine is so good that it is exported to one of the wine capitals of the world, France. Other major crops include wheat, oats, corn, rice, barley, rye, beans, potatoes, peas, and citrus fruits.

Fruit is a common dessert in Chile, but it is also served at breakfast along with milk or coffee and toast. Flan is a popular dessert. Lunch, the main meal, is served at about 2:00. Tea time is at 5:00 o'clock, where tea, or something stronger such as wine for the adults, is served with bread or cakes to tide everyone over until dinner. Dinner can be served anywhere from 8:00 p.m. to midnight.

Seafood is the main food in this country with a 2,600-mile coastline. Luckily, even poor people can afford to eat some of the treasures from the sea, such as abalone. Beef is popular too, but it is not raised to as great an extent as it is in other South American countries. Soup, salad, rolls, and a main course of seafood or beef are served. A favorite flavoring in cooking is the combination of garlic, oil, and paprika, called "color," which is orange-red. *Pebre*, a sauce made of onions, vinegar, olive oil, garlic, chili, and **coriander**, is as popular as catsup is in the United States. Some families like it mild and others like it very hot.

Uminitas — Corn Casserole

Yield: serves 4 to 6

4 cups corn kernels, freshly grated or frozen (thawed)
2 eggs, beaten
1 teaspoon all-purpose flour
salt and pepper to taste
4 tablespoons melted butter or margarine
1/2 cup shredded cheddar cheese

Equipment: Medium-size mixing bowl, mixing spoon, 8-inch baking pan

Preheat oven to 350° F.

1. Put corn kernels, eggs, flour, and salt and pepper to taste in mixing bowl and mix well.

2. Swirl melted butter or margarine around baking pan to coat bottom and sides. Add half of the corn mixture, 1/4 cup cheese, and remaining corn mixture. Sprinkle remaining cheese over the top. Bake for about 30 minutes, until top is bubbly and brown.

Serve hot as a side dish with meat, poultry, or fish.

Porotos Granados   *Beans with Vegetables*

Porotos granados is usually made with fresh or dried cranberry beans, called *porotos*. We suggest instead using more readily available cooked, dried, or canned navy beans.

Yield: serves 6

2 tablespoons vegetable oil
1 cup **finely chopped** onion
3 cloves garlic, finely chopped, or 1 teaspoon garlic granules
1 tablespoon paprika
1 teaspoon ground oregano
1 cup **trimmed**, peeled, and finely sliced zucchini
4 cups cooked dried navy beans (cooked according to directions on package; save liquid) or canned (**strain** liquid and save)
1 1/2 cups water, more or less as needed
1 1/2 cups **stewed** tomatoes, canned
1 cup corn kernels, fresh, frozen (thawed), or canned (drained)
salt and pepper to taste

Equipment: Large-size saucepan or **Dutch oven**, mixing spoon

1. Heat oil in saucepan over medium-high heat, add onion, garlic, paprika, and oregano and mix well. Fry until onion is soft (about 3 minutes). Add zucchini and beans and mix well.
2. Add enough water to reserved bean liquid to make 2 cups, and add to mixture. Mix well, and bring to a boil. Reduce heat to simmer and add tomatoes, corn, and salt and pepper to taste. Cook uncovered to reduce liquid but not dry out (about 30 minutes).

Serve as the main dish or a side dish with meat, poultry, or fish.

Argentina

If you like big juicy steaks, Argentina is the place for you. Cattle ranching is one of the biggest industries in Argentina. Argentina is a huge country at the southern end of South America, and by South American standards it is very prosperous. The land supports heavy agricultural production, and many modern methods are employed to increase it. Argentine cooking is very European, especially influenced by early Spanish and Italian settlers. Traditional old-world cooking procedures are followed using locally available ingredients. The cooking lacks the strong Native American influence found in most other South and Central American countries. The extensive use of squash in many types of dishes, from main course to desserts, is an exception, however, as squash is a distinctly Native American food. Another exception is a tea named *mate*, or *yerba*. It was brewed by the Guarani Indians originally and is an Argentine specialty, made of the leaves and stems of a South American holly tree. The leaves are used for at least ten brewings, with the fourth or fifth brewings considered the best. Some people add sugar and cream, but not the real lovers of this tea.

Other crops important to Argentina are wheat, corn, sugar cane, grapes, citrus fruits, and soy beans. The grapes are used to make wine, and Argentina is one of the largest wine producers in the world. Argentine beef is world famous. In the cities, restaurants have special grills called *parrillas*, where thick juicy steaks are cooked to order at very reasonable prices.

Carbonada   Meat and Fruit Stew

Combining meat with fresh fruit, as well as vegetables, is characteristic of Argentine cooking, as shown in the following recipe.

Yield: serves 4 to 6

2 tablespoons olive or vegetable oil
1 onion, **finely chopped**
3 cloves garlic, finely chopped, or 1 teaspoon garlic granules
1 pound boneless lean beef, cut into bite-size **cubes**
1 cup whole **stewed** tomatoes, homemade or canned
2 bay leaves
1 teaspoon *each* ground oregano and sugar
4 cups beef broth, homemade or canned
1 sweet potato, peeled, cut into bite-size cubes
1 potato, peeled, cut into bite-size cubes
2 peaches, fresh, peeled, **pitted** and sliced, 1 1/2 cups frozen (thawed), or canned, drained
2 pears, fresh, peeled, **cored** and **cubed**, or canned, drained
1 ear of corn, cut across the cob into 1-inch slices

Equipment: Large-size skillet, mixing spoon

1. Heat oil in skillet over medium-high heat, add onion and garlic, and fry until soft, about 3 minutes. Add meat, mix well, and cook for about 5 minutes until meat is no longer pink. Add tomatoes, bay leaves, oregano, sugar, beef broth, and potatoes, and mix well. Reduce heat to simmer, cover, and cook for 20 minutes until potatoes are tender.
2. Increase heat to medium-high, bring to a boil, and add peaches, pears, and corn. Mix gently so as not to mash fruit. Reduce to simmer, cover, and cook for 10 minutes more. Remove bay leaves and discard.

Serve *carbonada* as a one-dish meal.

The Spanish have many wonderful egg dishes and this recipe is no exception. It was brought to Argentina from Spain and is popular as a side dish or as the main course for brunch or lunch. It is usually served on a bed of rice.

Yield: serves 6

6 medium-size firm tomatoes
2 tablespoons butter or margarine
1 onion, **finely chopped**
1/2 cup chopped mushrooms, fresh or frozen (thawed), or canned, drained
1/2 cup finely chopped cooked ham
1/2 cup bread crumbs
salt and pepper to taste
1/2 cup shelled, green peas, fresh or frozen (thawed)
6 eggs
4 teaspoons Parmesan cheese
4 cups cooked rice (cooked according to directions on package)

Equipment: Tablespoon, small-size bowl, paper towels, medium-size skillet, strainer, nonstick or greased 8-inch baking pan

1. Cut tops off all tomatoes, about 1/2-inch down. Using spoon, carefully scoop out **pulp** and put in bowl. Turn scooped-out tomatoes upside-down to drain on paper towels.
2. Melt 2 tablespoons butter or margarine in skillet over medium-high heat, add onion and mushrooms, and cook for about 3 minutes, stirring continually until soft and cooked through.
3. Using a strainer, drain tomato juice from pulp. (Refrigerate juice to use at another time.) Add tomato pulp, ham, bread crumbs, and salt and pepper to taste to onion mixture and mix well. Cook to heat through (about 3 minutes more). Remove from heat, add peas, and mix well.
3. Preheat oven to 350° F.
4. Spoon mixture into scooped-out tomatoes, leaving about 1/2 inch of space at the top of each. Set filled tomatoes in baking pan. Break eggs, one at a time, and place one on top of each filled tomato. Sprinkle with salt and pepper to taste and Parmesan cheese. Bake in oven for about 20 minutes, cooking eggs to desired doneness. The tomatoes should be tender but still firm.

Serve stuffed tomatoes, while warm, on a bed of rice.

Uruguay

The cooking style of Uruguayans is similar to that of the people of neighboring Argentina in that European influence was far reaching and still predominates. Most of the usable land is devoted to pasture land. Wheat, corn, oats, barley, rice, sunflower seeds, and fruits such as apples and oranges are grown. Uruguay is self-sufficient in providing its own food. Beef is the most common food, but lamb or chicken are also eaten. Meat is served at all meals except tea time. It is cooked in many forms, roasted on a spit, grilled, pan-fried, and of course boiled into fine stews with fruits or squash. Tea time is a tradition that is still enjoyed. People eat little sweets to go along with their coffee or tea in the late afternoon. Dinner is served around 9:00 p.m., and so tea time is an important habit that bridges the hours from lunch to dinner. *Mate*, the tea mentioned in the Argentine section, is popular here as well. Since Argentina and Uruguay have such similar foods you can interchange recipes to fit your needs. A sweet that is popular in Uruguay and all over South America is called *dulce de leche* and is made from sugar and milk.

Dulce de Leche   *Milk Sweets*

There are many ways to make this sweet but none is easier than this following recipe.

Yield 20 candies

1 can (14 1/2 ounces) sweetened condensed milk
1/2 cup **finely chopped** nuts: pecans, peanuts, walnuts, or almonds

Equipment: **Double boiler** with cover, pie pan, wax-paper-covered plate

1. Fill the bottom pan of double boiler with about 3 inches of water. Bring to a boil over high heat.
2. Pour sweetened condensed milk into the top pan, cover, and set it over the pan of boiling water. Allow the water to boil for about 5 minutes, reduce to medium, and cook for about 3 hours. Carefully and frequently check the water level in the bottom pan to make sure it does not boil dry. Keep a kettle of hot water on the stove to add, from time to time, to the bottom pan.
3. When milk is thick, remove from heat and allow to cool at room temperature. Refrigerate for about 1 hour.
4. Put nuts in pie pan. Take a tablespoon of cooled milk, roll into a ball then roll in chopped nuts. Place balls side-by-side on wax paper. Cover and refrigerate.

Serve as a candy treat. They keep well for several weeks if refrigerated.

Bolivia

Bolivia is a landlocked country that had been part of the rich Inca Empire thousands of years ago. Today it is a struggling country, underdeveloped in almost every way. Most Bolivians are Native Americans, living much as their ancestors have for centuries. They grow potatoes, corn, rice, sugar cane, yucca, and **plantains**. Two important crops native to Bolivia and not found elsewhere are *quinoa seeds* and *oca roots*. These two foods provide the mainstay in many Bolivians' diet. Cheese sauce is used on both potatoes and oca. Quinoa seeds are roasted and boiled into porridge that has a nutty flavor. Chilies are used for spicing foods. Livestock raised include goats, pigs, cattle, and donkeys. Milk from goats and cows is made into cheese and creams.

The national food of the Bolivians is *chuno*, dehydrated potatoes. Spread out on the ground at the first frost, the potatoes freeze at night and thaw under the hot sun during the day, becoming soggy. They are then trampled on by family members, who squeeze out any moisture. The freezing, thawing, and stomping is repeated until nothing is left except hard little potato nuggets that can be stored for years without spoiling. This process was probably the first freeze-dry method of preserving food, dating back to the Inca Empire.

Along with potatoes, corn is the other important food. Combining them, as in the following recipe, is very common. We suggest adding vegetable oil instead of lard for a healthier dish. In Bolivia something similar to sour cream is made from soured fresh cream and buttermilk. We suggest serving commercial sour cream with this dish.

Papas y Elotes   Potatoes and Corn

Yield: serves 4 to 6

2 tablespoons vegetable oil
3 cloves garlic, **finely chopped**, or 1 teaspoon garlic granules
2 onions, finely chopped
1 3-inch fresh green chili pepper, **cored**, **seeded**, and chopped (available at most supermarkets and Latin-American food stores)
1 tablespoon ground cumin
1 teaspoon dried hot red pepper flakes, more or less to taste
salt and pepper to taste
4 cups chopped tomatoes, fresh or canned
1 tablespoon sugar
2 cups corn kernels, fresh (cooked, cut-off cobs), frozen (thawed), or canned (drained)
6 boiled potatoes (egg-size), quartered, fresh or canned
1 cup sour cream for garnish

Equipment: Large-size skillet with cover, mixing spoon

1. Heat oil in skillet over medium-high heat. Add onions, garlic, green chili, cumin, red pepper flakes, and salt and pepper to taste, and mix well. Cook for about 3 minutes until onions are soft.
2. Add tomatoes and sugar, mix well, and bring to a boil. Add corn and potatoes, mix well, reduce heat to simmer, cover, and cook for about 15 minutes, stirring frequently to prevent sticking.

Serve *papas y elotes* hot, in a bowl, with a side dish of sour cream to spoon over it and warm *tortillas* for sopping.

Saltenas   Meat Turnovers

On every city street corner in Bolivia vendors sell *saltenas* as a walk-and-eat snack. They're Bolivia's answer to the fast-food craze. The pastry is made with basic pie crust dough, and any ready-made crust can be used.

Yield serves 4

2 tablespoons vegetable oil
2 onions, **finely chopped**
3 cloves garlic, finely chopped, or 1 teaspoon garlic granules
1/2 pound ground lean beef
1/4 cup tomato paste
1/2 teaspoon ground hot red pepper, more or less to taste
1/4 cup **pitted**, sliced green olives
1 cup cooked rice (cook according to directions on package)
2 **hard-cooked eggs**, peeled, finely chopped
salt and pepper to taste
4 9-inch unbaked pie crusts, homemade or frozen (thawed)
1 egg, beaten

Equipment: Large-size skillet, mixing spoon, cup, fork, nonstick or lightly greased baking sheet, spoon or pastry brush

1. Heat oil in skillet over medium-high heat, add onions and garlic, and fry until soft, about 3 minutes. Add meat, mix well, and cook for about 5 minutes until meat is no longer pink. Add tomato paste, red pepper, olives, rice, eggs, and salt and pepper to taste and mix well. Cook for 3 minutes and remove from heat.
2. Have a cup of water handy. Place 4 pie crust rounds side-by-side on work surface and pile meat mixture equally on each, keeping to one half of crust. Leave a 1-inch margin along curved edge. Fold unfilled side over filling, joining curved edges to make a half circle. To seal edges together, dip a finger into cup of water and run it along inside curved edges. Using the back of fork **tines**, press edges firmly together. Using spoon or pastry brush, brush crust tops with egg. Make steam vents by poking each top about 4 or 5 times with fork tines. Place pastries side-by-side on baking sheet and refrigerate for about 30 minutes.
3. Preheat oven to 400° F.
4. Bake in oven for 10 minutes, reduce heat to 350° F., and continue baking for about 15 minutes more, until tops are golden brown.

Serve *saltenas* hot or cold as a snack or full meal. They are excellent to take on picnics or in a lunch box.

Brazil

Brazil is the largest country in South America. It is a land of many cultures, including the Native Americans who originally lived there and the Portuguese who began to arrive in 1500. Africans were brought as slaves, and other settlers from the four corners of the world, especially Europe, began to arrive in the twentieth century. The blending of these cultures contributed to the interesting and varied foods of Brazil.

Native Americans showed the Portuguese how to make **manioc** flour from **cassava** (yucca). It is still a widely popular ingredient and is kept on most tables just as salt and pepper are in the United States. Manioc can be used plain, just to sprinkle on food, or as a side dish when fried in a little palm oil and sprinkled with salt. Africans brought with them African palm, from which palm oil is gathered. Palm oil is widely used for frying in Brazil. It makes the food yellowish orange. The Portuguese imported many foods and began growing them in suitable climates. Ingredients in many dishes include **cilantro**, onions, chili peppers, garlic, bell pepper, and tomatoes. Food crops that are most important to Brazil are rice, coffee, sugar cane, corn, wheat, and many fruits.

Most countries throughout the world seem to have one national dish made with locally grown ingredients available to everyone. In Brazil the national dish is *feijoada*, a stew made by cooking a variety of meats together with black beans. For special feast days as many as 15 different meats are combined with the black beans. Sausage, pork, bacon, tongue, beef, and pig's feet or ear are basic ingredients, although for everyday eating no more than 4 or 5 meats are customary. Traditionally *feijoada* is served with a rice dish called *arroz brasileiro*, and orange salad called *laranjas*, and shredded greens called *couve a mineira*.

Feijoada   Meat Stew with Black Beans

Yield: serves 6

2 cups dried black beans (to **reconstitute** beans, boil in 6 cups water for 2 minutes, remove
    from heat, cover, set aside for 1 hour—beans will double in size)
3 to 3 1/2 cups water
1/2 pound sausage, cut into 1-inch pieces
1/2 pound *each* beef and pork, cut into 1-inch cubes (any cuts of meat)
3 slices bacon, cut into 1-inch pieces
1 jalapeno, or green chili pepper, **seeded** and **finely chopped (to handle peppers, wear
    rubber gloves or put hands in plastic baggies)**
1 tomato, finely chopped
3 cloves garlic, finely chopped, or 1 teaspoon garlic granules
salt, pepper, and ground red pepper to taste

Equipment: Large-size saucepan with cover or **Dutch oven**, mixing spoon, small-size skillet

1. Put drained, soaked beans with water in large saucepan or Dutch oven and bring to a boil over high heat. Reduce heat to simmer, cover, and cook for about 1 1/2 hours or until beans are tender; stir frequently.
2. Add sausage, beef, and pork, mix well, cover, and cook over medium heat for about 45 minutes. Stir frequently and add a little hot water if necessary to prevent sticking.
3. In small skillet, fry bacon over medium heat for 5 minutes or until crisp. Add jalapeno, tomato, garlic and mix well. Reduce heat to simmer and cook for 2 minutes. Add bacon and vegetables to meat mixture and add salt, pepper, and red pepper to taste. Mix well, remove from heat, and serve.

Serve over rice and garnish with orange slices.

Arroz Brasileiro   Brazilian Rice

Yield: serves 6

2 tablespoons vegetable oil
1 onion, finely sliced

1 green bell pepper, **seeded** and **finely chopped**
3 cloves garlic, finely chopped, or 1 teaspoon garlic granules
1 cup uncooked rice
2 1/2 cups boiling water
2 tomatoes, **peeled** and finely chopped
salt and pepper to taste

Equipment: Medium-size skillet with cover or **Dutch oven**, mixing spoon

1. Heat oil in skillet or Dutch oven over medium-high heat, add onion, green pepper, and garlic and mix well. Reduce heat to low and cook until soft (about 3 minutes).
2. Add rice, mix well to coat with oil, and cook for about 2 minutes. Add boiling water and salt and pepper to taste, increase heat to high, and bring to a boil. Reduce heat to simmer, cover, and cook for 20 minutes or until rice is tender.
3. Remove from heat, add tomatoes, and mix well. Cover and set aside for about 10 minutes. **Fluff** with fork before serving.

Serve *arroz brasileiro* as a side dish with *feijoada*.

Couve a Mineira   Shredded Greens

Yield: serves 6

6 cups water
3 pounds kale, collard greens, or spinach, washed, drained, stems removed, and **shredded**
1/2 pound bacon, **finely chopped**
salt and pepper to taste

Equipment: Large-size saucepan with cover, wooden mixing spoon, **colander** or strainer, large-size skillet, tongs

1. Put water in saucepan and bring to a boil over high heat. Add greens, and using wooden spoon, push down to cover with water. Bring back to boil, reduce heat to simmer, cover, and cook for 3 minutes. Drain greens in colander or strainer and rinse under cold water to stop cooking action.
2. Put bacon in skillet over medium-high heat and fry until crisp, about 3 minutes. Reduce heat to medium, add greens, and season with salt and pepper to taste. Using tongs, turn greens to mix with bacon and cook for about 3 minutes, until greens are cooked through.

Serve *couve a mineira* as a side dish with *feijoada*.

Laranjas   Orange Salad

Yield: serves 6

6 oranges, peeled and **pith** removed, cut in slices
1 teaspoon sugar
salt and pepper to taste

Equipment: **Serrated-edge** knife, medium-size platter

Arrange orange slices, slightly overlapping, on a platter and sprinkle with sugar and salt and pepper to taste. Refrigerate until ready to serve.

Serve as a side dish with *feijoada*.

Churrasco a Gaucha   Brazilian Barbecue

Along with China and Korea, Brazil uses more garlic in their cooking than any other country. This barbecue recipe uses its fair share of this popular flavoring.

Yield: serves 6 to 8

9 cloves garlic, **finely chopped**, or 3 teaspoons garlic granules
1 tablespoon red pepper flakes
1 teaspoon paprika
2 cups water
1/2 pound pork sausage link, either sweet or hot
1 chicken, cut into serving-size pieces
1/2 pound pork loin, sliced 1/2 inch thick
1/2 pound boneless beef, sliced 1/2 inch thick
salt and pepper to taste

Equipment: Small-size mixing bowl, large-size plastic baggie, charcoal grill, long-handled grill tongs or fork

1. *Prepare marinade:* make a **marinade** by mixing garlic, red pepper flakes, and paprika with water in small mixing bowl. Transfer to plastic baggie, add sausage, chicken, pork and beef, seal tightly, and **marinate** for 1 hour, shaking baggie several times to coat meats.
2. *Prepare grill:* light charcoal and allow time for coals to retain heat.
3. The grilling time varies depending upon the distance from the heat, thickness of meat, and the desired doneness. Use tongs or fork to place assorted meats side-by-side on grill rack. Roast all meats and chicken slowly on both sides and frequently sprinkle with remaining marinade. Add pork sausage and pork loin pieces first, since they take the longest to cook to well done, from 10 to 15 minutes per side, and then add chicken and beef. Add salt and pepper to taste. (Chicken is fully cooked and done when, poked with a fork, the juices that run out are no longer pink. Cook beef from about 5 to 10 minutes per side for medium, longer for well done.) Near end of roasting cut into pieces of meat to check the doneness.

Serve with *farova de ovo* and *molho a campanha.*

Farova de Ovo   Seasoned Eggs

Brazil is the world's largest grower of **cassavas**. **Tapioca** and manioc flour are made from cassavas. The starchy cassava is a tuber. Brazilians are very fond of manioc flour and sprinkle it on almost everything they eat. *Farova* is a famous Brazilian dish made with manioc flour. Manioc flour can be purchased at Latin- American food stores. If you cannot find it, try substituting unseasoned bread crumbs in the following recipe.

Yield: serves 4 to 6

4 to 6 tablespoons butter or margarine, more as needed
2 onions, **finely chopped**
12 pitted black olives
1/2 cup **diced** cooked ham
4 eggs, lightly beaten

1 cup unseasoned bread crumbs or **manioc** flour
salt and pepper to taste
1/2 cup chopped fresh parsley for garnish

Equipment: Medium-size skillet, mixing spoon

1. Melt 4 tablespoons butter or margarine in skillet over medium heat. Add onions, olives, and ham, mix well, and cook until onions are soft (about 4 minutes).
2. Add remaining butter or margarine and add eggs, stirring continually until eggs are soft scrambled (about 2 minutes).
3. Add bread crumbs or manioc and salt and pepper to taste and mix well. Reduce heat to low, cover, and cook through (about 5 minutes). Sprinkle parsley over mixture for garnish.

Serve as a side dish with *churrasco a gaucha*, Brazilian barbecue.

Molho a Campanha Cold Sauce to Serve with Barbecue

Yield: 1 1/2 to 2 cups

1 onion, **finely chopped**
1 green bell pepper, finely chopped
2 tomatoes, **peeled** and chopped
2 green onions, chopped
1/2 cup chopped parsley
1/2 cup white vinegar
3 tablespoons olive oil
salt and pepper to taste

Equipment: Medium-size bowl, mixing spoon

Put onion, green pepper, tomatoes, green onions, parsley, vinegar, and oil in mixing bowl and mix well. Add salt and pepper to taste and refrigerate.

Serve at room temperature as a condiment sauce for *churrasco a gaucha*.

Peru

The Spanish conquest of Peru killed off a large number of the original inhabitants, especially along the coastal region; thus the food tastes in Peru today, for the most part, are Spanish. Peru's western coastal region affords it many treasures from the sea, making fishing a major industry of this country. Fish stews and other fish dishes are commonly eaten. Street vendors sell food such as fruits, roasted pork, or deviled potatoes to people walking by. Markets are big open-air affairs. Vendors sit next to what they have to offer, such as a stack of tomatoes, corn, or squash. Peru's chief food crops are wheat, potatoes, beans, rice, barley, and sugar cane. They also grow coffee as an export crop.

The Native Americans still living in Peru, about 50 percent of the population, are very poor. Most Native American groups depend on farming and hunting to feed themselves and their families. Life for the middle class is not so hard. People who live in Lima eat a wider variety of foods and go out to restaurants for all kinds of specialities.

Potatoes are native to Peru, where thousands of years ago Inca and pre-Incan civilizations cultivated and developed more than 200 varieties. "Irish" potatoes were imported to Europe from Peru, so they're actually Peruvian potatoes! Peruvians cook potatoes in many interesting ways, blending Spanish flavors with cooking skills handed down from their pre-Columbian ancestors.

Llapingachos   Potato Cakes

Yield: serves 6

6 boiled potatoes, peeled and mashed, or 6 cups prepared instant mashed potatoes
1/4 cup butter
2 onions, **finely chopped**
2 cups shredded Cheddar cheese
salt and pepper to taste
2 to 4 tablespoons vegetable oil

Equipment: Large-size mixing bowl, mixing spoon, large-size skillet, pancake turner or metal spatula

1. Put mashed potatoes in mixing bowl and set aside.
2. Melt butter in skillet over medium-high heat, add onions, and fry until soft (about 3 minutes). Add onions, pan scrapings, and cheese to potatoes and mix well. Season with salt and pepper to taste. Divide mixture into 12 patties.
3. Heat 2 tablespoons oil in skillet over medium-high heat, add patties, and fry until golden brown on both sides, about 4 minutes each side. Add more oil as needed to prevent sticking. Keep in warm place until ready to serve.

Serve the patties warm or cold as a side dish or main dish. Peanut sauce, *salsa de mali,* is often served with the patties.

Salsa de Mali   South American Peanut Sauce

Traditionally *salsa de mali* is served with potato patties. In Peru it is made with fresh peanuts, but we suggest adding peanut butter for a smoother and quicker sauce.

Yield: about 2 1/2 cups

2 tablespoons vegetable oil
1 onion, **finely chopped**
1 clove garlic, finely chopped, or 1/2 teaspoon garlic granules
2 tomatoes, **peeled** and chopped, or 1 cup canned whole tomatoes (and juice)
1/2 cup chunky peanut butter
salt and pepper to taste

Equipment: Medium-size skillet, mixing spoon

Heat oil in skillet over medium-high heat, add onion, salt and pepper to taste, and fry until soft (about 3 minutes). Add garlic, tomatoes, and peanut butter, mix well to blend, and cook until heated through.

Serve *salsa de mali* warm over potato patties.

Ecuador

Ecuador is a small country in South America that sits right on the equator. It is hot in the areas close to the Pacific Ocean, but in the higher mountain regions it is cooler. There are three main regions of Ecuador, each producing its own food. Along the coast and rivers, fishing is the main source of food. Potatoes, corn, and barley grow in the fertile fields between the two ranges of the Andes mountains. In the jungle east of the Andes, bananas and **plantains** grow, along with other tropical foods such as **cassava**, which will grow even in poor thin soil.

The main food crops of Ecuador are bananas, barley, corn, rice, sugar cane, cacao, wheat, and vegetables. Cattle raising is done as well. Just as elsewhere, diet is affected by what food is available. The people who live in the mountains primarily eat corn, potatoes, and beans. Meat is rarely eaten by people living in the country. Coastal people have fish in their diets; it is cooked in stews along with peas or fried. Jungle dwellers prepare **plantains** by frying or roasting them. Soups and stews made with cassava are common, and fried rice with onion and herbs is frequently prepared.

Coconut Bars

In most Latin American countries sugar cane is plentiful, and sugar is added to desserts and candies with a heavy hand. In the following recipe the quantity of sugar seems excessive, yet it is exactly the amount specified. We suggest adjusting the quantity to satisfy your personal preference.

Yield: serves 6 to 8

4 cups grated unsweetened coconut, homemade (recipe page 208), frozen (thawed), or canned
5 cups sugar, more or less to taste
4 egg yolks (refrigerate whites to use at another time)
2 tablespoons butter or margarine (at room temperature)
2 tablespoons water

Equipment: Nonstick or greased 8-inch-square baking pan, wax paper, medium-size mixing bowl, wooden mixing spoon, baking pan large enough to hold 8-inch pan with water

Preheat oven to 325° F.

1. Line bottom of baking pan with wax paper, grease paper, and set aside.
2. Put coconut, sugar, egg yolks, butter or margarine, and water in mixing bowl and mix well to blend. Press mixture evenly in baking pan.
3. Fill larger baking pan with 1-inch water and place in oven. Set pan with mixture carefully into pan of water and bake for about 25 minutes, until top is crusty and the center is still moist.

Serve either warm or cold, as a dessert. A **dollop** of whipped topping can be added for a special touch.

Quindín — *Coconut Pudding Dessert*

Yield: serves 6

1/4 cup butter (at room temperature)
1 cup sugar
1/2 teaspoon cinnamon
8 egg yolks (at room temperature—refrigerate whites to use at another time)
1 cup half-and-half
1/4 cup grated coconut, homemade (see recipe page 208), frozen, or canned

Equipment: Large-size mixing bowl, electric mixer, mixing spoon, 6 buttered heat-proof custard cups, baking pan large enough to hold 6 cups

Preheat oven to 325°F.

1. Combine butter, sugar, and cinnamon in large mixing bowl, with electric mixer or mixing spoon, and beat until light and fluffy. Add egg yolks one at a time, mixing continually. Add half-and-half, mixing until mixture thickens and forms a ribbon when dripping off spoon (about 5 minutes).
2. **Fold** coconut thoroughly into egg mixture and spoon evenly into custard cups, filling each about 3/4 full.
3. Pour 1 inch of water into baking pan, place filled custard cups into water, and put in oven. Bake for about 50 minutes, or until firm and golden, remove from oven, and cool to room temperature.
4. Run a small knife around inside of each cup to loosen custard. Turn over cups, one at a time, on individual plates to release pudding. Refrigerate until ready to serve.

Serve puddings cold for dessert and add a **dollop** of whipped topping.

Colombia

Colombia, in the northwestern part of South America, is the South American link to Panama and the rest of Central America. The extensive coastal region is rich in fish and shellfish. Tropical fruits and vegetables flourish in the hot, humid, sea-level climate. On the mountain plateaus, where it is cooler, grow the agricultural treasures of Colombia. Coffee beans grown here are considered some of the world's finest and are exported throughout the world. Potatoes grow well in this area. Outstanding corn with huge white kernels and unusual purple corn with a delicate flavor and aroma grow on every available plot of land that can be cultivated. For many years, pockets of people lived in almost complete seclusion due to rough transportation over the mountains. Cooks developed their own styles, using what was available in the area. Colombian cooks are proud of their locally grown foods, preparing dishes simply, with a light Spanish touch, allowing natural flavors to come through as much as possible.

Mantequilla de Pobre   Poor Man's Butter

You may also know this by the name of a related recipe—*guacamole*, for which there is a recipe in the Mexico section (page 252) of this book.

Yield: about 2 cups

2 very ripe avocados, peeled, stone removed, **cubed**
2 tomatoes, **peeled, finely chopped**
2 to 3 tablespoons lime juice
1 tablespoon olive oil or vegetable oil
salt and pepper to taste

Equipment: Electric blender, potato masher, or wooden spoon; small-size mixing bowl, mixing spoon

1. Mash cut avocado in blender, or by hand with potato masher or wooden spoon
2. Put mashed avocados in a bowl and add tomatoes, lime juice, oil, and salt and pepper to taste. Cover and refrigerate until ready to serve.

Serve *mantequilla de pobre* as a spread on tortillas (Mexican flat bread), a heaping spoonful on a taco shell with shredded lettuce and chopped tomatoes, or as a salad or condiment with meat and poultry.

Humas Enolla   Corn Dish

Yield: serves 4 to 6

4 cups corn kernels, freshly grated or frozen (thawed)
1/2 cup all-purpose flour
4 to 6 tablespoons butter or margarine
1 onion, **finely chopped**
1 green bell pepper, finely chopped
2 pickled jalapenos, **seeded**, finely chopped
1/4 teaspoon ground red pepper, more or less to taste
1/2 cup half-and-half
salt and pepper to taste

Equipment: Medium-size mixing bowl, mixing spoon, large-size skillet

Preheat oven to 325° F.
1. Put corn and flour in mixing bowl, mix well, and set aside.
2. Melt butter or margarine in skillet over medium-high heat, add onion, green pepper, and jalapenos, mix well, and fry until onions are soft (about 3 minutes). Add corn,

stirring frequently, and cook for about 5 minutes, until corn is tender. Add red pepper, half-and-half, and salt and pepper to taste, reduce heat to low, and add more butter if necessary to prevent sticking. Cover and cook for 10 minutes more. Serve as a side dish with meat or fish.

Venezuela

Venezuela is an oil-rich nation on the northern coast of South America. Venezuelans are a blending of the original Native Americans who inhabited the area, Spanish, Africans, West Indies natives, and Europeans of every nationality. They have all contributed to the culture and food of Venezuela today. In small pockets of the Amazon region, Native Americans live pretty much as they have for hundreds of years, eating what they can forage from the forest, or grow by slash and burn farming techniques. Their lives remain untouched by modern society except for the occasional anthropologist, missionary, or government census taker.

In direct contrast to the isolated groups of Native Americans are the modern cities, such as Caracas, which thrive on oil money, but, although oil is important to the Venezuelan economy, most people in the country are involved in agriculture. Livestock raising is an important industry. The cattle produce tough meat, so special cooking techniques have developed to handle this problem, including boiling the meat for a few hours first, then roasting it with frequent bastings, or cutting the meat up into small pieces and using it in stews. Main food crops grown in Venezuela are sugar cane, rice, fruits, corn, cereals, and, of course, coffee, which is also a cash crop. Oil exports allow Venezuelans to import much of their food.

Pabellon Criollo *Sliced Steak with Rice and Black Beans*

The national dish of Venezuela is a symbol to the fine beef it once produced. *Pabellon* means flag, and the dish is tricolored like the Venezuelan flag. To serve *pabellon* properly the sliced meat must be arranged in the middle of a large platter with the cooked rice along one side and black beans along the opposite side; hence, a three-color effect.

Yield: serves 6

2 pounds skirt or flank steak
2 cups water
4 bay leaves
1/4 cup olive oil
1 onion, **finely chopped**
6 cloves garlic, finely chopped or 2 teaspoons garlic granules

2 cups **stewed** tomatoes, homemade or canned
salt and pepper to taste
4 cups cooked rice (cooked according to directions on the package—keep warm for serving)
4 cups cooked black beans, homemade (see page 232), or canned, heated through for serving

Equipment: Medium-size saucepan with cover or **Dutch oven**, sharp meat knife, large-size skillet

1. Put meat, water, and bay leaves in saucepan and bring to a boil over high heat. Reduce heat to simmer, cover, and cook for about 1 1/2 hours until meat is tender. Remove cover and set *pabellon* aside to cool in pan juices for about 1/2 hour.
2. Remove meat from pan, put on work surface, and cut into 1/4-inch-thick slices. Set aside any remaining pan juices and discard bay leaves.
3. Heat oil in skillet over high heat, add onion and garlic, and fry until onion is soft (about 3 minutes). Mix well. Add tomatoes, remaining pan juices, and salt and pepper to taste and mix well. Add meat and simmer until heated through, about 10 minutes.

To serve, mound meat in center of platter. Put cooked rice along one side and cooked black beans on the opposite side.

Panama

The tiny country of Panama has emerged as a focal point in the world of trade and commerce since the digging of the "Big Ditch," the canal joining the Atlantic Ocean with the Pacific. The majority of agriculture takes place on the eastern side of the country, where mountains give way to plains, making cattle raising and farming possible. Panama has large banana plantations, and other crops include rice, sugar cane, corn, and citrus fruits. The country is self-sufficient in basic foods but has to import more than it exports. Shrimping is a big industry along the Pacific coast. Many people fish for a living. Farmers for the most part own small farms and still work the land as their ancestors did before them, using primitive hand tools, trying to produce enough food to feed their families.

Native Panamanians are a mix of Spanish and Native American ancestry. Their cooking is a blending of the two cultures. Corn is ground and made into tortillas, and beans are popular food. Rice is a staple in the Panamanian diet. *Seviche*, fish cooked in lime juice, is popular. A stew-like soup called *sancocho*, with chicken, **cassava** root, **plantains**, corn, and potatoes in it, is very popular. In spite of the thousands of ships passing through the canal loaded with people from every country on earth, there is less foreign influence on Panamanian cooking than on the recipes of most other Latin American countries.

Citrus Squares

Yield: about 24 squares

2 1/4 cups all-purpose flour
1/2 cup confectioners' sugar
1 cup butter or margarine (at room temperature)
2 eggs
1/2 cup lime juice, more or less to taste
1/4 cup lemon juice
1 teaspoon baking powder
1 1/2 cups granulated sugar, more or less as needed

Equipment: Large-size mixing bowl, clean hands, nonstick or lightly greased 9-inch baking pan, oven mitts, medium-size mixing bowl, **whisk** or mixing spoon

Preheat oven to 350° F.

1. Put 2 cups flour and confectioners' sugar in large mixing bowl, add butter or margarine, and, using clean hands, blend until mixture is crumbly.
2. Transfer mixture to baking pan and pat evenly, covering the bottom.
3. Bake in oven until top is lightly golden, about 10 minutes.
4. Put remaining 1/4 cup flour, eggs, 1/2 cup lime juice, lemon juice, baking powder, and 1 1/2 cups granulated sugar in medium mixing bowl, and, using **whisk** or mixing spoon, mix until well blended. Taste and add more lime juice if too sweet or more sugar if too sour.
5. Using oven mitts, remove partially cooked dough from oven and cover completely with juice mixture. Return to oven and continue baking until top is set and golden, about 15 minutes. Remove from oven and cool to room temperature. Cut into about 24 squares, about 2-inches each.

Serve *citrus squares* as a cookie treat. Sprinkle top with confectioners' sugar just before serving. They store well, covered, in a cool, dry place.

Costa Rica

Costa Rica is known as a land of peace and democracy, and it is one of the most stable democracies in the region. It is a fertile country, and people successfully grow coffee, bananas, sugar cane, rice, corn, and cocoa. The coffee, which is of very high quality, sugar, and bananas are all exported around the world. Geographically, the country is a fishers' paradise, having 125 miles of coastline along the Caribbean Sea and over 600 miles along the Pacific Ocean. Seafood is an important part of the diet, and it is commonly served at dinner. Dinners usually consist of salad, soup, meat such as fish or roast beef, rice or corn, fruit juice to drink, and dessert, which may be ice cream with fruited jello, pudding, or cake. Salads may be palm hearts with a little vinegar and oil dressing or lemon juice. The corn grown has large white kernels, and it is never served on the cob but is ground up to make tortillas. Tortilla soup is a delicious way to start dinner.

Tortilla Soup

Yield: serves 6

2 to 4 tablespoons vegetable oil
3 corn tortillas, cut into 1/2-inch wide strips
1 onion, **finely chopped**
6 cloves garlic, finely chopped, or 2 teaspoons garlic granules
2 stalks celery, finely chopped
1 cup boneless, skinless, finely **diced** raw chicken
4 cups chicken broth, homemade or canned
1 cup canned **stewed** tomatoes
1 teaspoon *each* cumin, chili powder
1 tablespoon chopped fresh **cilantro/coriander**
1 bay leaf
salt and pepper to taste
1/2 cup sour cream, more or less, for serving
2 avocados, peeled, **seeded** and **cubed**, more or less, for serving
1/2 cup shredded Monterey Jack cheese, more or less for serving

Equipment: Large-size saucepan or **Dutch oven**, slotted mixing spoon, paper towels

1. Heat 2 tablespoons oil in saucepan or Dutch oven over medium-high heat, add tortillas, mix well, and fry until crisp. Remove tortillas with slotted spoon, drain on paper towels, and set aside.
2. Heat remaining 2 tablespoons oil in saucepan or Dutch oven over medium-high heat, add onion, garlic, celery, and chicken, mix well, and cook for about 3 minutes until onions are soft. Add chicken broth, tomatoes, cumin, chili powder, cilantro, and bay leaf and bring to a boil. Reduce heat to simmer, and, stirring frequently, cook for 30 minutes. Remove bay leaf; discard before serving. Add salt and pepper to taste.

To serve, put a few tortilla strips in the bottom of individual soup bowls, add a spoon each of sour cream, avocado, and cheese, and then add hot soup. Serve with remaining chips, sour cream, avocado, and cheese in separate bowls to add to soup if desired.

Pastelillos de Carne en Parillas — Meat and Banana Patties

Yield: serves 4

1 pound ground beef
1/4 cup bread crumbs
1 onion, **finely chopped**
1 teaspoon dried red pepper flakes
salt and pepper to taste
4 slices bacon
2 ripe bananas, peeled and sliced in half lengthwise
6 tablespoons melted butter

Equipment: Medium-size mixing bowl, 8 toothpicks, medium-size skillet, pancake turner or metal spatula, buttered 9-inch baking pan

1. Put ground beef, bread crumbs, onion, red pepper flakes, and salt and pepper to taste in mixing bowl, and, using clean hands, blend well.
2. Divide meat into 4 balls and shape into banana-shaped patties about 4 inches long. Coil a piece of bacon around each patty and secure with toothpicks at each end.
3. Set broiler rack 6 inches under heat and preheat broiler.
4. Put patties in the skillet, cook over medium-high, and heat until bacon and meat are cooked through on both sides, about 5 minutes each side. Reduce heat to medium if necessary.
5. While the patties are frying, put the banana halves, cut side up, in the baking pan. Cover with melted butter, and carefully set under the hot broiler for about 5 minutes, until heated through and bubbly. Remove from oven and put a half banana on top of each patty. Spoon baking pan drippings over banana patties.

Serve hot with side dishes of rice and beans as they do in Costa Rica.

Banana Bread

Yield: 2 loaves

3 1/2 cups all purpose flour
3 teaspoons baking powder
1 teaspoon *each* baking soda and salt
2 cups mashed bananas
2 tablespoons lemon juice
1 tablespoon grated lemon rind
1 cup sugar
1/4 cup shortening
3 eggs
1/4 cup milk

Equipment: Flour **sifter**, medium-size mixing bowl, small-size bowl, electric mixer or mixing spoon, large-size mixing bowl, 2 nonstick or lightly greased 9- x 5-inch loaf pans

Preheat oven to 350° F.
1. **Sift** flour, baking powder, baking soda, and salt into medium bowl and set aside.
2. Put mashed bananas in small bowl, add lemon juice, mix well, and set aside.
3. Using electric mixer or spoon, blend sugar and shortening until fluffy in large mixing bowl. Add eggs, one at a time, beating well after each addition. Stirring continually, alternate adding flour a little at a time, with milk. Add bananas and lemon rind and mix until well blended.
4. Pour mixture equally into 2 loaf pans, place in oven, and bake for about 1 hour until golden brown and toothpick inserted into breads come out clean. Cool for about 15 minutes before removing from pans.

Serve banana bread either warm or cold as a bread spread with butter, margarine, jam, or as a dessert with **dollop** of whipped topping.

Nicaragua

A fertile strip of Nicaragua, 40 miles wide, along the Pacific coast, is the agricultural area and the place where most of the population lives. Rice, corn, beans, bananas, cattle, and dairy products are produced in this region. Generally, the people cannot afford much meat. Red beans and rice are fried together with onions to make, perhaps, the most common dish in Nicaragua, eaten even for breakfast. It is called *gallo pinto*, painted rooster, because of its colors, not because chicken is used. Hot sauce is a table condiment available to add to any dish that might require some spicing up. Corn tortillas are the most common bread. They can be bought from vendors, ready made, and reheated at home. Fruits grow well in this region and are used in candies, puddings, and fruit drinks.

Fruit drinks are simple to make by combining water, fruit, and sugar together in a blender and switching it on high speed for less than a minute. Just don't forget to put the top on the blender! These drinks are made throughout Nicaragua but are common in other Latin American countries as well (see the recipe on page 250).

Maduro en Gloria   Heavenly Bananas

Bananas are plentiful, nutritious, cheap, and popular throughout Mexico, the Caribbean Islands, most of Africa, and Central and South America. Recipes for baked bananas are found in all of these countries. Sometimes they are called *banane celeste*. Sometimes fruit juice is added instead of coconut milk or cream, but whatever they're called and whatever liquid is added, the end result is heavenly.

Yield: serves 4 to 6

6 bananas, peeled and cut in half lengthwise
1/2 cup melted butter
1 cup cream cheese (at room temperature)
1/2 cup light brown sugar
1 teaspoon cinnamon
1 cup coconut milk or heavy cream

Equipment: Buttered shallow 9-inch baking pan, medium-size mixing bowl, mixing spoon, or food processor

Preheat oven to 350°F.
1. Put banana slices, cut side up, side-by-side in baking pan, and pour melted butter over them.
2. Put cream cheese, sugar, and cinnamon in the bowl and blend together, using the mixing spoon or in food processor.
3. Spread half the mixture over the cut side of bananas in the pan, and then layer each banana half with a remaining banana slice, sandwich-fashion. Spread remaining mixture over bananas and cover with coconut milk or cream.

4. Bake in oven for 20 minutes or until top is lightly browned and bubbly. Don't overcook.

Serve warm for dessert directly from the baking pan.

Ejotes Envueltos en Huevo — String Beans with Egg

Yield: serves 6

2 eggs, **separated**
2 pounds string beans, fresh, ends **trimmed** (**blanched** in boiling salt water for 3 minutes) or whole beans, frozen (thawed)
2 to 6 tablespoons vegetable oil
salt and pepper to taste

Equipment: Small-size bowl, **whisk** or fork, large-size bowl, electric mixer or **egg beater**, large-size skillet, tongs or slotted spoon, paper towels

1. Put egg yolks in small bowl and beat well with whisk or fork. Put egg whites in large bowl, and using electric mixer or egg beater, beat until stiff but not dry. **Fold** yolks gently into whites. Put beans in mixture and coat well.
2. Heat 2 tablespoons oil in skillet over medium-high heat. Using tongs or slotted spoon, carefully put the coated beans, a few at a time, in the skillet and fry, turning continually to brown on all sides (about 3 minutes). Using tongs or slotted spoon, remove beans from skillet and drain on paper towels. Add remaining beans in batches and add remaining oil as needed to prevent sticking. Sprinkle with salt and pepper to taste.

Serve beans warm as a side dish with meat or chicken.

Honduras

Bananas are the backbone of the Hondurans' economy; most Hondurans work either on the banana plantations or on their own small farms raising food with the help of primitive tools and oxen. Other food products exported include sugar, lobster, shrimp, coffee, and meat. Food crops include beans, corn, and rice.

In the cities a wider variety of foods is available, depending on income and cost of food. Dinner is served between 5:30 and 7:00 p.m. and usually consists of soup, rice and meat, fresh vegetable salad, and dessert of fruit or cake. Sometimes potatoes and bread and butter are served. The bread will usually be purchased from the local bakery, called *panaderia*. A typical diet of people who live in the country is exactly what they raise—corn, beans, and rice together with cottage cheese. Cottage cheese is locally made. Pork, eggs, fruit such as mangos, pineapples, papaya, and bananas are other common foods. Bananas are fried, and the corn is made into tortillas. Everything is made spicy with salsa, a chili sauce. Chili peppers come in all sizes and all degrees of hotness—the smaller the pepper the hotter it will be. Peppers grow extremely well in all Latin American countries where they are very popular. The mild large ones are stuffed with everything imaginable, such as this recipe for *chiles rellenos*.

Chiles Rellenos   Stuffed Chili Peppers

Cheese-stuffed poblano peppers are delicious, inexpensive, and easy to make.

Yield: serves 4 to 6

6 poblano chilies, fresh or canned, available at most supermarkets and Latin American food stores
1/2 pound Monterey Jack cheese, **finely chopped**
1 teaspoon cumin
3 eggs, beaten
1/2 cup milk
salt and pepper to taste

Equipment: **Egg beater**, nonstick or greased 8-inch-square baking pan, medium-size bowl, mixing spoon

Preheat oven to 350° F.
1. Cut chilies down one side, remove seeds, and rinse. Fill each chili with cheese and place them side-by-side in baking pan.
2. Add cumin to eggs and milk in medium-size bowl, and mix well. Pour mixture over stuffed chilies. Sprinkle with salt and pepper to taste.
3. Bake in oven for about 25 minutes, until eggs are set.

Calabacitas con Jitomate   Zucchini with Tomatoes

Honduran cooking is simple, made with whatever can be picked from the garden or is available at the market. Zucchinis and tomatoes always seem to be available, and the following recipe is a typical native dish. It is usually eaten with beans, rice, or potatoes.

Yield: serves 4 to 6

2 to 4 tablespoons vegetable oil
2 onions, chopped
3 cloves garlic, **finely chopped**, or 1 teaspoon garlic granules
1 pound zucchini, **trimmed** and cut into 1/2-inch-thick slices
2 cups chopped tomatoes, fresh or canned
2 canned pickled jalapeno chilies, **seeded** and chopped, available at most supermarkets and Latin American food stores
salt and pepper to taste

Equipment: Medium-size saucepan or **Dutch oven**, wooden mixing spoon

1. Heat 2 tablespoons oil in saucepan over medium-high heat, add onions and garlic, and cook until soft (about 3 minutes).
2. Add zucchini, tomatoes, jalapenos, and salt and pepper to taste and mix well. Reduce heat to low, cover, and cook for about 30 minutes or until zucchini is tender. Add more oil if necessary to prevent sticking.

Serve with meat, fish, or chicken as a side dish.

El Salvador

El Salvador was at one time part of the Mayan territory. It was invaded by the Aztecs and then the Spanish. The El Salvadorians are predominantly a mestizo people, that is, a mix between the Spanish and Native Americans. Just as the people have blended, so too has the cooking. A good example of this is the refried bean dish below—beans native to the area that are cooked in a Spanish way.

Even though it is small, El Salvador has a lot of people, and people put demands on the land to produce food. Sixty percent of the people living in El Salvador are farmers, living on what they raise—rice, corn, beans, tomatoes, onions, potatoes, peppers, chickens, and, for the more fortunate, pigs and goats. Export crops include coffee, shrimp, and sugar.

Life is hard in El Salvador. Many people do not get enough food every day. Long-term low-calorie intake results in shorter life spans. Sanitary drinking water is not available in some parts of El Salvador. People have to carry water from other regions to have something to drink. Compounding the problems of food and water shortages is the internal fighting (civil war) between the people who do not have money or power and those who do. This fighting has slowed the production of food and many farmers have had to leave their land to escape the fighting.

Frijoles Refritos

Frijoles refritos are very popular and frequently the main source of protein. A spoonful of beans can do wonders to cool one's mouth when the other dishes are hot and spicy. In the following recipe lard is always added, but we suggest adding vegetable oil instead.

Yield: serves 4 to 6

2 to 4 tablespoons vegetable oil
4 cups mashed pinto or red kidney beans, homemade (cooked according to directions on package) or canned
salt and pepper to taste

Equipment: Medium-size skillet, wooden mixing spoon

Heat 2 tablespoons oil in skillet over medium-high heat, add mashed beans, and cook until dry and firm (about 5 minutes). Stirring continually, add salt and pepper to taste and more oil if necessary to prevent sticking.

Serve warm or cold as a side dish with meat, poultry, fish, and eggs. Also, roll a heaping spoonful in a tortilla to eat like a sandwich.

In most sugar producing countries such as El Salvador, everyone loves their sweets very sweet. They cook with a special brown, cone-shaped sweetener called *piloncillo*, made of brown sugar, corn syrup, and water and use it to make praline-like candy, *nogada*. It is not unusual to see dozens of children selling homemade *nogadas* on the streets.

Yield: about 15 pieces

1 7-ounce *piloncillo*, available at some supermarkets and all Latin American stores
1/2 cup water
pinch of salt
1 3-inch stick cinnamon
1 tablespoon butter or margarine
1 teaspoon vanilla extract
1 cup halves or broken pecans

Equipment: Medium-size saucepan, wooden mixing spoon, **candy thermometer**, nonstick or buttered cookie sheet

1. Put *piloncillo,* water, and salt in saucepan and heat over low heat until dissolved, about 10 minutes. Add cinnamon stick, increase heat to rolling boil, mix well, and boil until a drop of mixture forms a soft ball in water, about 5 minutes. Candy thermometer should reach 236° F.
2. Add butter or margarine and vanilla. Beat by hand with wooden spoon until mixture starts to thicken. Stirring continually, add pecans until mixture is thick, about 2 minutes.
3. Quickly, before mixture hardens, drop by tablespoonfuls, side-by-side onto cookie sheet.

Serve *nogada* as a sweet treat. Wrap each in clear plastic and store in airtight container.

Guatemala

The cooking of Guatemala is an interesting blend of the old Mayan Empire, of which Guatemala was once part; the conquering Spanish; the British, from the time when the territory was part of British Honduras; and the Caribbean, from the laborers who came to work on the banana plantations. These peoples all added something different to the cooking style of Guatemala. The Mayans were sun worshipers, and a popular carryover from the Mayan culture is the use of *achiote*, the pungent seed of flowering, tropical annatto trees. The seeds give food a rich yellow to reddish orange  color and are added to many dishes, not only for the flavor but as a symbol of the sun and sunshine. The Spanish contributed their flavorings and cooking techniques, and in the cities the cooking has a definite international flavor, a reflection of the British influence. The cooks from the Caribbean enriched the foods in their own special way.

Main food crops include rice, corn, beans, wheat, fruits, and vegetables. Cash crops include bananas and coffee, which are grown on big plantations. Rural people are poor and have a hard time getting a balanced diet and clean water. Popular foods in rural areas are black beans, rice, and corn dishes such as *tamales* and tortillas. When they can afford it, meat is eaten. Small amounts appear in *tamales*. **Platanos** are fried then dressed up with cream and honey for a nice dessert treat.

Arroz Guatemalteo   *Guatemala-style Rice*

Yield: serves 4 to 6

2 tablespoons vegetable oil
1 onion, **finely chopped**
3 cloves garlic or 1 teaspoon garlic granules
1 cup uncooked rice
2 carrots, finely chopped
1 green pepper, **cored, seeded**, and finely chopped
2 1/2 cups water
1/2 cup green peas, fresh or frozen (thawed)
salt and pepper to taste

Equipment: Medium-size skillet with cover, mixing spoon

1. Heat oil in skillet over medium-high heat, add onion and garlic, and cook until soft (about 3 minutes). Add rice, carrots, and green pepper, and, stirring continually, cook for about 3 minutes more. Add water and bring to a boil. Reduce heat to simmer, cover, and cook for 20 minutes until water is absorbed and rice is tender.
2. Add peas and salt and pepper to taste, mix well, and **fluff** with a fork.

Serve rice as a side dish with meat.

Liquado Sandia   *Watermelon Smoothie*

Throughout tropical Central America fresh fruits are plentiful all year long. A refreshing drink is made by simply blending crushed ice and any kind of fruit you like. Watermelon, mango, and strawberry are the most popular. This recipe can be used for this entire region, including the United States since we often drink these, especially at heath food store cafes.

Yield: serves 2

2 cups crushed ice
1/2 cup sliced watermelon (or mango or strawberries) fresh, cut into pieces
sugar or artificial sweetener, more or less to taste (optional)

Equipment: Electric blender

Put ice and watermelon in blender container, cover, and blend until smooth.
Serve *liquado sandia* in a glass.

Mexico

Mexican cookery includes the oldest known indigenous cuisine in this hemisphere. Authentic dishes are essentially derived from the Mexican Aztecs with some traced back to about 7000 B.C. Corn (maize), beans, peppers (capsicums), and roots have existed for thousands of years and are still staples of the country. Tomatoes were cultivated around 700 A.D. Good crops were vital for the development of the complex agrarian society. Religious symbols took form in corn, the food that still dominates the Mexican diet. Ancient legends tell that humans were born from corn. For many, it still remains sacred, considered a gift from the gods. It is featured in many foods  including the staple, tortilla, a flat bread eaten at most meals, even breakfast.

There are regional differences in Mexican cooking. In northern Mexico, as in the southwestern United States, cattle and goats are raised, cheese is produced, and wheat is grown. In central Mexico, corn, beans, capsicums and roots, goat, pork, turkey, chicken, fruits, and vegetables are grown. Small patches of corn are even grown on steep mountain sides throughout this region. In the southern regions of Mexico and along the Yucatan peninsula, cooks integrate tropical fruits, vegetables, and seafood in a style derived from the ancient Aztec and Mayan cultures. Along the Pacific coast tropical fruits, vegetables, fish and seafood prevail. The flavor of the Orient has also affected the cooking because of the ships with Asian crews that have stopped and traded at their ports.

Mexico is not only divided by regions but even more so by class. The foods of the wealthy are very continental, with definite French flavors, sauces, and cooking techniques. Spain contributed a substantial amount toward the Mexican food that we know and love today. For example, the Spanish conquerors introduced frying. Beans became more flavorful with the introduction of frying from the Spaniards, but the exchange worked both ways. Many foods identified with certain countries were brought to Europe from Mexico, and Central and South America. Potatoes to Ireland and tomatoes to Italy are two examples of foods that originally came from Latin America but are now strongly identified with their adopted countries. Native Mexican foods that have traveled the world are pineapples, pumpkins, peanuts, sweet potatoes, squashes, and cocoa. Cocoa (chocolate) is a good example of how foods travel. The conquistadors found the Aztecs eating the cocoa bean which was in a chili chocolate sauce still eaten today in Mexico. The conquistadors brought it back to Spain. Sugar was added to the cocoa, making chocolate as we know it. Now cocoa beans are a vital export crop in West Africa and are shipped to the major chocolate-consuming countries in Europe and the Americas. Spain brought garlic, onions, cinnamon, and rice to Mexico, where they became part of many dishes. Mexican food, if properly prepared, is neither greasy or fatty. It is actually low in calories, high in nutrition, flavorful, and not necessarily hot (spicy).

Since prehistoric times Native American women of Mexico have soaked corn kernels in water and unslaked lime, ground this mixture to a paste, and hand-patted the dough into the famous edible plate, the tortilla. They're still stuffed and topped with a cornucopia of meats and vegetables, but they are now served on plates. Corn tortillas are the "staff of life" for all Mexicans. In almost every Mexican village, no matter how small, there is a bakery called a *tortillaria* that makes tortillas. Because of government price support, the tortillas are inexpensive and readily available to everyone. They are made with either masa harina (corn flour) or wheat flour. Corn flour tortillas are more popular in Mexico.

Yield: makes about 12

2 cups masa harina (corn flour)
1 teaspoon salt
1 cup warm water, more or less

Equipment: Medium-size mixing bowl, floured work surface, rolling pin or tortilla press, kitchen towel or wax paper, large-size cast iron skillet, pancake turner or metal spatula

1. Put flour and salt in mixing bowl. Add water, a little at a time, until mixture holds together to make a stiff dough. Divide into 12 equal balls and flatten each into a thin 6-inch circle with rolling pin or in a tortilla press. Stack under a towel until ready to fry.
2. Heat dry skillet over medium-high heat and fry tortillas one by one. When they bubble and are light brown, about 2 minutes, turn them over and cook other side for about 1 minute. When done, wrap in wax paper or kitchen towel.

Serve tortillas warm for the best flavor and stack them in a towel or napkin to keep them soft and warm. In Mexico, tortillas are eaten as bread.

Guacamole   *Avocado Sauce*

Avocados, often called "poor man's butter" for their creamy rich meat, make a great substitute for high-cholesterol foods such as sour cream, mayonnaise, and butter (although avocados do have a high fat content). Avocado trees are native to Mexico, Central, and South America and are especially rich in vitamin C. Avocados are used in and on everything from soups to desserts. When buying avocados, press the skin slightly, if it gives, the avocado is ripe; it should be soft, not mushy. The nut inside should not rattle when the fruit is shaken. If the avocado is still very firm when you buy it, it will ripen at room temperature in a day or two. To prepare avocados, slice lengthwise, rolling knife around the large nut in the center, and twist halves apart. The meat can be eaten right out of the shell-like skin with a spoon or it can be peeled, sliced, **diced**, and mashed. If the avocados are very ripe, they are easy to mash, using the back of a fork or potato masher. After peeling an avocado, sprinkle the meat with lemon juice to prevent browning. The following recipe is for Mexico's most popular avocado dish, *guacamole* (see also related recipe for *mantequilla de pobre* in the Columbia section of this book, page 239).

Yield: makes 2 cups

2 avocados, peeled, pit removed and **finely chopped** or mashed (in Mexico it is usually chopped)
1 tablespoon lemon juice
1 tomato, finely chopped
1 onion, finely chopped
salt to taste
1/4 teaspoon hot red pepper sauce, more or less to taste

Equipment: Medium-size bowl, mixing spoon

Put avocados in mixing bowl, add lemon juice, and mix well to keep avocado from browning. Add tomato, onion, salt to taste, and red pepper sauce. Refrigerate until ready to serve.

Serve *guacamole* as an appetizer with tortillas, on shredded lettuce as a salad, or as a side dish condiment with meat.

Salsa   Red Tomato Sauce

Mexican cooking includes many sauces, which are either added to or served with most dishes. They are usually made with tomatoes, herbs, spices, chilies, and peppers. Both chilies and peppers have been used for centuries.

Yield: about 2 cups

2 tablespoons vegetable oil
1 onion, **finely chopped**
1 clove garlic, finely chopped
2 ripe tomatoes, **peeled, seeded**, and chopped
1 pickled jalapeno chili pepper, **cored**, seeded, and finely chopped, available at most supermarkets and Latin American food stores
1/2 teaspoon sugar
1 tablespoon chopped fresh **cilantro/coriander**, or 1/2 teaspoon ground cilantro/coriander
salt and pepper to taste

Equipment: Medium-size skillet, mixing spoon

1. Heat oil in skillet over medium-high heat, add onion and garlic, and, stirring continually, fry until onion is golden (about 3 minutes). Add tomatoes, jalapeno, and sugar and bring to a boil. Reduce to simmer, mix well, and cook for about 5 minutes, until mixture is well blended.
2. Add coriander and salt and pepper to taste and remove from heat. Cool to room temperature and refrigerate.

Serve *salsa* in a small bowl as a condiment to spoon over other Mexican dishes. It is also a great dip for tortilla chips.

Huevos Rancheros   Ranch Style Mexican Eggs

Many of you may have had srambled eggs with a little *salsa* thrown on top and been told you were eating *huevos rancheros*. The following recipe is how *huevos rancheros* are actually served in Mexico.

Yield: serves 4

2 tablespoons vegetable oil
8 tortillas, homemade (see recipe on page 252), or in packages, available at most supermarkets and all Latin American food stores
2 tablespoons butter or margarine, more or less as needed
4 eggs
1 onion, **finely chopped**
salt and pepper to taste
2 cups refried beans, available at most supermarkets and all Latin American food stores
1 cup *salsa*, homemade (see previous recipe), or bottled

Equipment: Medium-size skillet, pancake turner or metal spatula, paper towels

1. Heat oil in skillet over high heat, add tortillas, and fry on both sides until crisp. Drain on paper towels, stack, and set aside in warm place.
2. Melt butter in skillet over medium-high heat, add onion, and fry until soft. Mix to coat. Add eggs, one at a time, and fry until just set. Sprinkle with salt and pepper to taste.
3. Put a tortilla on each individual plate and top each with an egg. Spoon *salsa* over the yolk and spoon refried beans to one side.

Serve eggs with extra warm tortillas, *salsa*, and refried beans on the side.

Arroz a la Mexicana   *Mexican Rice*

After the invasion of the Spanish conquistadors, Native Americans began using foods the Spaniards brought with them, such as rice and lard. Before the Spaniards the Native Americans used neither fats nor oils in their food. Mexican rice is a blending of Native American and Spanish cookery. The Spanish brought rice to Mexico and the Native Americans enlivened it with tomatoes and chilies.

Yield: serves 4 to 6

2 tablespoons vegetable oil
1 cup uncooked long grain rice
1 clove garlic, **finely chopped**
1 teaspoon salt, more or less to taste
1/2 cup finely chopped onion
1/2 cup finely chopped tomato
1/2 teaspoon ground cumin
3 cups chicken broth, homemade or canned
1 cup frozen peas (thawed)

Equipment: Medium-size saucepan with cover or **Dutch oven**, mixing spoon

1. Heat 2 tablespoons oil in saucepan or Dutch oven over medium-high heat, add rice, and brown slightly, stirring continually.
2. Add garlic, salt, onion, tomato, cumin, and chicken broth, mix well, and bring to a boil. Reduce heat to simmer, cover, and cook for about 30 minutes, until rice is tender.
3. Remove cover, add peas, mix well, and heat through.

Serve as the main meal or as a side dish with *picadillo*; recipe follows.

Picadillo   Spiced Ground Meat

There are many ways to make *picadillo;* it can be mildly seasoned or fiery hot. *Picadillo* is eaten with rice and beans, as crispy taco filling, or rolled in tortillas.

Yield: serves 6 to 8

2 tablespoons vegetable oil
1 cup **finely chopped** onions
2 pickled jalapeno peppers, **cored**, **seeded**, and finely chopped, available at most supermarkets or Latin American food stores
1/4 cup vinegar
2 pounds lean ground beef or pork or combination
1/2 cup raisins (optional)
4 cups chopped whole tomatoes, canned
salt and pepper to taste

Equipment: Large-size saucepan or **Dutch oven**, mixing spoon

1. Heat oil in saucepan or Dutch oven over high heat, and add onions, jalapenos, 2 tablespoons vinegar, ground meat, and raisins, and mix well. Reduce heat to simmer and continue cooking until meat is lightly browned, stirring to keep crumbly.
2. Add tomatoes, remaining vinegar, and salt and pepper to taste, and mix well to blend. Bring mixture to a boil, mix well to prevent sticking, and reduce heat to simmer, and cook until thickened (about 20 minutes).

Serve *picadillo* hot over rice or beans.

Polvorones   Mexican Wedding Cookies

A box or basket full of *polvorones*, wedding cookies, makes a wonderful homemade gift to give friends, especially during the holidays. Individually wrap cookies in brightly colored waxed tissue paper, twisting the ends of the paper to hold cookies. (Waxed tissue is available at most craft shops.) The cookies are not only delicious but festive.

2 cups all-purpose flour, **sifted**
1/2 cup confectioners' sugar
1 cup finely chopped pecans
1 teaspoon vanilla extract
1/2 cup butter or margarine (at room temperature)
1 tablespoon ice water, more or less as needed
confectioners' sugar for garnish

Equipment: Large-size mixing bowl, wooden mixing spoon, nonstick or plain cookie sheet

Preheat oven to 350° F.

1. Put flour, confectioners' sugar, and nuts in large mixing bowl and mix well. Add vanilla and butter, and using clean hands or wooden spoon, blend until mixture forms a soft ball. Add a little ice water if mixture is too crumbly.
2. Pinch off about ping-pong-ball-size pieces of dough and roll into balls between the palms of your clean hands. Place side-by-side on cookie sheet, allowing about 1 inch between balls. Bake for about 12 minutes, until set and golden. Remove from oven and generously sprinkle with confectioners' sugar.

Serve the cookies as a sweet treat with milk.

North America

The climate, terrain, vegetation, and soil of both Canada and the U.S. are as varied as the people who have immigrated to their shores. The cooking of both nations reflects the mixed heritage of its many settlers. The majority of early Canadian settlers were French and British. Since their arrival many other Europeans have found a new way of life in Canada. In recent years large settlements of Asians have immigrated to Canada and have settled along the Pacific coast, adding their culture to the country.

In the United States the soil is rich, with fruitful orchards, fertile plains, and enormous herds of cattle roaming grasslands that are as large as some of the countries of the world. The agricultural and marketing technology is the finest in the world. Labor-saving household appliances have made the task of cooking a breeze, comparatively. Yet in spite of it all, U.S. cooking is simple and direct. It is unsophisticated and straightforward, concerned with content rather than form. The U.S. has regional cooking and cultural differences, making it an interesting place to live, travel, and eat.

Although Mexico is usually considered part of North America, we have included it under the Latin American section because its cooking and culture are more closely related to the countries of Latin America than to Canada and the U.S. There is, however, considerable cultural overlap between Mexico and its northern neighbors, and Mexican food, especially *salsa*, is popular throughout North America.

Canada

Canada, often called "the great white north," is known more for volumes of snow than for its food. Settler cooking was simple; it depended upon what the people could catch, hunt, raise, and store. Fortunately, there was an abundant supply of wild game, birds, and fish. Canadians cooked wholesome stews and thick and nourishing soups of dried beans and peas and salted and smoked fish and meats. Old world cooking skills of France and Great Britain were used by the settlers to prepare the natural foods of their new homeland.

Canada has regions that are known for different agricultural products. British Columbia grows exceptional fruits and nuts. Wild blueberries, wild mushrooms, along with a delicious asparagus-like fern called the fiddlehead, grow in the province of New Brunswick. Alberta raises prized grain-fed beef. Ontario is known for wild rice, and Quebec is known for cheese and maple syrup; some of the finest wheat grows on the western plains. Along with wheat, Canada is a leading exporter of fish and shellfish. With almost endless coastlines and thousands of clean lakes, the Canadian fishing industry is probably the world's richest. Most people mistakenly think Canadian and American food are the same because the countries are close to each other. This may be true for popular fast foods in big cities, but it is not the case for Canada's heritage foods, which are rooted in its two founding cultures, the English and French. French Canadian and English Canadian cooking are very different from each other and from American cooking as well.

Habitant Pea Soup   Pea Soup

Cold weather and steaming pots cooking on the stove conjure up warm and caring feelings; they just seem to go together. Thick soups, chowders, stews, and hashes reflect not only the extreme Canadian weather but a way of life. If Canada has a national dish, it has to be *habitant pea soup*. It is thick and wonderfully rich, originally created by and named for the hard-working French Canadian farmers.

Yield: serves 6 to 8

10 cups water
2 cups yellow or green dried split peas
1/2 pound lean salt pork or 2 cups **diced** smoked ham
1 ham hock
2 bay leaves
1 onion, **finely chopped**
2 carrots, diced
1 cup finely chopped celery (with leaves)
salt and pepper to taste

Equipment: Large-size saucepan with cover, mixing spoon

1. Heat water and peas in saucepan over high heat. Bring to a boil for 2 minutes, remove from heat, cover, and set aside for 1 hour.
2. Add salt pork or smoked ham, ham hock, bay leaves, onion, carrots, and celery to pea mixture and bring to a boil over high heat. Reduce heat to simmer, cover, and cook for about 1 1/2 hours until peas are tender, stirring frequently. If necessary, skim off fat. If using salt pork, remove from soup, cut into small pieces, and return to soup. Remove ham hock and discard. Add salt and pepper to taste.

Serve hot in individual bowls. Pass saltines or crusty bread for dunking.

Blueberry Corn Fritters

Yield: serves 4 to 6

1 1/2 cups all-purpose flour
2 teaspoons baking powder
2 eggs, separated
3/4 cup milk
1 teaspoon salt
2 tablespoons sugar, more or less to taste
3/4 cup cream-style canned corn
1/2 cup blueberries, fresh or frozen (thawed and drained)
2 to 8 tablespoons butter or margarine

Equipment: Flour **sifter**; 1 large-size mixing bowl; electric mixer, mixing spoon, or **whisk**; medium-size bowl; large-size skillet; metal spatula or pancake turner

1. Put flour and baking powder in sifter.
2. Combine egg yolks, milk, salt, and sugar in large mixing bowl and mix well. Slowly **sift** in flour mixture, stirring continually, using mixer, spoon, or whisk, until smooth and lump-free. Add corn and blueberries and blend well.
3. Put egg whites in medium bowl and beat with mixer or whisk until stiff. Gently **fold** whites into batter using whisk or mixing spoon.
4. Melt 2 tablespoons butter or margarine in skillet over medium high heat. Drop batter by tablespoonful into pan, flatten slightly with back of spoon. Make each fritter about 3 inches across. Cook about 5 minutes on each side, until golden brown. Add more butter or margarine if necessary.

Serve *fritters* warm with maple syrup or blueberry jam. They're excellent to serve for breakfast or brunch with bacon, sausage, or ham and eggs.

Maple Syrup Shortbreads

Canadian forests provide a wealth of wonderful products. None is more precious than one of nature's greatest gifts, maple syrup. Millions of gallons of this amber goodness are harvested each year. The sap of the stately sugar maple begins to run at the first breath of warm weather, and it is as cold and clear as spring water, flowing for only a few brief weeks in early spring. Harvested drop by drop, it takes 40 gallons of sap to yield only 1 gallon of pure maple syrup.

Yield: makes about 36

1/2 cup (1 stick) unsalted butter or margarine (at room temperature)
1/4 cup sugar
1 cup all-purpose flour
3/4 cup firmly packed brown sugar
1/2 cup pure maple syrup
1 tablespoon butter or margarine (at room temperature)
1 egg (at room temperature)
1 teaspoon vanilla
1/2 cup chopped walnuts

Equipment: Large-size mixing bowl, mixing spoon or electric mixer, greased 9-inch baking pan, medium-size mixing bowl

Preheat oven to 350°F.
1. *Prepare cakes:* cream butter and sugar together in large mixing bowl, using spoon or mixer, until light and fluffy. Add flour, a little at a time, mixing continually, and blend well. Do not form into ball. Pat mixture into baking pan. Bake in oven until light brown (about 25 minutes), remove from oven, and set aside.
2. *Prepare topping:* in medium bowl blend brown sugar, maple syrup, and butter. Add egg and vanilla and mix until smooth. Pour evenly over shortbread and sprinkle top with walnuts. Return to oven and bake until topping sets, about 20 minutes. Cool before cutting into 1 1/2-inch squares.

Serve *shortbreads* as a snack; they keep well in an airtight container and also make lovely special-occasion food gifts.

Canadian Apple Cake

Two Canadian products that are both plentiful and popular are apples and maple syrup; this recipe contains both.

Yield: serves 8 to 10

1 1/2 cups **sifted** all-purpose flour
1/2 cup sugar
2 teaspoons baking powder
1/2 teaspoon salt
1/2 cup vegetable shortening
1/2 cup milk
1 egg, beaten
3 apples, peeled, **cored**, and finely sliced
1/2 teaspoon ground cinnamon
2 tablespoons butter or margarine
2 tablespoons maple syrup

Equipment: Flour **sifter**, large-size mixing bowl, knives or pastry blender, mixing spoon, greased 8-inch-square cake pan

Preheat oven to 375° F.
1. **Sift** flour, 3 tablespoons sugar, baking powder, and salt in mixing bowl. Cut in shortening with 2 knives or pastry blender. Add milk and eggs, using mixing spoon, and mix to form soft dough.

2. Spread dough smoothly in cake pan and put overlapping slices of apples in rows on the dough. Mix remaining sugar and cinnamon and sprinkle over apples. Dot with butter or margarine. Bake for about 50 minutes or until toothpick comes out clean when inserted in cake. Remove from oven and pour maple syrup over top.

Serve *Canadian apple cake* while slightly warm, cut into squares or wedges.

Hot Apple Cider

Yield: serves 12 to 20

2 quarts apple juice
2 quarts cranberry juice
1/2 cup light brown sugar
3 sticks cinnamon
1/2 tablespoon ground cloves
1 lemon, sliced into rings
2 oranges, cut into quarters
3 tablespoons whole cloves

Equipment: Large-size saucepan, mixing spoon

1. Heat apple juice, cranberry juice, brown sugar, cinnamon, ground cloves, and lemon slices in saucepan over high heat. Bring to a boil and mix well. Reduce heat to simmer and cook for 15 minutes.
2. Poke whole cloves, polka-dot-fashion, into the skin side of orange wedges. Add to cider and continue cooking for 5 minutes more. The cloves and orange wedges add to the flavor as well as provide a decorative garnish.

Serve warm apple cider in cups. It's a great cold weather party beverage.

United States

Throughout the United States people from similar cultures, sharing common interests, often settled near one another in regions, communities, and neighborhoods. They find comfort and a sense of belonging by keeping the same cooking and eating customs they grew up with. Neighborhood "mom and pop" restaurants were the first to share the foods of their heritage. Today regional and community cookouts, cook-offs, and festivals are taking place all over the country showcasing the foods that reflect this country's cultural diversity. For example, throughout the Great Lakes region there is a large Scandinavian population who prepare dishes much as their ancestors have done for centuries. They still use the old Nordic way of preparing fish by boiling it with vegetables. Today a family or community gathering wouldn't be complete unless a "fish boil" is prepared and served. In the south central states, people by the thousands come to small Louisiana towns to sample crawfish prepared the Cajun way. There are festivals for everything, from garlic tastings and *grunion* runs in California to Italian and Greek food festivals on the streets of New York. Every ethnic group and every region in America is anxious to share foods they love and proudly show off.

Boston Brown Bread

Boston brown bread is traditionally eaten with Boston baked beans. The bread is not baked, but the batter is poured into cans and steamed. Two empty cans with one end smoothly removed, thoroughly washed (labels removed), and dried are needed for this recipe. The size of the cans should be: 2 1/2 cups-size (3 1/4 inches wide x 4 1/2 inches high). This recipe would be easy to prepare right in the classroom. Yum!

Yield: makes 2 loaves

2 cups buttermilk
1/2 cup dark molasses
1 cup seedless raisins
1 cup rye flour
1 cup whole wheat flour
1 cup white, fine ground cornmeal
3/4 teaspoon baking soda
1 teaspoon salt
1 tablespoon butter or margarine (at room temperature)

Equipment: **Egg beater** or electric mixer, large-size mixing bowl, wooden mixing spoon, **sifter**, 2 clean cans (2 1/2-cups size, one end removed), wax paper, aluminum foil, string or tape, wire rack to fit inside large-size saucepan with cover, oven mitts, wax-paper-covered work surface

1. Put about 2 quarts water in tea kettle and bring to a boil over high heat.
2. Using egg beater or mixer, mix buttermilk and molasses for about 5 minutes until well blended. Add raisins.
3. Put rye and whole wheat flours, cornmeal, baking soda, and salt into flour sifter and **sift** into buttermilk mixture, a little at a time; stir continually until well blended.
4. Spread softened butter or margarine over inside bottom and sides of cans. Pour mixture equally into the prepared cans. Cover each can loosely with greased wax paper (greased sides down), allowing room under the wax paper for the bread to rise. Cover wax paper loosely with a large piece of foil, pulling it tightly around the outside of each can but puffing it up over the opening. Tie or tape foil securely to sides of each can. Place filled cans on rack in saucepan. Set saucepan on stove and add enough boiling water to reach about 3/4 of the way up sides of cans. Set on high heat and bring water to a boil. Reduce to low, cover, and steam bread for 2 1/2 hours.
5. Using oven mitts, carefully remove cans, one by one, from water, and place on work surface. Carefully remove foil and wax paper from hot cans. Turn cans upside down, turning bread out on wax-paper-covered work surface.

To serve, allow the bread to cool before slicing into about 1/2-inch-wide pieces. Refrigerated, the bread keeps well, if wrapped, for about 10 days.

Apple Pie

Nothing is more American than the Fourth of July and apple pie. This has been said more times, in more places, in more songs, and in more movies and stage plays than one can imagine. Ever since Johnny Appleseed headed west, dropping his seeds on the way, apples have been the all-time All-American favorite food.

Yield: serves 6 to 8

1 1/2 cups light brown sugar
2 1/2 tablespoons all-purpose flour
1/4 teaspoon salt
1/2 teaspoon *each* ground cinnamon, ground nutmeg, and ground cloves
5 tart apples (such as Granny Smiths) peeled, **cored**, and finely sliced
2 tablespoons butter or margarine
1 teaspoon vanilla extract
2 unbaked 9-inch pie shells in oven-proof pie pans, homemade or frozen (thawed), one shell to be used for lattice top (see recipes below)

Equipment: Small-size bowl, mixing spoon, fork

Preheat oven to 350° F.

1. Combine brown sugar, flour, salt, cinnamon, nutmeg, and cloves in small bowl and mix well.
2. Layer apple slices in pie shell and sprinkle with dry mixture, starting with apples and ending with mixture. Dot top with butter or margarine and sprinkle with vanilla extract.
3. For **lattice** top, cut dough into 1/2-inch strips and place half the strips from left to right, about 1-inch apart, over apples. Repeat with remaining strips, placed from top to bottom at right angles to the first. Wet ends and press together with pie crust edge. Using fork tines make track marks around edge, sealing lattice top with bottom crust.
4. Bake in oven for about 45 minutes, until top crust is golden brown. If pastry edge starts to brown too quickly, cover with a strip of aluminum foil.

Serve warm or with ice cream for a grand dessert.

Pie Crust

You've heard the expression "easy as pie?" Well the following two pie crusts are foolproof, easy, and quick to make.

Yield: 1 9-inch crust

1 1/2 cups flour
1/2 cup vegetable oil
1 teaspoon salt
1/4 cup cold water

Equipment: Spoon, 9-inch pie pan, aluminum foil, uncooked dried beans or rice for weight

Preheat oven to 450° F.

1. Put flour, oil, salt, and water in pie pan, and, using clean hands, blend the mixture into a ball. Pat dough out to cover bottom and sides of pie pan. Using fork, prick bottom 3 or 4 times.
2. To prebake pie crust before adding filling, cut a circle of foil to cover bottom and weigh it down with uncooked dry beans or rice.*
3. Bake for about 10 minutes, remove from oven, remove beans or rice and foil, return to oven, and bake until golden brown, about 10 minutes more. Remove from oven, cool to room temperature, and fill with favorite filling.

3-Minute Goof-proof Pie Crust

The easiest way to make pastry is to add cream cheese to flour. No water is needed because cream cheese provides sufficient moisture. Cut in butter, **knead** to blend, and the job is done—perfect and delicious pastry every time. Blending the ingredients in a food processor takes less than 1 minute, and about 2 minutes more are needed to shape the dough into the pie pan.

Yield: 1 9-inch pie crust

1/2 cup cream cheese at room temperature
1 cup all-purpose flour
1/2 cup cold butter or margarine, cut into pea-size pieces

Equipment: Large-size mixing bowl or food processor, fork, pie pan, aluminum foil, uncooked dried beans or rice for weight, oven mitts

1. Put cream cheese and flour in food processor or bowl and mix until mixture looks like cracker crumbs, about 10 seconds if you are using a food processor. Add butter, and, if using your fingers, blend well but don't overmix (about 1 or 2 minutes). If using a processor, process on and off, in short spurts for about 10 seconds. Wrap ball of dough in foil and refrigerage for about 1 hour.
2. Transfer mixture to pie pan and lightly **knead** into a flat disk, about 1 minute, just until dough holds together. Pressing with your fingers, spread dough out evenly to cover the bottom and up the sides and over the rim of pie pan.* Prick crust about 6 times with fork.
3. Preheat oven to 400° F.
4. Line crust with foil and fill with dried beans or rice for weights. Put in oven and bake for about 20 minutes, until dough is almost dry. With oven mitts, remove from oven, and carefully remove weights and foil. Return to oven and bake for about 15 minutes more, until crust is light golden around edges.

To serve, fill with your favorite filling.

Hopping John

There are many southern dishes that never made it north. One is *hopping john*, an old southern dish that is pure comfort food. A bowl of *hopping john* has nourished many people through hard times. That's why it's high on the list of southern food favorites. As the legend goes, eating a bowl of *hopping john* on New Year's Eve means good luck for the coming year.

* If you are making pie crust for the apple pie recipe, stop here.

Yield: 8 servings

4 cups black-eyed peas cooked, with liquid, homemade or canned
1/2 cup water
1 cup smoked ham, **cubed**
2 cups cooked rice
salt and pepper to taste
1 or 2 shakes liquid hot red pepper sauce (optional)
1/2 cup **finely chopped** onion, for garnish

Equipment: Medium-size saucepan, mixing spoon

> Put cooked peas with liquid, water, and ham in saucepan, mix well, and heat over medium heat for about 5 minutes until well blended. Add cooked rice and salt and pepper to taste, mix well, and heat through.

Serve *hopping john* in individual bowls sprinkled with chopped onion. Have hot red pepper sauce on the table for those who like theirs fiery hot.

Peanut Brittle

During the Civil War, an infant was left an orphan after his slave mother was killed. The infant grew up with a love for the soil, reading, learning, and determined he would help make the world a better place to live. The man who overcame unbelievable obstacles to pursue his dream was Dr. George Washington Carver. He received world acclaim while head of the department of agriculture at the Tuskegee Institute in Alabama. He was a genius in scientific agriculture, making hundreds of useful products from peanuts and sweet potatoes, such as the following well-known peanut candy.

Yield: serves 6 to 8

1 tablespoon butter or margarine, more or less as needed
1/2 cup shelled, skinned peanuts
1 1/2 cups sugar

Equipment: Nine-inch-metal pie pan, 12-inch square aluminum foil, small-size heavy bottomed saucepan or skillet, wooden mixing spoon

1. Line bottom and sides of pie pan with foil, wrapping foil over the pan's top edge to secure the foil. Grease foil generously with butter or margarine. Lay peanuts on foil and shake pan to spread evenly over bottom.
2. Melt sugar in saucepan or skillet over high heat, but do not mix until sugar begins to melt, about 3 minutes. Reduce heat to medium and stir continually with wooden spoon until all sugar is dissolved. Carefully remove pan from heat and pour hot mixture over peanuts, using wooden spoon to make sure they are well covered. Cool to room temperature, peel peanut brittle from foil, and break into serving-size pieces. To crush peanut brittle, first wrap it in foil and completely cover with a clean kitchen towel. Using a mallet or hammer hit the wrapped candy until it is crushed to the desired consistency.

Serve *peanut brittle* as a candy treat. Store in a covered jar and crush some for the following recipe.

Tuskegee Ice Cream

Dr. Carver loved peanuts and worked wonders with them. Credit for creating the following delicious recipe, called *Tuskegee ice cream*, goes to Dr. Carver as it appeared in a printed pamphlet dated 1925.

Yield: serves 6

1 quart vanilla or lemon ice cream, slightly softened (at room temperature)
1/4 pound peanut brittle, finely crushed

Equipment: Medium-size mixing bowl, mixing spoon, aluminum foil

Put ice cream in the mixing bowl, add peanut brittle, and mix well. Cover with foil and refreeze.

Serve *Tuskegee ice cream* in individual serving dishes or in ice cream cones.

Pecan Pralines

Pecan trees thrive throughout the south, and there are many wonderful ways of using the nuts. *Pecan pralines* are popular and easy to make.

Yield: makes about 4 dozen

2 cups granulated sugar
1 cup firmly packed light brown sugar
1 cup milk
2 teaspoons white corn syrup
1/2 cup butter (do not substitute)
4 cups pecans, broken in small pieces

Equipment: Medium-size heavy-bottom saucepan, wooden mixing spoon, 2 tablespoons, wax paper covered work surface

1. Put granulated and brown sugars in saucepan, add milk, corn syrup, and butter, and, stirring continually, bring to a rolling boil over medium-high heat. Reduce heat to low and cook for about 20 minutes, stirring frequently. Add nuts, mix well, increase heat to medium, and cook until mixture barely drops off spoon when lifted up, about 20 minutes; stir frequently to prevent sticking. Remove from heat.
2. Quickly and carefully drop candy by tablespoonsful onto wax paper. Use the second spoon to scoop the candy off the first spoon. Each drop should form about a 2-inch patty. When cool, remove from paper and store in airtight container or wrap each in plastic wrap.

Pralines make wonderful gifts to give friends and family.

Beef Jerky

It was necessary for the early pioneers traveling across the United States and Canada to preserve food and find a way to carry it in a very limited space. Jerking meat was the answer; it preserved the meat and was compact and easy to carry. Explorers such as Lewis and Clark considered jerking meat just another necessary chore and seldom wasted much time or imagination on it. They simply strapped out long strips of meat, laid them upon rocks, or hung them from bushes to sun dry. Frequently they assisted the process by building smudge fires under the meat, which also helped to keep flies off.

Jerky became popular, and is still a favorite trail and snack food. *Jerky* can be made from deer, elk, buffalo, or beef. Originally sun dried, the oven can effectively dry beef with similar results. Set the oven to the very lowest heat; remember, you're not cooking the meat, just drying it out—hence, the name, "dried beef." The **marinade** for the following *jerky* recipe is to flavor the meat, not **tenderize** it. Worcestershire sauce and hot red sauce can be added, more or less to taste. This recipe can also be used as a dish from Africa or South America, as it is a common food throughout the world.

Yield: 10 to 20 pieces

1 to 2 pounds lean beef, such as round steak, fat **trimmed**, put in freezer for about 30 minutes to firm. Slice with grain (not across grain) in strips, 1/8-inch thick.
1 capful liquid smoke
3 teaspoons garlic granules
2 teaspoons *each* ground oregano and thyme
2 teaspoons salt
1 tablespoon pepper
2 teaspoons soy sauce

Equipment: Glass or plastic bowl, wire cake rack, aluminum foil

1. Mix liquid smoke, garlic, oregano, thyme, salt, pepper, and soy sauce in bowl. Using your clean hands, rub mixture on meat strips making sure to coat each piece. Refrigerate for 1 hour.
2. Preheat oven to lowest heat, about 150° F.
3. Place strips side-by-side on wire rack and put in oven (place a sheet of foil on shelf under meat rack to catch drippings). Make a wedge of rolled foil to keep oven door open about 3-inches to release moisture. Keep meat in oven at least 12 hours or overnight.
4. In the morning check the meat: if it's brittle, it's done. If it bends without breaking, leave it in for another couple hours. When dry, store in an airtight container.

Serve *beef jerky* as easy-to-carry, quick-energy snack.

Monte Cristo Sandwich

Eating out is an important family group activity in the United States. It is a shared experience with others, often bringing happy memories of childhood to later years. An example of such an outing may be a day of shopping with grandma, stopping for lunch at a charming restaurant, being served by waiters in freshly starched white aprons, bringing plates beautifully garnished with watercress, the largest glistening strawberries, and a memorable sandwich called the *monte cristo*. It was the creation of a chef at a now long-gone San Francisco restaurant. The place and the *monte cristo* received world fame and acclaim, and the wonderful memory of both linger on.

Yield: serves 2 to 4

6 thin slices white bread, crusts removed
4 tablespoons mayonnaise
4 thin slices cooked turkey breast
2 thin slices American cheese
4 thin slices baked ham
3 eggs
2 tablespoons milk
2 tablespoons vegetable oil
4 tablespoons sour cream for serving
4 tablespoons strawberry jam for serving

Equipment: Small-size shallow bowl, large-size skillet or griddle, pancake turner or metal spatula

1. Place 2 bread slices on work surface and lightly spread each with mayonnaise. Top each with 2 slices of turkey, trimming overhang if necessary. Spread 2 more bread slices lightly with mayonnaise on both sides and place over the turkey. Top each with 1 slice of cheese and 2 slices of ham, trimming overhang if necessary. Spread 1 side of each remaining bread slice with mayonnaise and place, mayonnaise side down, over ham. Press lightly on sandwiches to compact and cut each diagonally into 4 triangles.
2. Put eggs and milk in small shallow bowl, and mix well. Heat oil in skillet or on griddle over medium heat until a drop of water sizzles on contact. Dip each triangle into egg mixture, turning to coat all surfaces. Fry, turning to cook all sides evenly, until golden brown (about 10 minutes). Lightly coat skillet or griddle with more oil if necessary to prevent sticking. Remove sandwiches and drain on paper towels.

Serve *Monte Cristos* hot, accompanied with little individual dishes of sour cream and jam to spread on the sandwiches.

Index